S^{The}ongwriter
GOES TO
★ ★ ★ ★ ★ War

S^{The}ongwriter

GOES TO

★ ★ ★ ★ ★ War

The Story of Irving Berlin's
World War II All-Army Production of
THIS IS THE ARMY

Alan Anderson

Foreword by
Mary Ellin Barrett

Pompton Plains, NJ

First Limelight Edition November 2004

Published in 2004 by:
Amadeus Press/Limelight Editions
512 Newark Pompton Turnpike
Pompton Plains, NJ 07444
www.limelighteditions.com

Manufactured in the United States of America

Library of Congress Cataloging-in-Publication Data

Anderson, Alan, 1917-
   The songwriter goes to war : the story of Irving Berlin's World War II all-Army production of "This is the army" / Alan Anderson. — 1st limelight ed.
       p. cm.
   ISBN 0-87910-304-3 (hardcover)
   1. Berlin, Irving, 1888- This is the Army. 2. World War, 1939-1945 — Music and the war. I. Title.

ML410.B499A53 2004
792.6'42 — dc22

                               2004017690

To my dearest Nancy

Contents

Foreword

Mary Ellin Barrett

I first met Alan Anderson more than sixty years ago at the final dress rehearsal of *This Is the Army*, July 3, 1942, on the eve of what would turn out to be one of the most remarkable opening nights in Broadway history. I was the daughter of Irving Berlin, the show's creator, excited at being made part of a great occasion, an event I knew was of unprecedented importance in my father's life. Alan was an Army sergeant and the show's stage manager. Fleeting glimpses of an attractive young man in uniform—blond, with a quick smile, a down-to-earth manner and some urgent message, no doubt, to deliver to "Mr. B.," as Irving Berlin was known to the men of his company. Seeing this pleasant fellow in his early 20s, and being a teenager myself, I had no idea of the prodigies he was performing. "What does a stage manager do?" I asked my father. "He makes things work," was the reply.

And how they worked! Opening night the curtain goes up on a stage full of soldiers delivering the opening chorus, and then takes off number by number, skits and songs kidding Army life, a military vaudeville show ... two beautiful new Berlin ballads, "I'm Getting Tired So I Can Sleep" and "I Left My Heart at the Stage Door Canteen" ... GI's tapping out a hot swing tune, getting their laughs dressed up in crinolines for "Ladies of the Chorus" (left over from *Yip! Yip! Yaphank*, Berlin's soldier show of the first world war). And then at the end of the second act, a small, black-haired man in an old doughboy's uniform stands alone on stage, hat in hand, mouth open, ready to sing. The house explodes in a roar. It is ten minutes before Irving

Berlin is permitted to deliver his theme song and the evening's number one showstopper, "Oh! How I Hate to Get Up in the Morning." When the soldiers line up one last time for the finale, the curtain comes down on something much more than a Broadway hit, something memorialized by the words of one critic: ". . . at once delightful entertainment and a song of American democracy . . . because [it] does not try to capitalize on patriotism, it is one of the most truly patriotic works I have ever encountered. . . . Because it always keeps a sense of humor and never tries to be emotional, it is one of the most moving events in theatrical history."

Where did this khaki stage marvel come from and where did it go? That is the wonderful story Alan Anderson has to tell in The Songwriter Goes to War, a long lost tale of frontline show business that only he at the center could have attempted—and finally has. How the show was put together sets the tone: a determined songwriter asking the impossible and getting it; a motley crew of recruits, some with experience, many more just full of pluck, molded into a musical comedy team; blacks and whites together in the first and only integrated division in the US Army.

Episode by episode the saga unfolds. The show, originally slated to play a modest month on Broadway, make some money for the Army Relief Fund and disband, keeps going and going: a coast-to-coast tour of the US, a pause in Hollywood to make a movie version (more millions for Army Relief), then overseas, it's globe-circling tour ending only when the war itself ended.

It's a new way of looking at World War II, from a new angle, through the prism of a particular enterprise that is at once familiar and unfamiliar, a "backstage" story that ultimately involves transporting a full-scale Broadway musical revue to Great Britain in the blitz, the Italian front lines, the Persian desert and the jungles of New Guinea. From all levels of show business, performers were taking their talents to the edges of the battleground—from the smallest USO troupe to the great stars of stage, screen, radio and concert halls. But nothing could compare to the mind-boggling logistics of *This Is the Army*: the scenery, the costumes, the lights, the setting up, taking down, moving on, with a cast of 150 to be billeted and fed, under the dual command of Army brass and the civilian Mr. Berlin, not always in perfect accord. (One riveting episode in Naples almost ends in a court martial.)

In Anderson's relaxed, colloquial, carefully-detailed telling, the story builds, immersing the reader in this wartime world, its community, its mores, its lingo. Irving Berlin, the leading man, springs to life. You can see him moving quickly, in or out of uniform, the producer, busy with every aspect of his enterprise, guiding and watching out for his "boys." You can hear his raspy voice getting a general on the phone to straighten out some ill-advised order that is screwing up the show, or hear the jumbled sound of the piano behind a closed door as he works on a new song . . . and reworks . . . and reworks. It is the father I knew yet did not know, could not know, as the men of the *TITA* company knew him.

What varied, interesting characters these men are! Bob Sidney—the show's principal choreographer, brilliant, funny, defiant of authority (other than Mr. B.'s), openly gay. Ezra Stone—radio's Henry Aldrich, the brash, talented director who becomes Berlin's adversary in a painful falling out. Milton Rosenstock—the conductor and master musician, a flamboyant personality who sometimes needs reining in. Pete Feller—Alan's scrappy best buddy, who boasts, whatever the challenge, "I can do it!" Marc Daniels—the unfortunate lieutenant in charge of a bunch of show folk in uniform, who pulls rank at the wrong time.

And always there is Alan himself—making things work, apparently unflappable (even when inwardly seething), homesick for his young wife and baby son, the eyewitness laying it out place by place, scene by scene, from the everyday nitty gritty to the most highly charged moments: the night in London when General Eisenhower comes backstage to congratulate the cast and tell them he is recommending that they be sent on to theaters of war to entertain and bolster morale for their fellow soldiers; the performance in Santa Maria, the little town north of Naples, where the show plays for the first time to war-weary men trucked in straight from the front.

The Songwriter Goes to War is a memoir, as personal as it is informed, an insider's recollection of a small but unique piece of theatrical and World War II history. It's a story I've always hoped would be told, one in which, as that songwriter's daughter, I take great pride. I thank Alan Anderson for writing it.

Acknowledgments

I begin with gratitude to my sister, Hesper. Nancy and I were living in Sonoma, California, when Hesper moved from Los Angeles to Napa and announced that she was going to start a writer's group. She had run one before to great success. I mentioned having made a couple of attempts on a book about Irving Berlin's show *This Is the Army*, and she promptly suggested that I begin again with her group. Treat it as a memoir rather than as history, she said. It was that suggestion, followed by Hep's few but very wise reactions to my Tuesday night readings over the next four years, that produced *The Songwriter Goes to War*.

In 1979, the minute I was eligible for Social Security I retired from being an advertising writer at J. Walter Thompson—and promptly started to look for something to write. By 1985, I had started to write a history of the extraordinary experience I'd had as a soldier in World War II, when, by chance, I was chosen by Irving Berlin to become the production stage manager and First Sergeant of an all-Army show he had written and produced called *This Is the Army*. While at work on the book, and again by chance, I met Berlin's eldest daughter, Mary Ellin Barrett, whom I had not seen since she was fifteen and came backstage with her father after the final dress rehearsal of the show on Broadway. She was very pleased in 1985 that I was writing about the show and greatly encouraged me from then on.

Linda Emmett, Mary Ellin's younger sister, as editor of a comprehensive compilation of her father's songs, has helped me invaluably with details about Berlin's work.

The manuscript would never have become a book had it not had an agent who believed in it enough to find it a home. Barbara Hogenson, most dauntless and gracious agent, undertook this pursuit. She survived a series of encounters without a trace of discouragement and finally met with enormous success when she put the first draft in the hands of Mel Zerman, who then turned the torch of Limelight Editions upon it. I shall be forever grateful for their confidence and devotion.

Mel sold Limelight in the middle of the book's production, and I and my memoir were fortunate to be passed into the hands of John Cerullo.

Zinn Arthur, one of the talented singers in the show, was, quite on his own, responsible for a full pictorial account, by supplying a wide variety of photographs of our overseas adventures. Zinn died before I could finish the book, but I am grateful that his daughter, Robin, and son in law, Chris Probst, have helped fully realize Zinn's visual contribution.

Thanks, too, to Bert Fink and his staff at the Irving Berlin Library and The Rodgers and Hammerstein Organization for their part in telling the story in a great many irreplaceable photographs.

I wish I had managed to tell the story sooner, when more of those who were part of the journey were still alive. But it has been gratifying to be encouraged by Bob Sidney, who played a vital role in the show. His professional strength never wavered, and Mr. B.'s faith in him was enormous.

I've also enjoyed the support of Seymour Greene, a surviving company member and very expert trombonist, who keeps cheering me on. And there are unseen hearts and minds that have supported me through these years. For instance, Emily King Michie, who read every word, smoothed out many small knots and bumps, and made the words flow more smoothly.

I shall ever regret that my dearest lifetime love, Nancy, did not see the book in print. She did live to see the contract arrive, however, and I can still feel the warm flush of pride and shared happiness of her arms around me. She had spent many hours in these last years waiting for me to leave my writing desk to be by her side.

Preface

It was mid-afternoon on a hot August day in 1985 and I was half finished with the mowing job on our two-acre lawn. The roar of the tractor precluded any contact with the outside world, so I had a habit of glancing toward the house periodically. This time I was surprised to see my wife, Nancy, standing on the front steps with both arms swaying back and forth over her head like seagrass in the wind. Something important. I promptly stopped the machine and watched her pantomime a phone call, with left hand to ear and right hand to mouth. That was followed by a vigorous beckoning motion. I threw the tractor into high speed and followed her command. As I hustled past her into the house, she quickly elaborated on her message.

"Irving Berlin is calling!"

I hurried toward the kitchen phone, my mind juggling. I hadn't talked to him for thirty years and I had been waiting for weeks for a letter in response to mine. I hadn't expected a phone call, but come to think of it, I shouldn't have been surprised—he always liked to deal with things using the most direct method. I couldn't take the time to go to my study and turn on my tape recorder. "Damn," I said as I reached for the phone.

"What?" Nancy said from behind me.

"I wish I had my tape recorder." I threw my hands up in frustration and picked up the receiver.

"Hello?"

"Is this Mr. Alan Anderson?" A woman's voice.

"Yes."

"Irving Berlin wants to talk to you."

"Good," I said, wondering if I should recognize the voice. I picked up the grocery list and a pencil so I could take notes. The next sound was unmistakable. His voice—high-pitched, somewhat strained. The last time I'd heard it was in the fifties when I had run into him in a theater lobby.

"Hello, Alan?"

"Yes. Hello. How are you?" I said, stumbling through my words.

"I'm ninety-seven," he said. And that was all. Clearly that was the answer to my question. I was reminded of a line in *Valley Forge*, one of my father's plays in which one soldier says in reassurance to another (and I quoted to Berlin), "You? Die? Never! You're the skinny kind that lives forever."

"I hope not," he replied. I'd better say something—but he beat me to it. "Why do you want to write a book about the show? Nobody cares about that anymore. You'd be wasting your time."

My heart sank. As soon as I heard those words I realized that I should have expected them. My letter to him was to tell him that I was all excited, having decided to write a book about *This Is the Army*, the all-Army musical variety show he had written and produced during World War II that had played across the country, had been made into a movie by Warner Brothers and then played to our soldiers all around the world. Besides writing and producing it, he had starred in it through the entire run, except for a few weeks when he was obliged to fulfill some obligations in Hollywood. I had been with the show for every performance for three and a half years as the production stage manager and first sergeant of the Army company.

"Nobody cares about that anymore. You'd be wasting your time."

This was similar to the responses he'd made forty years earlier whenever anyone wanted to call public attention to the show or to him.

How could it surprise me this time around? Did I suppose that he had changed—that he might encourage me?

I took another approach. If he realized how many people are intrigued by the story, it would surely change his opinion. "Everyone I talk to," I said with confidence, "thinks it's a great idea!"

"Everyone who knew about the show is dead."

"Not quite," I assured him. "I've been in touch with about half the guys and they're all enthusiastic."

"They just want to see their names in print." He had a point there. The show had been an experience to them unlike any other in their lives, as it had been for me, and they would love to have the story told with their names in it.

"Yeah, well, maybe," I admitted. "Of course, they all feel it's their story, too. I've also talked to a couple of publisher friends about it and they think it's a great idea."

"They just want to make money out of you," he said.

"I'd be happy if they could. That would mean it was a hit!" I laughed. "Maybe they'd give me a little of it."

No response to that—nothing had changed in forty-five years. He didn't want anyone to do a book about his show or about him. His paranoia about publicity had started when he was courting Ellin Mackay and every newspaper had dogged them daily. It had taught him that when someone writes about you, it never comes out the way you want it or the way it happened. Nevertheless, I plunged on with one more attempt. "The thing is," I said with confidence, "the story is unique and the uniqueness is largely due to you."

"What do you mean unique? It was just a show."

"No one in the whole world could have done that show and no one else could have induced the Army to send it around the world and keep it going—but you!"

"Maybe," he admitted, and I thought I had him. But he found a way around that one, too. "It's over. It was so long ago—forget it. Everybody else has."

I couldn't speak. I didn't want to upset him. We had been good friends. When he spoke I realized he felt the same thing. "I can't stop you if you want to do it," he said. "But I can't help you with it."

"I understand that," I replied, feeling reassured. This was almost encouragement. He seemed to apologize a little, blaming it on his age.

"I'm almost a hundred, if I make it."

"You'll make it," I said firmly. "You'll outlive us all."

He gave a sort of half laugh, half derision, and then he choked me up. "How is that boy of yours, and your beautiful wife?"

"They're both fine," I said. "I'm glad you remember them."

"I do," he said.

"That boy" was the first child born to a member of the *This Is the Army* company. Being born in New York when I had been three thousand miles away had given Berlin the idea for a song, "What Does He Look Like?" about a soldier whose son is born when he is away at war. Berlin dedicated the song to "that boy" and gave us a copy of the original sheet music. It was sung in the movie version of the show.

"I wish you could meet that boy now," I said. "I'll tell him you asked. He'll get a kick out of that."

"Say hello to your beautiful wife," he said, and then finally, "I'm glad we talked." And he was gone. The receiver clicked and I was hearing "All Alone" in my head.

I decided I had to do the book. After all, I was right about a couple of things. First, he *did* make it and then some. He died on September 22, 1989, at the age of one hundred one and four months. And second, he *will* outlive all of us who shared that extraordinary adventure with him. And I can't resist remembering it for one last time before the curtain falls.

C h a p t e r 1

THE WAR
—*Sep 2, 1940: USA agrees to provide Great Britain with 50 sub-marines.*
—*Sep 17, 1940: Hitler announces postponement of invasion of England.*
—*Oct 9, 1940: Increasing U-boat successes in North Atlantic removes some escort ships from anti-invasion duty.*
—*Jan 2, 1941: The USA announces plans to build 200 utilitarian freighters, Liberty Ships, to carry war materials to our allies.*
—*Jan 4, 1941: The Greeks begin to falter against the increasing Italian forces.*
—*Jan 24, 1941: US Secretary of the Navy advises Secretary of War Henry Stimson of the possibility of an attack on Pearl Harbor.*

I was first aware of the name Irving Berlin in 1925 when I was eight years old and I read it on the label of a ten-inch 78 RPM record.

That summer Dad had surprised us by buying a phonograph. He and my mother listened to it almost every evening. Mostly they played classical music but sometimes they played popular. The dark varnished wood cabinet was a little taller than I was, so I had to stand on a footstool to work it. I watched them enough until I could do it alone. You had to wind it up for each record using the crank on the side. When you raised the hinged top it locked in place and you could put a record on the turntable, turn on the machine, and lower the playing arm gently so the needle just touched the record.

Of the popular music, I found myself listening over again to songs with labels that read, "Words and Music by Irving Berlin." The lyrics and the melodies stuck in my memory, lines like "What'll I do, when you, are far away? What'll I do? What'll I do?" And another one, "I'll be loving you always, with a love that's true always." He wrote a lot of songs and, of course, as I got older, I heard him a great deal.

One day, seventeen years later, something quite extraordinary happened: I met Irving Berlin in person—right in front of me. And for just a second a wind-up Victrola and 78 records flitted through my mind.

It happened when I was a corporal in the United States Army, on temporary duty with a Special Services office called the Theater Section and I was working with several other soldiers. One of my associates, Corporal Mike Wardell, suddenly rushed into my office and said in a loud whisper, "Anderson, if you don't want to get your butt in a sling, you'll get into Dixie's office on the double!" Dixie was our name for our commanding officer, Captain Richard E. French. I slipped into my blouse, buttoned it fast and charged down the big open room to Dixie's office. The door was partly open and I heard voices. Knowing Dixie's behavior, I knocked gently. The peremptory response was unquestionably my boss. Having worked with him for several weeks, I knew it was not an invitation. It was an order.

"Come in, Anderson!"

I pushed the door open and faced Dixie, who was seated at his desk, his lips tight, his jaw clenched. But my eyes were drawn immediately to his guest—a civilian—a slim, rather short man, looking very trim and handsome in a three-piece suit with very subtle pin stripes, white button-down shirt, dark tie. He rose, smiling and put out his hand to me.

"Irving Berlin," he said.

As we shook hands, I could feel a broad, involuntary smile taking over my face as I said, quite dazed, "How do you do, sir?"

We were standing in a room in an Army office building at 90 Church Street in lower Manhattan. Like Mike Wardell, I was a corporal, a noncommissioned officer, with two stripes on the arms of my olive drab uniform, an enlisted man in the United States Army. It was February 10, 1942. Technically we had been at war with Japan and Germany for nearly ten weeks, ever since December 7, 1941, Pearl

Harbor Day. Dixie—Captain French—indicating his rank by the two silver bars on each shoulder, was the only commissioned officer in the room. The other noncommissioned officer present was my immediate boss, Staff Sergeant Ezra Stone.

In terms of age, success, wealth and leverage Irving Berlin, the lone civilian, unquestionably outranked us all. I'd been surprised when he rose to greet me. Dixie would not have risen in my presence unless there was a fire in his pants. Also surprising was to see this famous man in this small, plain office, furnished in Army utility drab. Irving Berlin belonged in a far more inviting background.

I knew quite a bit about Dixie and Ezra, having been on duty with them for a little over two months. Dixie, a reserve officer before the war, had been called for active duty from his civilian role as a business manager in the Broadway theater. Dixie undoubtedly recognized that he was outranked as a civilian by all those who filled artistically creative positions in that world. For instance, Staff Sergeant Ezra Stone, who had been a director in the theater, represented just such a complex affront to Dixie's superior Army status. Dixie's response as a captain was to bully the lower army ranks under his command. We observed that he was also an obsequious coward with his superiors. Being in service, we all learned the distinctive indications of rank, between commissioned and noncommissioned officers: shining silver or gold shoulder emblems worn by the commissioned officers; simple fabric stripes on the arms of the "noncoms." We also learned that those of higher rank who were confident in their roles could be gracious with all ranks.

However, I had discovered that Ezra held a special role, because through his father he had a personal relationship with Major General Irving J. Phillipson, the boss of us all, including the lowly captain. Such were the forces at play in this meeting between Dixie, Berlin, Ezra and me.

Irving Berlin, at fifty-three, was unquestionably the most popular American songwriter alive, with an unmatched number of hit songs to his credit, including such unforgettable gems as "Alexander's Ragtime Band," "Always," "All Alone," "Cheek to Cheek," "Easter Parade," "Heat Wave" and "God Bless America." The list went on and on.

Ezra Stone, all of twenty-two years old, had already been the director of two successful Broadway plays. He was even more widely known across the country for a weekly evening radio show in which he had starred for several years, *The Adventures of Henry Aldrich.* Henry was a teenaged cut-up, whose mother began each program with a commanding, "Henry! Henry Aldrich!" To which in an adolescent's cracking voice, Henry cried out, "Coming, Mother!"

My own theater experience at twenty-two consisted of three years as a stage manager on Broadway, working with well-known directors and stars. My father, Maxwell Anderson, had been a successful playwright as long as I could remember, and while I would never have dreamt of following in his theatrical footsteps, I discovered that I liked being a stage manager.

"How do you do, sir?" Starry-eyed as I was, my use of "sir" to Mr. Berlin's greeting was quite automatic for me after ten months of Army service. He said something in reply I hadn't expected.

"I'm glad to meet you, Alan. I'm a great admirer of your father."

My response was an honest reflex—"So am I"—then I thought this might have sounded like a smart-ass answer. But in fact I was honestly proud of my father, knowing he was one of the two most prestigious playwrights in the country. Indeed, he had written and produced more successful plays than any other American alive, including Eugene O'Neill. Not only had he won a Pulitzer Prize, he was the winner of the first two New York Drama Critic's Circle Awards and was well-known for many Hollywood movies made from such plays of his as *Elizabeth the Queen, Winterset* and *Key Largo,* among others.

Like most children of famous parents that I had known, I often felt uncomfortable when people praised my father. But this time it was coming from another man for whom I felt enormous respect.

"He's a great man," said Mr. Berlin.

"Thank you, sir. I think he would say the same about you." And as I said that, I was thinking about how long my father and I had been listening to his music.

"I doubt it," he replied, smiling.

"I'd like to call him tonight to tell him I met you. I hope you don't mind."

"Not if you'll tell him what I think of him," he replied.

"It's a deal, sir!" I was enjoying myself. I was also thinking how excited my wife would be when I called her with the news.

Mr. Berlin sat again, his eyes still fixed on mine. I could feel Dixie's fidgety, seething annoyance. That he should be totally ignored in his own office! I knew it to be characteristic of him, and it occurred to me as it had before that a wiser, more confident man would have taken pride in such subordinates.

While Berlin seemed oblivious to the Captain's discomfort, Ezra and I were sharing our enjoyment of it. Mr. Berlin went on to explain to me why he had come all the way down to our humble offices, but Dixie cleared his throat and sought desperately to find a new course for the conversation.

"Uh, well—!" he said, as though we should now get on to important things.

But Berlin wasn't finished. He continued to address me. "You're too young to know it, but I did an Army show in World War I and I've been in touch with General Marshall to let him know that I would like to do another Army show right now. I'm glad to tell you he thought it was a good idea." Seeing an opportunity for himself, Dixie jumped in.

"Well, I'll certainly do everything I can—"

Berlin was not listening. He was still talking to me. "I don't have a title yet. I guess we could call it *Yip! Yip! Yaphank the Second* for the moment." He gave Ezra an appreciative glance.

"Ezra has agreed to be my director. Now," and he looked me straight in the eyes, "let's get down to business. Ezra told me some of the Broadway shows you stage managed. And I see you've done musicals. How about you being my stage manager on this show?"

Before I could respond, Dixie tried again. "You can have anyone you want, Mr. Berlin." Berlin frowned slightly at this interruption but he continued looking at me, waiting for my answer.

"I'd like that very much, sir!"

"Uh—" from the captain.

"Good! Then that's settled," Berlin said, and looked at Ezra for confirmation.

Dixie's mouth kept opening and closing like a landed fish, but he couldn't say anything and just shook his head in frustration. Not wanting there to be any doubt about my interest, I said, "Thank you very much for the opportunity, Mr. Berlin."

He rose then, smiling at me. "I'm glad to have you, Alan." He picked up his fedora and, starting for the door briskly, said to Ezra, "Let's get together tomorrow in my office. Let me know when you can make it."

Everyone was standing now. "Yes, *sir*," Ezra replied. "I'll get all the guys together this afternoon and work out a schedule for you to look at."

"Thank you," said Berlin. Then he turned to Dixie. "Thanks, Captain. I'm sorry I missed Rosenstock. I'll call him tomorrow." I was glad that he indicated he was considering Corporal Milton Rosenstock for music director. The captain was looking for a leave-taking strategy—perhaps a handshake between the host and the guest of honor—but Berlin was leaving and Dixie had to address his back.

His "Anything at all, sir. Just let me know what you need," produced a final blow to his self-esteem when Berlin replied, "I'd like to deal with Ezra personally since he's going to be the director." In terms of show business, what Berlin said made perfect sense. But of course it didn't make sense to Dixie. Dixie took one more chance to stay in the picture. He attempted to repair the damage.

"Stone can keep me apprised of plans."

Berlin didn't appear to be listening as he said, "Take me down to my car, will you, Ezra?"

"Yes, *sir.*" Ezra followed Berlin into the elevator.

As the elevator door closed, Dixie said loudly, "Report to me when you get back, Stone!"

We could hear Ezra's reply from the descending elevator. "Yes, sir!" I thought I heard the slightest break into falsetto in Ezra's final word, an echo of "Coming, Mother!" I looked away quickly to avoid Dixie's eyes. Ezra was safe from attack but I was a vulnerable target. I started away quickly.

"Get back to work, Anderson!" I pivoted to him and threw him a salute.

"Oh, go to hell!" He ignored my salute, went into his office and banged the door.

☆ ☆ ☆ ☆ ☆ ☆ ☆ ☆ ☆ ☆ ☆

I was still reeling from Berlin's hiring me for the show he was planning—*Yip! Yip! Yaphank the Second*, or whatever he would call it. I suddenly realized he would never have chosen me if I hadn't left college and started a career in the theater. It got me thinking about the series of events that delivered me into Berlin's hands.

When I finished my sophomore year at Columbia, I had said to my father that I wanted to apprentice at the Suffern County Summer Theater. Of course he said fine, and I fell in love with stage managing and Nancy Swan that summer of 1937. Nancy had apprenticed there for two years as an actress—she was good and she was beautiful! And we were in love. That wiped out everything else for us, including the state of the world. We were thinking about nothing but each other and our activities as apprentices in the County Theater.

My father would talk to me about Chancellor Adolf Hitler and the danger he represented to Europe, and, as he put it, to the civilized world. I'm afraid that a lot of young people didn't want to face the fact that we should be helping England and preparing ourselves for the possibility of war. But after that first summer, I got a job as a fifth assistant stage manager on Broadway and Nancy started college at Barnard. In the back of my mind I didn't even want to hear what Dad was saying, because I was so excited about being in the theater.

The following year Nancy was a sophomore and I was a head stage manager on Broadway, and when that show ended, I had another show. Then in the fall of 1940, Nancy was starting her junior year at college and I had just been hired for my fourth Broadway stage managing job. On October 20, I received a letter of "greetings" from President Roosevelt. Nancy's heart sank; my father and I were resigned.

On November 1, I slipped an engagement ring on Nancy's finger. We decided to set the date as soon as we could convince her mother that it was a wonderful idea. Dad and my stepmother, Mab, both said hooray and gave Nancy a big hug. My kid sister, Hesper, jumped up and down and said, "I want to be a flower girl!"

"You betcha!" I said, and she ran into my arms.

Gulia Snow, Nancy's mother, was very dubious about the practicality of marrying someone who worked in the theater. I pointed out to her that some people made a lot of money in the theater and I was aiming to be one of them. She finally gave in and managed to accomplish a great deal in a short time by borrowing a beautiful apartment in the Hotel Carlyle from old friends and sending out all the invitations.

I don't remember much about St. Patrick's Day, except that it was our wedding day. There were quite a lot of relatives and friends. And as to ceremony, I remember being asked if I would take this angel person next to me to love honor and obey under various circumstances, to which I heartily agreed.

I came down to earth for a moment realizing that my kid sister had never appeared as the flower girl and learned that she had been diagnosed as a measles patient. Two days later I went to bed in Dad's house with measles. A few days later, Nancy joined me in the sickbed with the same disease. I got up and took care of her night and day. Then I had to leave her in bed while I reported to duty as a private in the US Army at Fort Dix, New Jersey.

Shortly after assignment to C Company barracks building, I began basic training. When Nancy was well enough, she drove our Plymouth down to Fort Dix and we found a room and bath for her above Captain Simpson's garage in Lavalette, New Jersey, right across the road from the Atlantic Ocean. We chose it because it was a few blocks from Nancy's mother and stepfather's summer family retreat. She would have family close by and the warm summer beach to speed her recovery. Lavalette was a forty minute drive from my tent area at Fort Dix so we were together for many weekends at the beach that summer.

When I finished basic training, I filled out a questionnaire about my various skills. My experience in theater and photography were both ignored, but my admission that I could type with two fingers was not. I was promptly assigned to join two other privates in the Public Relations Office at Fort Dix Headquarters, in the job of writing stories for the local newspapers about our newly inducted fellow selectees. Once written, we mimeographed and mailed copies to the *Trenton Times* and the *Newark Star Ledger.* Our boss was Major Aage Woldike, who was also the head of intelligence for Fort Dix. After two months, the Major promoted me from private to corporal, increasing my monthly salary by about ten dollars. As fall approached the Major encouraged me to think about further promotions. I applied to Officer's Candidate School at Fort Monmouth, New Jersey. My goal, if I was accepted, was to become a commissioned officer specializing as a combat photographer.

An extremely intelligent and delightful young man, Private William

Agar, joined the PR group shortly after me. His father, Herbert Agar, was a prominent historian and like my father, a Pulitzer Prize winner. Bill and his girlfriend, Nan, became Nancy's and my close friends. We very shortly persuaded them to follow our example and get married. We were invited to the wedding and I was Bill's best man. When I signed up for Fort Monmouth, Bill followed my example to attend OCS, except that he chose the infantry in Fort Benning, Georgia.

In September the beach life ended. Nancy and I rented a tiny house in Browns Mills, right next to Fort Dix. It was in the damp chill of the pine barrens of New Jersey, but we were close to each other and I could be with her every night. In October, Bill left for Georgia and I was still waiting for a response from Fort Monmouth. Finally, on Monday, November 17, I received orders to report to Fort Monmouth on December 9, 1941, my 24th birthday. Nancy notified our landlord.

On Wednesday, December 3, when I walked into the PR office at 9:00 a.m. one of my fellow writers said with considerable excitement, "Get in there, quick, Anderson. Boss wants you!"

The Major's door was open. He saw me and gestured me to join him, and barely taking time to return my salute, leapt up and thrust a telegram in my hands.

"You'd better read this right away, Alan." I started reading, totally mystified. The orders read in part:

CORPORAL ALAN ANDERSON WILL PROCEED TO FORT JAY, GOVERNOR'S ISLAND, IN TIME SO AS TO ENABLE HIM TO ARRIVE NO LATER THAN 9 A.M., DECEMBER 4, 1941 . . .

I looked up. "But that's tomorrow, sir!"
"I know that, Anderson," he said, smiling.
I went back to the message and read the rest of it out loud:

". . . FOR TEMPORARY DUTY IN THE THEATER SECTION, 2ND CORPS AREA, MORALE OFFICE, MAJOR GENERAL IRVING J. PHILLIPSON."

I looked up at him puzzled.

"Major General? Theater Section? "But what about the Signal Corps, sir?"

"Don't worry, it says temporary duty. They'll take you when you finish. The orders are from the CO of 2nd Corps. Who do you know, Anderson? You've been hiding something." He grinned at me.

"Well, I was in the theater. Whatever 'Theater Section' means, it may have something to do with that."

"Well, you did a good job here. I'll miss you."

"Thank you, sir. I enjoyed working for you."

He put out his hand. "Good luck. I'll see you when you get back."

I said good-bye to my pals, put on my coat and hat and hurried to our little house.

☆ ☆ ☆ ☆ ☆ ☆ ☆ ☆ ☆ ☆ ☆

Nancy called her father before we left. She informed me that her father and Betty would love to have guests at their Lexington Avenue apartment.

I was on the Lexington Avenue subway platform at 7:00 a.m. the next morning and arrived at Battery Park before 8:00, within a short walk to the Governor's Island ferry. I had enough gear with me to stay overnight if I had to. I didn't know whether I would be living on or off the base.

I walked up the ramp from the ferry at 8:20 and was looking right at a sign that read "Fort Jay, Administrative Offices." I found a soldier at a desk just inside who directed me to the stairs.

"Second floor, room 220, down the hall on your right."

There was a freshly lettered sign on the door: "Theater Section, Morale, 2nd Corps Area." I went in and found a corporal sitting at a desk talking on the phone. He finished his conversation and hung up and I showed him my telegraphic orders. He looked at the message briefly and handed it back.

"He's waiting for you," he said.

"*The General?*" I must have turned a little white.

"No, no, no!" he laughed. "Lieutenant Kingsley."

"Oh," I said. I didn't know a Lieutenant Kingsley. The only Kingsley I knew was Sidney Kingsley, Pulitzer-winning playwright, good friend of my father. I knew him.

"Leave your bag out here. I'll watch it for you." He opened the door and said, "Anderson is here, sir."

A voice said, "Good. Send him in." It was a peculiarly familiar voice, somewhat high and nasal. I stepped inside and met him coming around his desk.

"Sidney! I'll be damned! You're a lieutenant?" And we were shaking hands and smiling at each other warmly. "What are you doing here? Oh, my God, you must be the Theater Section!"

"Part of it," he said. "As a matter of fact, I made up the name. I hope I didn't mess up your life getting you up here from Dix."

"No! Well, not much. I mean, what's it all about? How did you get in the Army? Aren't you—?"

"Too old for the draft? Yeah. I was appointed. It's sort of a special job I got roped into by General Phillipson. And you're married, aren't you?"

"Phillipson?" I glanced at my orders. "Yes, and very happy."

"So am I."

"Happy?"

"And married too."

"To whom?"

"Madge Evans."

"You're kidding!"

"Nope."

"I've had a crush on Madge Evans for years. I've seen every picture she's done! It's all right. Nancy knows all about it. Of course your wife doesn't. Sidney, that's wonderful."

"She's a wonderful lady. Your Dad told me about your marriage.

He's crazy about your wife. I called him to find out where you were stationed."

"How come?"

"I needed an experienced stage manager who was in the Army."

"You're kidding? For temporary duty? I was just about to be a combat photographer."

"Well, maybe you can go back to that when you finish this job."

"Maybe? What's going on?"

"I'll tell you." He sat and gestured for me to do the same. "Actually, I helped this friend of mine start the Theater Section. He's the one who sent your orders."

I read from the piece of paper I'd been carrying all day. "You mean, 'Major General Irving J. Phillipson, 2nd Corps Area' is your friend?"

"I've known him two or three years—he's a theater buff—and he asked me if I could help him organize Army theater units at all the camps and forts in the 2nd Corps Area. That's New York, New Jersey and Delaware."

You mean soldiers put on their own shows?"

"Exactly."

"Sounds like a good idea."

"You see, all of a sudden there are thousands of guys reporting to camps all over the country, leaving home, and they have a lot of time on their hands in the beginning. It's a morale problem. They've left home, their lives are all screwed up, they're waiting to be assigned somewhere. That's what the morale sections are for. And the theater sections will be specialists in setting up theater activity. That's where you come in—and all the guys in the next room. Come on, let's go in and introduce you."

Sidney got up and talked while he put on his jacket. We left his office and walked down the hall to a meeting room.

"They're a great bunch. We've got Staff Sergeant Ezra Stone from Camp Upton—"

"Ezra Stone? *The Adventures of Henry Aldrich?*"

"That's him. He's really in charge of the group."

He opened the door and we walked into a conference room with a long table and a chalk board, five or six guys at the table. The plump guy at the end of the table stood up and came toward me. The voice was unmistakable. Henry Aldrich!

"Hi, Alan, welcome. I met your Dad once—a great man." It had the ring of honest admiration.

Next to him, a good looking guy with a mustache, dark hair and a deep growl. "Anderson, I hope you're in shape. I'm gonna work your ass off." It turned out to be Corporal Peter Feller, theater technician supreme.

Reacting to Pete came a high, buoyant laugh from bumptious, enthusiastic Milton Rosenstock, graduate of Juilliard—our music man.

"Don't let him scare you," Rosie assured me. "Pete barks that way to keep his crew under control. Now it's a habit."

The introductions continued to reassure me about the "section": Carl Fisher, blonde, good-looking guy, company manager for George Abbott; Dave Breger, already-famous young cartoonist creating a good-natured view of the transition of young civilians into young selectees.

Suddenly the atmosphere changed. A middle-aged captain entered the room. Ezra barked, "Ten-shun!" And we were all on our feet. The Captain—the two bars on each shoulder gleaming as he approached us—managed to look stern and uncertain at the same time. He emitted a grudging "At ease," and Sidney introduced me.

"This is Alan Anderson, Captain. He's just arrived from Dix. I told you about his background as a stage manager." And then to me, "Captain French is our commanding officer, Alan." The Captain nodded toward me without change of expression or proffering a hand. As I looked at him, I realized we had met when we were both in civvies.

"How do you do, sir," I said. "I think we met once at Sardi's with Vic Samrock?" Victor Samrock was the business manager of a show I was with at the time.

"Oh, did we?" he asked without conviction. Then without enthusiasm, "Welcome aboard." He turned to Ezra as I was saying to his back, "Thank you, sir." Then I remembered. It was at Sardi's bar and when French left us, Vic turned back to the bar and said with a grimace, "What a horse's ass!"

Without further comment, the horse's ass said, "Ezra, I want to go over a couple of things with you!" and started for the door.

"Back in a few minutes, guys. We'll set up a schedule for the day."

"Come on, Stone!"

"We'll be here!" Pete growled, and we all sat again. Sidney, sitting next to me, explained the relationships. "Phillipson needed someone with enough rank to provide you all with whatever you need to do your job. That's what Dixie is here for. Excuse me, Captain French."

"That's what he was called," I said. "Dixie! Wasn't he a business manager with John Golden?"

"That's our Dixie," said Carl. "Here to help us out!"

"Where'd he get the name Dixie?" I asked.

"He talks so much about being born in Virginia," Carl replied, "so as long as I can remember, he was Dixie. But," Carl cautioned me, "not to his face. In fact, he seems to have a lot of names not used to his face. I think his father wanted to make a man out of him, so he sent him to a military school. Then he was a Reserve Officer and a few months ago they yanked him back to duty. Phillipson was looking for officers with theater backgrounds for his headquarters." Now that I'd met everyone, I had one selfish question. "Sidney, while we're on this temporary duty, where do we live?"

"Up to you. You can sign up for barracks space or you can request living expenses and live off base, as long as you're here whenever you're wanted."

Sidney left us. Ezra rejoined us before lunch and laid out the day's activities.

I spent the afternoon working with Pete on an inventory of scenery and electric equipment.

At five o'clock, Ezra blew a police whistle he loved to carry around and everyone quit work and got together in the meeting room so Ezra could give us any new assignments for the next day. Ezra said, pointing at my barracks bag, "Hey, you can't lug that all over town in the rush hour. Come on, I'll drive you home. It's not that far out of the way."

I accepted. I made a quick call to Nancy while Ezra was getting the car. I thought I should warn her that the honeymoon had not yet been put on hold.

I tossed my bag on the back seat and climbed into Ezra's very comfortable Chrysler convertible. My relaxation diminished. Ezra drove like a guy who expects the car to do the right thing no matter what he does. It was a big car but he moved around in traffic as though it were a motorcycle. I ventured a question as we swooped onto the East River Drive. "How come they put the Theater Section on an island? Doesn't it slow things down?"

He didn't answer immediately. He was in the process of tipping his head way over on one side. I thought maybe he had a sinus problem. But I guess he was watching the road.

"I brought that up with Dixie. All he said was, 'We're lucky to get what we have.' I may have to go over his head."

"How would you do that?"

"I'll call Phillipson." His head came back and then tipped again.

"You call the General?" He was staying in his lane. I guessed we were okay.

"Yep," he said and then tipped again.

"You know him? I mean, you're friends?"

Ezra took a deep breath. "Long story," he said. "I was working for George Abbott directing, casting. I'd been with him for almost two years. I was also doing my weekly radio show. Dad and I figured I was gonna get drafted before long, so he said, 'You might as well get into something that you like.' The long and the short of it was Dad had a friend who was a judge, who had taken Dad to dinner. They had a great time. Anyway, two phone calls later—" Ezra's head tipped again and I started watching the street. And then the head came back. I decided to stop worrying. "—Dad and I had a meeting with Phillipson and I made him a proposition: if I enlist, he gives me the job of organizing entertainment at Camp Upton and I put on shows for all the guys who are being ripped out of the family bosom. Phillipson says, 'That's exactly what I'd like to do. But,' he says, 'there's one catch. The Morale Branch has no budget for putting on shows.' That's when I proposed—I guess you could call it a bribe—I offered to give the Morale Branch the major share of my radio salary every week. All the Army has to do is give me Thursdays to do the radio show. Phillipson jumped at my offer, with one limitation: 'If we are suddenly in an emergency,' he said, 'or if we go to war, all bets are off. Agreed?' 'Of course,' I said. In the meantime, Sidney had made his proposal to Phillipson and so Upton became the model for what Phillipson wanted to do in every camp."

We suddenly swung into the curb. "Here we are—955."

As I thanked Ezra and opened the door, he said, "I'm glad you reminded me. I'm gonna call Phillipson tomorrow morning and say, please get the Theater Section the hell off Dixie's island."

We finished out the week. Dixie left at noon on Saturday with an order to Ezra: "You can leave at 5:30, but be sure you're on time Monday."

When I got home, Nancy said my sister-in-law Meg and my brother Quentin wanted us to spend the rest of the weekend with them. We threw some warm clothes in a bag and drove out to the country in time for a late dinner.

On Sunday morning, December 7th, Nancy and I slept a little late. It was sunny but cold. We both put on warm country clothes. After breakfast, we needed down jackets for a walk to the pond. There was a skim of shining ice. Three more inches and we could go skating.

When we got back I helped my brother Quentin bring in more

wood for the big fireplace as Meg served our lunch—good lentil soup
and ham sandwiches. Dad called—he and my mother-in-law lived
right next door—suggesting we climb High Tor later.

As we finished lunch, I turned the radio to WQXR for a little classical music. Suddenly, Schubert's "Unfinished Symphony" was interrupted by a voice that was intense, even frantic:

> "Attention! This is a news flash: Japanese war planes struck Pearl
> Harbor at 7:47 a.m., Hawaiian time."

Suddenly we were riveted to the message.

> "A huge and totally unexpected attack was made by six Japanese
> aircraft carriers and one hundred fifty to two hundred bombers and
> fighting planes against our whole fleet in harbor, sinking a large
> number of ships. First estimates are that as many as two thousand
> lives have been lost and as many more injured. President Franklin
> Delano Roosevelt spoke to the nation briefly, declaring war on Japan
> and Germany, describing the extent of the treacherous attack and
> characterizing this December 7th, 1941, as 'A Day that Would Live
> in Infamy.'"

Another voice then came on:

> "Further official word from the Office of the Chief of Staff, General
> George C. Marshall, ordered all servicemen and women who were
> not on their base to report immediately to their headquarters in uni-
> form."

I was aware that Meg, in great urgency, was on the phone, asking
Mab and Dad if they had heard the news. Evidently, they had
not. From Meg's excitement it was clear that they had all been praying
that we would get into the war before Hitler had occupied all of

continental Europe, leaving our British allies to face him alone. I felt the same but with conflicted emotions.

Nancy turned to me, her hand to her mouth in consternation. I put my arms around her.

"What will happen?" she asked trembling.

"Darling," I said. "We don't know what will happen yet." She buried her face in my chest.

Meg and Quentin were still talking to Mab and Dad. It was good news for England and for civilization. Now Congress would give the President anything he asked for. I pulled away enough to look in her eyes.

"We have to go into town. I have to get into uniform, folks."

"Of course," she said, her eyes frightened.

"I'll get our bag." Meg suddenly saw Nancy's face as I started for the stairs and she hurried to her.

When I came down I called Dad. "Sorry to miss the climb up the Tor. Give our love to Hep and tell her we're sorry not to see her." Meg and Nancy were clinging to each other. Nancy dropped her arms and made a try at smiling. "I'm all right. We have to go into town."

I gave my brother Quentin a hug. He didn't know how to handle it. The Anderson male thing.

I asked him to call our brother Terry.

"I will," he said with a smile that said take care of yourself.

Nancy and I rode in silence for a while, nothing but the sound of the car as we went down Route 9W.

"You have to put on your uniform. Then what do you have to do?"

"Well, since I'm living off base, I think I just have to report at eight o'clock in the morning."

"And then what?"

I didn't say anything for a minute.

"I don't know, darling. I guess we won't know anything for a while. But we're all on temporary duty. We'll have to wait and see. I may have to go back to Dix."

She didn't say anything.

"At least we don't have to leave each other tonight."

She moved close to me, her head on my shoulder.

Chapter 2

THE WAR
—Dec 7, 1941: In concert with the attack on Pearl Harbor, the Japanese
raided Guam, Wake and Midway Islands.
—Dec 8, 1941: Great Britain and other Allied nations join the USA in
declaring war on Japan. The Japanese mount air attacks on the
Philippines and continue to broaden attacks in the South Pacific.

The next morning, December 8, the alarm clock went off and I jumped up quickly, feeling I should get over to Fort Jay and find out what was happening.

Leaving Nancy asleep, I got into uniform, had some cereal and coffee, and went up to say good-bye. She mumbled, half awake, reaching up for a kiss. I gave her one. "I'll call you when I find out what's happening."

"Don't worry about me," she said. "I love you."

"I love you," I said. I pulled the blanket up around her chin and closed the door quietly.

Wearing my backpack in case I had to stay in camp, I started for the 1 subway station. Everyone gave me a look on the subway. They'd heard the news. A couple of people smiled.

Pete and I were the first ones in the office. Pete and Katie had married two weeks after us and they were staying with her widowed mother in Greenwich Village. I knew that he had just left Katie, too, and was probably wondering just when he'd see her next.

Pete's first words were a growl. "Well, Anderson, what'll you bet?"

I had already learned that talking tough was Pete's way of dealing with emotion. Mine was to joke about it if I didn't want to deal with it head on.

"I know," I said. "I'll bet they send us all into battle under the command of that great warrior, Captain Dixie French."

"They'll sure as hell cancel our temporary duty," Pete said. "There'll be no more Theater Section."

"Nope," I agreed. At least not for any of us young enough to go overseas. Pete lit a cigarette. I loaded my pipe and lit it.

"Seriously, Pete, what'll you do?"

"Maybe sign up for the engineers—build bridges. How about you?"

"Maybe I can still get into OCS for combat photography."

"Good God, Anderson—right up front with nothing to shoot but a camera!"

I shrugged my shoulders. "I suppose I'd rather shoot pictures than bullets."

The rest of the guys started coming in. By 8:30, everyone including Dixie was present and accounted for. Wardell came out of Dixie's office.

"Everybody into the meeting room—on the double!"

We all went in, giving Mike a few verbal jabs in reaction to his self-importance.

Lieutenant Kingsley was there before us with his usual cheerful smile. It occurred to me that both officers were too old to be sent overseas or anywhere near combat.

We all stood quietly. Dixie walked in quickly, tense and nervous. He was always uncomfortable when he had to assume a command position. Ezra was the only one who kept playing the old game. The moment that Dixie entered, Ezra blew a loud blast on his favorite whistle and then squeaked, "Ten-shun!" We all obeyed. The whistle so grotesquely overplayed the situation, all I could think of was Gilbert and Sullivan. Everyone attempted to stifle any reaction they felt. Dixie took Ezra and all of us by surprise. Dixie found the nonsense so extreme that he smiled and shook his head.

"You know, you are such a monstrous little fat jerk you're almost funny. Now, let's get to work because we've got plenty of it. I have something to read to you. The following order was on my desk this morning:

To Captain R. E. French, copy to Lieutenant S. Kingsley, Theater Section, 2nd Corps area, oh six hundred hours, 8 December, 1941. In view of the catastrophic attack on our forces in the Pacific Theater, we anticipate an immediate substantial acceleration in the nationwide draft and enlistment program. It is imperative that we meet this emergency, with a response equal to every demand for equipment and personnel. This will require a doubling or tripling of our efforts to fulfill this mammoth responsibility to provide entertainment for the added thousands of men in uniform each day."

Dixie looked up at us to see if we were surprised. Most of the faces showed great surprise and there were murmurs reflecting the same reaction. The captain looked down at the paper and continued reading.

"We expect to receive, as soon as possible, an appraisal of additional personnel and equipment requirements necessary to fully satisfy your increased activity. Signed, Major General Irving J. Phillipson, Commanding Officer, 2nd Corps Area, 90 Church Street, New York, NY."

"USA," Ezra added a split second later.

Dixie was no longer vulnerable. Evidently he had decided not to give Ezra the enjoyment of a reaction.

"Wrong, Sergeant. Your friend General Phillipson appears to have found that unnecessary. Now, may I continue?"

"Yes, sir," said Sergeant Stone.

Dixie continued, speaking calmly now. "Obviously we will have to work even harder now—as the general suggests: three times as hard. Lieutenant Kingsley and I will be discussing this challenge with you in the days ahead. Let's start today to aim in that direction: tripling our output. Thank you."

"Sir?" Ezra said quickly.

"Yes, Sergeant?"

"May I ask all of our gang to remain right now so we can discuss our immediate action?"

"Yes, Sergeant. Thank you."

Captain French departed. Kingsley stayed with the rest of us.

"I'll be good after this," Ezra said. "It looks like we've got a lot of work to do." He sat down, pulling a pad and pen in front of him. Everyone settled into chairs around the table. "First of all, Dixie doesn't know this, but I got hold of the General last night and he told me the orders that Dixie just read to us. So I said that in that case, it would double our efficiency if we could be in Manhattan and no longer at the mercy of the ferry schedule. Phillipson's going to find something. Incidentally, our temporary duty has been extended. It will now read 'until completion of duty.' "

"Are you kidding?!" said Pete, speaking for all of us.

"He also reminded me, although I was well aware of it, that this is the end of my radio show. I'll be with you guys seven days a week."

"What's Morale going to do without your money?" Rosie asked.

"It seems Washington is going to eliminate the Morale Division sometime soon and create a new one with its own budget."

The meeting ended on a high. A number of us made phone calls with the news and everyone felt like getting to work.

Two weeks went by. We were working our tails off and no one complained. Everyone got away for Christmas day and for New Year's Eve.

The draft rate accelerated rapidly. Ezra's commanding officer at Camp Upton, Captain Rankin, phoned Ezra and said he was receiving more and more men with entertainment skills and suggested Ezra come out there twice a week to go through the induction papers to decide which talent should be reassigned to which camp.

On Saturday, January 10, our whole office was loaded into Army trucks and moved to the fourth floor of 90 Church Street in lower Manhattan. Under Pete's supervision, all our theatrical equipment was transferred to a huge storage building just a block away. By Monday afternoon we were in our new offices, the phones were ringing, and we were taking orders. We occupied a whole suite on the fourth floor. Dixie had an office next to the elevators. Sidney Kingsley had an office near General Phillipson on the sixth floor. The rest of us had cubicles in one big room. We accomplished at least triple the work just by moving. We could increase that more with extra help. Dixie was actually looking happy. He found that he could run up to Sardi's Restaurant in a staff car for a martini lunch.

A week later a new notice appeared on the bulletin board, signed by General Phillipson. It read:

> WE HAVE BEEN NOTIFIED BY WASHINGTON THAT AS OF JANUARY 20, THE MORALE BRANCH WILL BE DISSOLVED AND REPLACED BY THE SPECIAL SERVICES DIVISION. SPECIAL SERVICE WILL HAVE ITS OWN BUDGET AND TABLE OF ORGANIZATION. FURTHER INFORMATION ON HOW THIS WILL AFFECT YOUR ASSIGNMENT WILL BE FORTHCOMING.

Pete and I read the notice on the way to lunch.

"This means," I said, "that Dixie will be able to give us ratings commensurate with our responsibility."

"Good luck!" said Pete. "You know what he'll think we're commensurate with!"

"Maybe Ezra can go over Dixie's head!"

"That wouldn't be cricket."

Pete glared at me. "Do you want to be commensurate or not?"

I couldn't argue with that.

☆ ☆ ☆ ☆ ☆ ☆ ☆ ☆ ☆ ☆

It was the last week of January 1942. Ezra was rehearsing a new show written by a couple of guys in his Upton group, an Army comedy

called *We're Ready* that was to open on Friday the 30th at the Fort Jay
Theater, on the island from which we had so recently escaped. Ezra
stuck his head into my cubicle on Thursday morning.

"Hey, if you want to take Nancy to Fort Jay this weekend to see the
show, let me know. I thought you might be feeling nostalgic about the
good old ferry ride."

Nancy and I had to have dinner with her mother on Friday so we
went to the Saturday show. We went backstage afterward to tell the
guys how much we liked it and I got talking to Stanley Saloman, one
of the actor-singers.

"Hey, Sarge," Stanley said as we were leaving. "You'll never believe
what happened yesterday afternoon on the ferry!"

"What? You mean before the opening performance?"

"Yeah. Some of the guys and I got out of the truck and we were
standing at the rail when this little guy walks past us. He's all dressed
up in a dark blue three-piece suit, wearing a fedora and a black overcoat. He was real natty. And then he turns around and comes back. He
sees all the uniforms and he says, 'By any chance, do you fellows know
anything about the soldier show that's opening tonight at Fort Jay?'
'Yes, sir,' I said. 'We happen to be in the show.' And then I says, 'Are
you coming to see it?' 'I thought I would, yes,' he said. 'Does it have
any songs?' 'Yeah, some,' I said. Well, we chatted back and forth and
then he says, 'How would you fellows like to do a big show—on
Broadway?' So we all said, 'Are you kidding? We'd love it, but how do
you figure we can do that?' So he says, 'Well, I'm thinking of doing
one. I write songs, see. My name is Irving Berlin.' Well, we almost fell
off the damned boat! Irving Berlin! 'You're Irving Berlin?' I said. I could
hardly believe it. So he says, 'Well, give a good show tonight. I'm
anxious to see it.'

"So he leaves us and we're peeing our pants. We've got Irving Berlin
in the audience for our opening show. Who the hell isn't gonna be
nervous with him sitting out front? Thank goodness, I think we gave a
good show in spite of being nervous, just knowing he was out there.

But we gave it everything we got."

"Jaysus, Stanley, did you tell Ezra?"

"No. I haven't seen him. He came to the dress, but I don't know where to get him."

I called Ezra at home on Sunday morning.

"Hey, Ezra, guess who was at your opening according to Stanley Saloman?"

"You got me. Mayor LaGuardia?"

"Irving Berlin."

"You're kidding!"

"I went back to see the guys and Stanley told me. They met him on the ferry going over and then he came backstage just long enough to tell them they were great. But here's the strange thing: On the ferry he asked them how they'd like to be in a Broadway show, because he was thinking of doing one."

"You're kidding! You're sure it was him?" Ezra said.

"I didn't see him. Tell you what: if we had a picture of him we could show it to Stanley and be sure."

"I'll find one."

Ezra found a picture on the cover of a musical score: Berlin sitting at the piano, looking over his shoulder at us. But by then *We're Ready* was playing in Fort Dix, New Jersey.

Three days later Ezra was in his office in Upton when the *We're Ready* outfit returned. Ezra went to the door and yelled to Stanley as he was climbing down out of the show truck. Stanley came in a minute later and looked at the picture lying on Ezra's desk.

"Is this the guy who came to the show?" Ez said.

"Sure! That's him. It looks like the same suit!"

Ezra called the Abbott office in New York and got his ex-boss on the phone.

"George, do you know Irving Berlin?"

"Of course I know him."

Ezra told him the ferry boat story and Abbott said, "Wait a minute!

Berlin did a show in the First World War. Maybe he's thinking of pulling it out of the trunk."

"What do you mean 'trunk'?"

"I don't know if it's true, but I've always heard he keeps a copy of everything he ever wrote—whether they get published or not—in a trunk, and that when he starts working on a show he takes a look at the old stuff in case he finds a number that fits into the new show."

"Thanks," Ezra said. "George, if you hear any gossip about his doing a show, let me know, will you? Maybe he'd do something for us."

"Good luck, kid!" Abbott said. "Win this thing and come back. I need you," and he hung up.

☆ ☆ ☆ ☆ ☆ ☆ ☆ ☆ ☆ ☆ ☆

Our work became routine. By the end of January we had theaters at thirty camps doing shows, and several more on the way. Several were smart enough to imitate what Ezra had started at Upton: doing adaptations from Broadway or writing their own shows and then taking the productions to other camps.

At 4:30 p.m on Friday, February 6, 1942, Dixie called Wardell into his office. "Cover my phone, Wardell. I've got to leave a little early. Tell the men to keep working until the decks are clear. See you Monday."

"Right, sir."

At 5 p.m. Dixie's phone rang. Wardell answered. "Captain French's office."

The caller said, "Is Ezra Stone there?"

"I think so, sir. Can I tell him who's calling?"

"Irving Berlin."

He held the phone closer to his ear. "Sir?"

"Irving Berlin. I'm looking for Ezra Stone. I was told he would be at this number."

"Oh! Sure, Mr. Berlin! Just a moment, please."

Wardell covered the mouthpiece and yelled, "Ezra!"

"Yeah?"

"Phone call—on the Captain's line—for you!"

"Can you take a message? I'm just on my way out."

"It's Irving Berlin!"

"Cut the crap, Wardell. See you Monday."

Wardell clamped his hand over the mouthpiece. "I'm not kidding, Ez, for Christ's sake!"

Ezra started running and talking at the same time. "Why didn't you say so?" He was puffing a little when he grabbed the phone from Mike.

"Hello?"

"Ezra? This is Irving Berlin."

"How do you do, sir? Sorry it took so long. I'm afraid I didn't believe it was you!"

"In the flesh."

"Yes, sir. What can I do for you? I'm afraid Captain French left a little early. I guess he had something pressing."

"That's all right. You're the one I wanted to talk to. General Phillipson gave me this number."

By now, all of us had heard who was on the line and we were bunched around Dixie's door, listening.

We heard Ezra say, "At your office?" Pause. "Right away." Pause. "Seventh Avenue and 52nd? Six fifty-nine. As soon as I can, sir." Pause. "Right. I'll be there."

He hung up and looked up at all the faces.

"It was nothing."

"Bullshit," Rosie said, "What did he say?"

"He wants to talk to me—right now." Ezra was walking to his cubicle to get his stuff. We were all following him.

"About what?" Rosie said.

Over his shoulder, "About an Army show or something."

"Holy shit," said Rosie. "What's 'or something'?"

"I don't know. I'll tell you Monday."

"The hell you say! Call us tonight!"

"All right—unless it's a military secret."

"Bullshit!"

"See you Monday, guys." The elevator door closed. We could hear his last line. "*Maybe* I'll call!"

We stood there watching the elevator indicator swing slowly to "one."

"Let's go have a drink!" Rosie said. We all agreed.

Chapter 3

THE WAR
—*Jan 23, 1942: The Japanese land in New Britain, Borneo, and the Solomon Islands.*
—*Jan 29, 1942: In Africa, Germany's Rommel retakes Benghazi and moves eastward, pushing back the British 2nd Armored Brigade.*
—*Jan 30, 1942: US positions on the Bataan Peninsula under increasing pressure as Japanese make amphibious landings.*

We never heard from Ezra over the weekend.

Monday morning when he came in, he went straight into Dixie's office and closed the door. Everybody went about their business. About an hour later, Ezra came out and asked Mike Wardell to try to get everyone for a meeting in the conference room at noon.

"I'll call Kingsley."

"Pete Feller is at Fort Tilden going over blueprints."

"Call him. Tell him to try to make it."

At noon everyone was sitting at the big table where I'd first met them, including Pete. "Fellas," Ezra said, "I'd better start off by telling you that this could be good news. You remember when Irving Berlin went to see *We're Ready* and he talked to Stanley about doing a soldier show? Well, it's all true. He wants to do what he calls a sequel to a show he did in World War I when he was at Upton called *Yip! Yip! Yaphank.* And he's looking for a new title."

"Irving Berlin was at Upton?" Carl said.

"In 1918. He got drafted and the General found out he was a song-writer and asked him to do a show to raise money."

"So that's what he wanted to talk to you about?" Rosie said.

"Yes. But I wasn't the first one he talked to. He's talked to General Marshall's office in Washington, and the chief of staff of the whole god-damn Army thinks it's a great idea!"

We were all amazed. We also couldn't help wondering where we came in.

"What kind of a show?" Carl asked.

"A big variety show—an all-Army show—involving at least three hundred soldiers, if it is to be like the first one. That includes everyone—orchestra, stagehands, singers, dancers, comedians—everybody."

Rosie asked our question. "How about us?"

"Well, that's the big question. He needs help. When he did the first show, he was in the Army and he directed and ran the whole thing. But this time, he needs to find everybody involved in producing and performing in it. To start with, he doesn't want to do it unless he can have at least three hundred men. I had to promise him I could deliver that."

"And you said you *could?*" Rosie asked.

"Sure. You know why? Because," Ezra took a big breath, "You see, Marshall, or at least his aides, contacted Phillipson and told Phillipson to give Berlin whatever he wanted. Phillipson contacted Berlin and said he just happened to have an Army organization of experienced theater men who could put the whole thing together, and that's when he gave him my name and the phone number here. After my meeting with Berlin, I told Phillipson what I had promised Berlin and he said, 'No problem.' "

"So who's going to set up the production?" Carl, our business managing expert wanted to know.

"We are, with Berlin's okay on every decision. So far Berlin asked me if I would direct the show."

"What did you say?" Rosie asked.

"What would you say?"

"Chicken," Pete said.

"I told him about you, Pete, and Alan. By the way, Alan, I told him about your father. I hope you don't mind."

"No," I said. "Not if it helps."

"He seems to be impressed. I told him about our man from Juilliard—Rosie. He liked that a lot. And Eddie Barclift for dance director, Johnny Koenig for scene and costume design, and I told him about the whole machinery we had in the Theater Section for finding talent. After that he said again, 'That's the one thing you have to promise me: that you can get me three hundred soldiers with the experience we need.' So I promised. 'In fact,' I said, 'you will have enough men that you can choose from the pool and pick just the three hundred men you want.' So we shook hands on it.

"The funny thing was, when we were talking about me being the director, he showed me a letter from Garson Kanin who's a first lieutenant—been in the reserves—and said he would love to direct the show. Berlin turned him down. Kanin's done a lot more than I have—had a couple of Broadway hits—and he's a great guy."

"How come?" Rosie asked.

"What I figured out is, Berlin knows from experience that to have a show done your way you've got to be in charge. He doesn't want stars and he doesn't want commissioned officers. He wants enlisted men so that nobody will pull rank. No Broadway stars, no Pentagon stars, either."

"Yeah, but he's got to work with the Army. He's already needed generals."

"Generals he has no trouble with. They're so flattered by having Berlin ask them for something, they'll give him anything! They're smart enough to know that Berlin is a civilian general of the highest rank."

"Okay, so what's next?"

"As I understand it, Berlin wants to have a meeting with each of you before he decides on assignments."

"How does Dixie feel about all this?" Carl asked.

Ezra looked at the door and then said quietly, "Overwhelmed. I hate to admit it, but I was almost sorry for him. He wants me to try to get Berlin to keep him involved. I think he's afraid we're going to get out of his control and he won't be able to take the credit for what we do."

"So are you going to talk to Berlin about him?" said Pete.

"I'm not that sorry!"

☆ ☆ ☆ ☆ ☆ ☆ ☆ ☆ ☆ ☆ ☆

We didn't hear anything for a few days and then came the meeting I've already described. That beautiful Tuesday afternoon, February 10, 1942, when I had my introduction to the guy whose songs I heard on a Victrola as an eight year-old.

Berlin was on the job every day, meeting with everyone in the Theater Section. He had Rosie come uptown to his office so he could play some of the numbers for him.

Then just as suddenly, he stopped with a phone call to Ezra who came out of his cubicle looking worried. Rosie and I were standing in the aisle. "We've got a problem, fellas."

"Yeah?"

"Berlin just called me. He's having trouble working on the show. When he did the show in 1918 he was in the Army, living with the guys day and night. He knew what they were feeling, how they reacted. What he wants is to move the whole operation out to Upton so he can be surrounded by Army soldiers. He wants to hear them talk, get them into conversations. He says it's the only thing that will help him write the show."

"Why not?" said Pete, joining us. "Makes sense."

"He's right," Rosie agreed and then produced a joyful guffaw. "Wait'll Dixie hears that!"

"I don't want him to hear it yet," Ezra said. "I'll tell you what: I'd better call the General, but not from here. I'm going down to the lobby to call from a pay phone. Cover for me with Dixie. Anybody got any change?" We gave him some quarters and then we all went with him to the elevator. He pushed the button.

"What'll we tell him?" I said.

"I don't know." The door slid open. "Think of something." As the door started to slide shut he had another idea. "Tell him I got a better offer!"

"Thanks a lot!" Rosie yelled.

"I'll be at my desk," Pete said.

"Me, too," said Rosie.

"Thanks, guys," I said.

Five minutes later, Captain Richard E. French came out of his office and went to Ezra's cubicle. A moment later he was looking at me.

"Where's Stone?" he said crossly.

I rose hastily. "Isn't he in his office, sir?"

"Of course he's not in his goddamned office, Anderson. Why would I ask where he is if he were in his goddamn office?!"

"Oh, I remember, sir. He said he had to go out to phone his father. His father lives in Pennsylvania."

"I know where his father lives, goddamn it!"

"He was under the impression that you didn't like having him make long—"

"Oh, shut up, Corporal!"

"Sergeant, sir."

"Not for long, if you go on giving me a pain in the ass!" He marched back to his office and slammed the door.

☆ ☆ ☆ ☆ ☆ ☆ ☆ ☆ ☆ ☆ ☆

Ezra returned from the pay phone looking cheerful. "It's all set. Phillipson's going to contact Baird and have him set up our move."

It didn't take long for Major General Phillipson to convince Colonel C. W. Baird, the commanding officer of Camp Upton, that he could earn Brownie points in Washington if he would invite Mr. Berlin to put his whole show together at Upton. Baird was very enthusiastic. Berlin happened to be with us when the call came through, so we heard Berlin's responses to Baird.

"Wonderful! I'm glad you called! . . . When? . . . Well, I'd like to be out there as soon as possible. I want to finish revising and writing some new songs right there with all the guys around me. I haven't been around soldiers since 1919 so I'm a little out of touch, although I imagine that some of my lyrics will still be appropriate. For instance, 'Oh! How I Hate to Get Up in the Morning!' I don't imagine that's out of date. . . . Good! The sooner the better. Oh, and by the way, there are a few things I'll need out there. . . . Uh, yes, I'll make a list. . . . No, I'll bring my own piano. . . . Thank you, Colonel. I'll wait for your call."

He turned to us, "Well, that was quick! You guys better help me put together a list of what we'll need."

"Yes, sir," Ezra assured him.

Berlin put on his inveterate fedora. Call me as soon as you've figured out the move. And, Rosie, don't forget the Buick!" The door closed behind "General" Berlin.

"What the hell is the Buick?" Pete asked. We all turned to Rosie who gave us his gutsy guffaw. He obviously loved the story.

"It's his special piano. There's a guy in Brooklyn that invented them. Now he's got four of them. One at home, one in his New York office, one in California and the fourth is the Buick. He travels with that."

"What's special about it?" Pete asked. "Does it write the songs for him?"

"No, you jerk! It plays in all keys. He found out it was easiest for him to compose in F-sharp, so he plays on the black keys where F-sharp is centered and the singer is hearing the key he needs to work in." Pete still wasn't satisfied.

"Do all composers need special pianos?"

"Of course not. But Mr. Berlin says he never could take the time to learn how to read or write music. He said he had too much to do. He wrote down some words and then he worked out a melody that went with them. When he was satisfied, he memorized the song and played it for his pianist friend, Helmy Kressa, who wrote down the music as he played. And if Helmy is in California and he's in New York, they do it over the telephone. The point is, when we go to Upton, the Buick goes with us.

We learned a lot more about our new general as the days went by. One thing was about his working habits. Habitually he worked at night, rose late in the day, saw friends or associates in the afternoon or early evening and then went to his piano. In 1918 he was twenty-nine years old, and all of a sudden he got his draft notice. As the war went on, they started drafting older men. Berlin found himself a private in the United States Army where his bedtime was 9 p.m., and he was blown off his Army cot by a bugle at 5 a.m., just when he was used to hitting the sack. Then he would put on his olive drab uniform, wrap his legs in puttees, button his woolen jacket tight around his neck, pull his cap onto his head, and stagger into formation in the morning cold, his eyes bleary with lack of sleep.

It hadn't been long before he followed his normal habit of putting his innermost thoughts into song and wrote, "Oh! How I Hate to Get Up in the Morning." And he meant every blessed word! Including, "Someday I'm going to murder the bugler, someday they're going to find him dead. I'll amputate his reveille, and step upon it heavily, and spend the rest of my life in bed."

Actually, he had been saved an act of murder because his CO, Major General J. Franklin Bell, the commanding general of Upton, learned that he had a songwriter under his command. Bell interviewed his new private and asked if he could put his talents toward doing a show that would earn money.

"When parents come to Yaphank to visit their beloved sons, they have no decent place to stay. We'd like to build them some facilities and we need about thirty-five thousand dollars to do it. Do you think you could raise some of that money?"

Berlin had leaped at the opportunity. The first thing the general did was make him a sergeant, and the next thing, after Berlin had admitted that he composed best at night, was to excuse him from all duties or schedules, including reveille. He wrote several more songs and got some Broadway friends to supply comedy sketches and various other necessary talents, like set and costume design. Berlin was performer, director and producer of the show. *Yip! Yip! Yaphank* was scheduled for eight performances but had been such a hit that it ran for thirty-two and could have gone on. Instead of the General's more modest hope of $35,000, it took in $83,000. A few months after this successful venture, the war ended and Berlin took off his uniform and resumed his normal habits.

☆ ☆ ☆ ☆ ☆ ☆ ☆ ☆ ☆ ☆ ☆

General Phillipson didn't waste time moving us to Upton. He issued formal orders, sending copies to Upton, to Washington, and to the Theater Section, which of course included Captain French and Lieutenant Kingsley.

The next day, when the orders reached Dixie's desk, he came roaring out, shaking the infamous document under Ezra's nose. "You're responsible for this!" he bellowed, his complexion dangerously flushed. "Making Berlin think he'd be better off putting the show together way the hell out at Camp Upton instead of right here at the heart of the biggest show town in the world!"

Ezra got as far as "Sir, Mr. Berlin said—" which doubled Dixie's fury.

"Mr. Berlin said! You stupid, fat, ugly little bastard! You know damn well he would have been far better off right here at the center of operations for the Corps Area—" he gasped for more air, "instead of going way the hell out there in the boondocks, where there's nobody who knows a goddamn thing about putting on a show!"

He started for his door, but *that* tore it. Before Dixie could get there, Ezra's rebuttal rang in his ears: "No one who knows about putting on a show, *with the possible exception, SIR, of every one of us fat little bastards!*" And with that, Ezra turned on his heel and went to the elevator, leaving Dixie to slam his own door.

Silence on the fourth floor of 90 Church Street.

☆ ☆ ☆ ☆ ☆ ☆ ☆ ☆ ☆ ☆ ☆

Moving to Upton would make problems for some of us. After an extensive six-week search, our intrepid wives, Nancy and Katie, who had become close friends, had found small but adequate apartments across the hall from each other. The $35 monthly rent for each fit nicely into our sergeant's pay, augmented by their minimal pay from their jobs with Elmo Roper's polling company. The apartments were on East 47th Street, precisely on the land that was later occupied by the United Nations building. Pete and I had been enjoying our honeymoons while commuting daily by public transportation to the Theater Section. We knew it was too good to last. However, there was every prospect that we would have our weekends together—for a while. And then if the show really did open in New York for four weeks, we'd be together with our wives every day.

☆ ☆ ☆ ☆ ☆ ☆ ☆ ☆ ☆ ☆ ☆

Two weeks later Ezra drove Mr. B. and me out to Yaphank, Long Island. We pulled up in front of the headquarters building promptly at 11 a.m., and Captain A. H. Rankin, the Post Special Services Officer, was just as promptly waiting for us. Rankin proved to be an amiable man who clearly respected what Ezra had accomplished at Upton and was obviously pleased to be hosting Irving Berlin.

Rankin led Mr. B. and all of us on a walking tour. He added Corporal Dave Supple to our group as note-taker. Dave had experience as a stagehand and a court stenographer when he was inducted, and Pete Feller had grabbed him for the "Upton Opry House."

Rankin described the camp layout to Berlin briefly and then took us to the CCC (Civilian Conservation Corps) barracks, where we were to house our three hundred men. The barracks were a leftover from President Roosevelt's New Deal of the '30s. They had been kept in reasonably good shape. Building T-11 had been chosen as our headquarters. For Mr. B. it had a bedroom, bath, and workroom with space for the Buick; also, a meeting room, bunk space and bath for Ezra, Rosie, Pete, and me. Berlin wandered about examining the rooms, looking out the windows at our surroundings.

"What are all those tents and buildings next to us?" Berlin asked.

Rankin joined him at the window. "The barracks are for your company. The tents you see are part of the reception area where a lot of the new recruits are housed while they're with us."

"Perfect," said Mr. B. "I'll get a chance to talk to the guys who are just getting into uniform and starting training."

"Absolutely." Rankin was enjoying his role as host.

Berlin looked at Rankin with a smile. "Do they have a bugler?"

"Oh, yes! But if he bothers you, I can move him further away."

"That's okay" Berlin said, smiling. "I've got earplugs."

"Are you going to use that song again?"

"You bet I am! When can we move in?"

Rankin looked around. "We'll need a week or two to spruce up these buildings. They haven't been in use for some time. But if you think the arrangement is okay . . . "

"It's perfect, Captain," Berlin said. "We'll take it!" And then he turned to Rankin. "There's just one thing missing."

"Yes, sir?"

"Lunch!" That was another thing we had learned about our new boss: he was slim, but he had a hell of an appetite.

☆ ☆ ☆ ☆ ☆ ☆ ☆ ☆ ☆ ☆ ☆

The next three weeks, while the CCC barracks were being fixed up, we were busy in New York. Berlin had pulled out all his scores from *Yip! Yip! Yaphank* and he was starting work on new songs. While we wrapped up our Theater Section assignments, Ezra requested Phillipson's authority to start searching the whole country for talent for the new show. Phillipson cleared this with Colonel Frank

McCarthy, General Marshall's aide, who had been appointed to work with us. As soon as we had the authority, Ezra got us together to compose a letter to go out to every Army installation in the country requesting that we be sent a resume of every Army man who had indicated an entertainment skill among his experience qualifications. Berlin called Ezra at 90 Church to say that the letter was great. And then he said, "By the way, Ezra, the letter should include the title of the show."

"What do we do for a title?" Ezra asked him.

"I just finished a song," Berlin said. "Listen to the first verse." In his squeaky-husky voice, he sang over the phone. Ezra turned the phone so we could hear. "'This is the Army, Mister Jones—no private rooms or telephones; you had your breakfast in bed before, but you won't have it there anymore.' How do you like it?" asked Mr. B.

"It's great," Ezra said. "But we still need a title."

"That's the title! *This Is the Army*. Okay?"

"Sounds great!" said Ezra.

"Ask the boys," said Berlin.

"Hey, guys, Mr. Berlin suggests *This Is the Army*. What do you think?"

"Great!" we all said.

"Good," said Berlin and hung up.

Replies started pouring in to the letters that went out by telegraph. We sorted them by skill and experience. We then submitted each qualifying name for a vote by each member of the Theater Section qualified to judge that individual skill. Ezra and Berlin would check every final choice after which orders for transfer were issued from Colonel Baird's office and countersigned by Phillipson's office. Men soon would start arriving at Upton with orders to report to *This Is the Army* Detachment for temporary duty.

It was already the middle of April and much had to happen by July 4th: songs had to be written, sketches written, men auditioned and rehearsed for the various roles for which Ezra and Mr. B. chose them. Once the songs, numbers and sketches were selected, set and costume designs had to be created; and, finally, constructed, built or sewn; rehearsals had to be conducted of the orchestra, the soloists, the chorus, the sketches, and the continuity—all of which had to be ready for the opening night on July 4, 1942, at a theater yet to be chosen. Nothing to it! Four weeks in New York City, all the profits sent to Army Emergency Relief Fund, and the men could return to their regular duty.

"Before you know it, Anderson," said Pete, "you'll be a lieutenant in the Signal Corps Photographic Division, ready for duty! And Berlin will be back in Hollywood with Bing Crosby, Fred Astaire and Ginger Rogers."

"And then," I replied, "Katie and Nancy will be waiting for letters telling them how much we miss them and unable to tell them where we are."

Pete looked at me for a moment. "Okay, Anderson, I shouldn't have brought it up. We've got work to do."

Chapter 4

THE WAR

—*Mar 11, 1942: General MacArthur leaves the Philippines making his celebrated assurance: "I shall return."*

—*Mar 27, 1942: Britain's RAF and the American volunteer aviators are forced to abandon Burma.*

—*Apr 9, 1942: Bataan Peninsula position collapses: 75,000 men taken prisoner including 12,000 Americans. The Death March commences.*

Irving Berlin was packing his bag for Camp Upton. Ezra and all of us were cleaning out our desks in the Theater Section at 90 Church Street. Pete Feller and two helpers were rushing with last minute shipments of equipment. Kingsley was organizing a replacement staff to continue our Theater Section functions.

Suddenly, Dixie's door swung open, banged against the wall, and he was facing us with a triumphant, twisted smile. "Hold it up, fellas, right where you are! General Phillipson has a little additional job for you right here in dirty old New York, so just forget about lollygagging on the beaches of Long Island!"

It seems the Mayor of New York, Fiorello LaGuardia, otherwise known as "The Little Flower," had called a meeting with military commanders: General Phillipson, representing the Army, and the commanders of the Third Naval District, the US Marine Corps and the New York area Coast Guard. Our flamboyant mayor—opera buff and theater lover—had had a brainstorm. Because everyone connected with Broadway entertainment—movie theaters, concerts, operas, radio shows, football and baseball managements—had done so much for all the servicemen and women who were in uniform in the New York area, he felt it was payback time. Let's have all the military services put on a show for all those generous civilians. We'll call it *Entertaining the Entertainers.* And who did the Mayor call? Among others, his pal, Major General Phillipson. And who did the General call? Captain R.E. French, the keeper of the seals—the seals that bark and flap and roll over for the crowd—Ezra and his gang!

Like everybody in New York, we all knew who "The Little Flower" was, because he ran the city so well and he was legendary for reading the Sunday funnies on radio. It would interrupt the work we were to start, but since the message came from the General, an appeal would be difficult.

"Have you told Mr. Berlin about this?" Ezra asked Dixie innocently.

"No, Sergeant, I haven't. *You're* going to have to take care of that since the order came from your pal, the General. And I suggest you call him right away."

Fiorello had already booked the Metropolitan Opera House and set the date for April 27 at 11:30 p.m., so that the performers in all the Broadway shows—even those who were working—could be there. April 27 was less than two weeks off.

Ezra was caught in the middle. General Phillipson called and asked him to let Berlin know there would be a slight delay. Poor Ezra! We listened to his side of the conversation. It wasn't hard to imagine Mr. B's.

"Hello, Mr. Berlin? It's Ezra. Have you heard from General Phillipson? . . . Oh, well, I was hoping he'd called you. . . . No, I won't be leaving today. . . . No. . . . That's why I hoped the General had called to explain. There's something the General wants us to do before we move out to Upton. . . . Well, it's another show. . . . No, it's nothing like that. It's just one performance. . . . No, sir, it has nothing to do with you or with *This Is the Army*. It's for the, uh, Mayor of New York."

Ezra went on to explain that the Mayor had decided the armed forces ought to thank all those who had done so much for us. "He thinks we ought to produce it as our thanks. . . . That's right, sir. He thought you'd be in favor of it, I guess." Ezra listened for quite a while, then he said, "But, Mr. Berlin, I can't tell the Mayor or the General that they are sabotaging your show. Someone with a little higher rank would have to do it. And the trouble is, my only leverage is through

General Phillipson and he loves Mayor LaGuardia!... But, sir, it won't take that long. It will all be over on April 27th, then we can get right out to Upton and start tryouts and casting and you can get acquainted with today's GIs." And then he was listening again.

"Believe me, this show isn't going to take the punch out of *This Is the Army*. I guarantee you, no one will remember the Met show two days after it's over."

"I'll keep in touch with you every day, Mr. Berlin." He listened for a moment and then he hung up.

"What did he say?"

"He said, 'I'd better not say what I'm thinking. You're too young to hear it' — and he hung up."

☆ ☆ ☆ ☆ ☆ ☆ ☆ ☆ ☆ ☆

The whole Theater Section was involved in producing the Met show.

For two weeks we all worked incredibly hard. Ezra called Mr. B. regularly to ask how he was doing and whether he wanted to play something for someone. Everything was rehearsed in bits and pieces. There was no way to have a complete run-through of the show.

Finally we were ready and the curtain went up on *Entertaining the Entertainers* at 11:50 (twenty minutes late), on April 27. The first half hour almost sent everyone home. It took that long for the bands and glee clubs of the Police and the Fire Departments and the Department of Sanitation to get off the stage. The Navy Band then came on and picked up the spirits. The Ellis Island Coast Guard almost lost them again with a demonstration of flag signaling. And then the show took hold of them with a series of sketches and comedy song and dance numbers. They were sitting up straight, suddenly clapping and roaring with laughter. Before the laughter had ended, Rosie and his jazz band broke into a wild medley of fine jazz that brought the house down. There were cheers and endless curtain calls before the house lights went on and everyone could stagger, gratefully, home to bed.

☆ ☆ ☆ ☆ ☆ ☆ ☆ ☆ ☆ ☆ ☆

General Phillipson expressed his appreciation to all of us for getting a superb show together on short notice and his great thanks to Mr. Berlin for his patience. Mr. B. was almost able to smile. The general then issued orders to move the Theater Section gang to Camp Upton immediately to assist Mr. Berlin in preparing *This Is the Army* in time for that opening performance on July 4th, 1942, at the Broadway Theatre in New York City.

Nothing to it! Just write, cast, design, build, rehearse, and open in— eight weeks!

While we were busy with the Met show, the mail continued to pour in to Upton from Army bases all over the country, from dancers, singers, musicians, actors, magicians, acrobats. Every couple of days, trusty Corporal Wardell went out to Upton and brought the replies to 90 Church. We marked the ones we wanted, Wardell took the "yes" pile back to Upton, and Upton sent telegraphic transfer requests. An impressive talent pool for *TITA* (*This is the Army*) was piling up at the CCC barracks.

☆ ☆ ☆ ☆ ☆ ☆ ☆ ☆ ☆ ☆ ☆

On Wednesday, April 29, two days after the curtain closed on the Met show, Ezra drove Mr. B., Pete, Rosie and me to Camp Upton. We arrived at our CCC barracks just in time to see a Brinks armored truck pulling up in front of Barracks Building T-11, our home and office for the next month.

With a clipboard in hand, the driver jumped down and approached us as we got out of Ezra's Chrysler.

"Mr. Berlin?" He looked us over doubtfully. The three of us turned and pointed to Mr. B., who was just emerging from the front passenger seat.

What precious cargo was being delivered under armed guard?

"I'm Mr. Berlin," said our dapper leader, standing by the car. As the driver approached Mr. B., he answered our question with one of his own. "Where do you want your piano, Mr. Berlin?"

That was it! The "Buick," the mysterious piano Rosie had described, had arrived by armored truck! It traveled in a handsome wooden case with large rubber-tired wheels. We watched almost reverently as it was moved inside to Mr. B.'s study. We all crowded into the room as the hinged door of the moving case was unlocked and swung open. A built-in ramp was put in place and the Buick rolled majestically into its new home under Mr. B.'s instructions. Next, the piano bench was brought in. The boss pulled it into position and sat down to demonstrate the magical key-change lever. Above the keyboard a gold-lettered label bore the identity of this extraordinary instrument: Calvin L. Wesser, Monarch Piano, New York, Upright Grand.

A bizarre idea suddenly struck me: If any of Mr. B's four special pianos got into the wrong hands and fingers, they might compose one of *his* songs! Mr. B. did not want to risk losing control of any aspect of his work, hence, the armored truck. Even though it would be hard to slip a piano in your pocket and run off with it, he felt safer having it under lock and key until it was literally in his hands.

For the next thirty days Mr. B.'s fingers were on the black keys day and night, working, reworking, trying the results out on us. Now and then he stopped to sleep, or to eat. It proved impossible to anticipate when Mr. B. would get hungry—and when he was ready to eat, nothing else would do—so Captain Rankin arranged with the officers' mess to deliver food to the boss when he got hungry. For the rest of us, we ate when the mess hall was serving food.

With each new song, Mr. B. would want Ezra, Rosie, the dance directors, whoever might be involved with the song or dance, to drop everything and listen. And then he would want an answer. What do you think? Is it okay? Or do you like this ending better? Then Johnny Koenig, our set and costume designer, would want Mr. B. to look at some sketches for the opening number, for the Navy number, for the ballet; or one of the directors would want Mr. B. to hear a voice, hear a gag, a reading, watch a special act.

In the meantime, Ezra and I had chosen my first and second assistant stage managers: Jus Addis, first assistant, Hayden Rorke, second assistant—and they joined me in arranging auditions of the talent that was arriving every day from bases all across the country. Then Mr. B. (by now we all referred to him by this title), Ezra, Rosie, Pete, the choral director, and the dance directors, Bob Sidney and Eddie Barclift, decided who was up to singing what, who would dance in what numbers, who would be in the orchestra, what stage hands we would use. We had six rehearsal pianists. Mel Pahl was also an arranger and he worked primarily with the dancers. Morty Kahn and Murray Newman worked with the soloists. Morty was Mr. B.'s favorite; the others filled in wherever needed. They could play anything, any rhythm, any key, any tempo.

Berlin had chosen three songs from *Yip! Yip! Yaphank* to be used in *TITA:* "Oh! How I Hate to Get Up in the Morning," "Ladies of the Chorus" and "Mandy." He had written an astonishing nine new songs between January and the end of March, which left him with another seven or eight to do. By walking around Camp Upton and getting into conversations with enlisted men and officers (mostly the former), hearing them, seeing them, he got a sense of what the songs should be about, what kind of jokes the men laughed at, what they missed in being away from home.

Mr. B. struggled with "What the Well-Dressed Man in Harlem Will Wear." He had a lyric and the melody line but he wanted it to work with dance, tap, whatever the boys could come up with. One night he kept us all wakeful until early morning, trying it and trying it again. And when he had it, he woke Ezra and we were all awake. Ezra dragged the phone to the piano and Mr. B., sitting at the keyboard, called Helmy Kressa, waking him to sit by his phone with his music paper. Mr. B. then played and sang in Yaphank, Long Island, and Helmy, with his ear next to his home phone, wrote down the music score at his home.

"Did you get it, Helmy? . . . Are you sure? . . . I'll play it once more and you can check it."

And he did the whole thing again. "Is it right, Helmy? . . . Every note? . . . Great! Good night!"

And then Mr. B. turned to us. "Is it all right? What do you think?" It took several minutes of reassurance from everybody to have him finally look happy. "It's gonna be great!" he said, and went to bed. We all sighed in relief as Ezra looked at the closed door.

"I hope nobody blows a bugle tomorrow morning! Let's go to bed, guys."

"Yeah!" said Rosie.

Mr. B. slept until noon. Captain Rankin had been as good as his word. General Bell had let him sleep in 1918. We'd better do the same thing in 1942!

Ezra drove Berlin into town on Saturday afternoon to be with his family for twenty-four hours. Pete and I hitched a ride to East 47th Street in the backseat of Ezra's Chrysler. Nancy and Katie were waiting for us.

"I was afraid he'd decide to work seven days a week," Nancy said, as she and Katie greeted us.

"I don't think so, honey. He loves to see his family on the weekends."

When we arrived late on Sunday afternoon to pick up Mr. B., he came down to the door and said, "Ellin wants you guys to have a cup of tea before we go."

Ellin Berlin served everyone tea and Mr. B. finished a sandwich to keep him going. His wife was a charming hostess and we were conscious of the family warmth that was in those rooms. She could be amusing and relaxed with us all, asking about our families and about our work on the show. When we left and we were all chatting on our way back to Upton, I couldn't help thinking: four guys who feel lucky in love.

Our small group started out in building T-11 with Mr. B. and the Buick. The next barracks building housed the rest of the creative people on the show: the dance directors, set and costume designers, orchestral arrangers, rehearsal pianists, my assistant stage managers. And as the days went by, we were very quickly filling three more barracks, as we chose all the performers, musicians, stage hands, costume tailors, makeup artists, publicity men, box office men. The only Army members of the show that were chosen solely by Mr. B. were the music pluggers. They were crucial to the Irving Berlin Music Publishing Company because as soon as the show was announced to the public they would promote the songs with the radio stations and music stores. The income this would produce, plus the ticket sales for the show, would earn many thousands of dollars for the Army Emergency Relief Fund. The group of song pluggers worked out of Mr. B.'s office under the direction of Captain Walter Schumann, who had worked with Berlin for years as a civilian. Schumann had been a reserve officer before the war began in Europe and had been called for duty. Through the influence of General Phillipson, he had been assigned to Mr. B. and the *TITA* Detachment. They were vital in helping the songs popularity and assuring the substantial success for Mr. B.'s support of the Army Emergency Relief Fund. Through no fault of their own, the song pluggers were to be at the center of an argument between Mr. B. and Ezra Stone several months later.

☆ ☆ ☆ ☆ ☆ ☆ ☆ ☆ ☆ ☆ ☆

Organizationally, in Army terms, *This Is the Army* was a group of detached soldiers, the grouping officially known as the *This Is the Army* Detachment, with an official detachment number, 0665-A. Captain Rankin assembled a separate cadre of soldiers assigned to the *TITA* Detachment for administrative purposes. This cadre was made up of administratively trained soldiers, necessary until such time as the *TITA* Detachment could handle its own administration. None of them were to be in the show. The cadre included an acting first sergeant, two drill sergeants, a supply sergeant and a company clerk. Officially, Rankin was their commander as well as ours.

In show business terms, Irving Berlin was our producer, our boss. Working under the producer were Ezra as the director; Rosie, the orchestra conductor; Pete, the technical director; Edgar (Nelson) Barclift and Bob Sidney, dance directors; Johnny Koenig, set and costume designer; and I was the production stage manager with four assistant stage managers. Bob Sidney wasn't drafted until February 7, so he was a newcomer at Upton who very soon became one of the most important creative figures in the show, staging all the big chorus numbers and most of the dance numbers.

We began to develop the show from the song and dance numbers that Berlin was writing; the specialty acts that we found among our talent pool; and the sketches which were taking shape from the writing talents Ezra had in the Opry House group at Upton, plus writers that Berlin brought in from Broadway.

As the show numbers began to come together, the next step was to begin rehearsing, right there in Upton. Bob Sidney and Barclift started working with the dance numbers. Rosie, with Joe Lipman's assistance, began to put together his orchestra, using some of the musicians from Upton and a great many more from the talent pool. In 1918, with *Yip! Yip! Yaphank*, Berlin had brought in a few civilians and he did so again for the Broadway production: choral director Lynn Murray, two or three orchestral arrangers, and Broadway's Hassard Short to supervise the lighting for the opening. His engagement of these Broadway veterans was our first inkling of the nervousness that our dear Mr. B. exhibited as the opening night drew closer.

Rehearsals at Upton were very limited because of space requirements. But the restrictions served to shake down a lot of talent auditioning, shifting the best voices and the best dancers to the most demanding performances, and saving the best sketches and dropping the weaker ones. Rosie honed his orchestra down to a forty-four-man group of superb quality—men who came to us from well-known bands, including Tommy Dorsey's, Jimmy Dorsey's, and a wide variety of both popular and classical orchestras.

Because we were a detachment with no organizational chart that would make us eligible for a given number of noncommissioned officer rankings — sergeants, corporals, etc. — we had no way to reward those who had the greater responsibility or who deserved the greatest credit for their creative contribution to the show. Actually, because these men were all in the US Army, we had been in a position to choose any talent we desired, regardless of what they would have been paid as civilians. It allowed us to assemble a production that no producer would have been able to afford financially!

Every morning, our cadre of non-*TITA* guys would take over. Our men had to fallout (line up in platoons) in front of each barracks building, have a roll call, and then be dismissed for breakfast. After breakfast, they were marched to a drill field to do some routine marching training, including handling of rifles. At 10:00 a.m., the show would take over. The rehearsal schedule was posted on the bulletin board at T-11. At that point, Bob Sidney, Eddie Barclift, Rosie, Lynn Murray and Ezra would work with the men until 4:30, with a one-hour lunch break at 12:30. Before supper and in the evening, you could hear the sounds of violinists practicing their bowing, soloists exercising their voice range, drummers working their wrists with paradiddles, trumpets being lipped, trombones sliding, the reeds of clarinet and oboe, the deep throat of the bass fiddles — and it was only the beginning.

Everybody was hungry for the real work space, be it dance floor, rehearsal stage or orchestra pit.

Finally, the casting was complete, all parts were filled. It was June 3 — one month and a day from Opening Night. We posted a list of the names of everyone in the TITA company who should pack their gear, ready for a morning train to Penn Station, New York. The phones were busy that evening making calls to families. My phone message carried a special weight. June 3rd was also Nancy's birthday.

"We'll be together every day until the show closes."

"You'll get tired of me!"

"Oh, sure. It'll be awful."

"Do you think Irving and Ellin talk this way?"

"I think he's still pretty crazy about her."

"Can you imagine having someone write those songs for you?"

"I could try, but I don't make any promises!"

"Just come! It's a great birthday present!"

While we were loading the trucks in the morning, the Brinks armored truck arrived at T-11 to pick up the Buick. Now we knew it was the real thing!

"It's O.K., Sarge, they're going to 'This Is The Army'."

Cartoon by Robert Day

Chapter 5

—*May 6, 1942: The brave defense of Corregidor ends with the surrender of 15,000 US and Filipino troops. The Japanese begin moves against the Aleutian Islands to divert Americans from Midway area.*

—*June 4, 1942: US torpedo-bombers attack Japanese ships. We sink four of their carriers within 24 hours.*

—*June 17, 1942: New Allied line in North Africa broken by German forces. Withdrawal of 8th Army HQ is necessary. Tobruk is now isolated.*

It isn't easy to move a piano from Yaphank to Broadway, but it's considerably more difficult to move a company of over three hundred men, each one with two barracks bags, pack, rifle, bayonet, Army belt, canteen and steel helmet.

In one month our detachment had grown from about ten young soldiers and a fifty-three year-old civilian to an oversized, temporary company of three hundred ten men, and the same remarkable civilian. He had under his command what Ezra had promised him: even more than three hundred hand-picked men! A mongrel group still known as the *This Is the Army* Detachment, #0665-A, assigned to Special Services Division. Mission: temporary duty performing a show for four weeks on Broadway to raise funds for the Army Emergency Relief Fund, to assist needy families of servicemen.

It required five special coaches on the Long Island Rail Road to move us to Manhattan.

When the men got off at Pennsylvania Station, they were *on their own* for living quarters and food. No more barracks or mess halls were available. In lieu of the CCC barracks and the mess hall, the Army was obliged to pay what they call "rations and quarters" of $2.35 a day. We were free to squander this munificent sum as we chose. That adds up to $70.50 per month. Not much in New York City for rent and three meals a day.

The majority had either their own funds, family help, were sharing with someone, or improvisations we'll never know about. The Andersons and the Fellers still had their honeymoon apartments on East 47th Street.

Army salaries are based on rank. Initially, the ranks in our detachment were just what they held when they joined us, which meant that most of them were privates. A few were corporals or sergeants. Ezra was a staff sergeant. Chester O'Brien had to relinquish his rank of first sergeant when he joined us, but Mr. B. assured us that he would seek help in Washington when the show opened. In the meantime, we still had the administrative cadre that Rankin had assigned us in Upton. They would remain with us on a temporary basis.

In the case of commissioned officers, having left Camp Upton and Captain Rankin, we would need a commanding officer with a high enough rank to obtain the facilities from the Army that we needed to function. The CO would also need another officer for administrative assistance. Phillipson's office found us both. The commanding officer was a genial, rugged, ex-cop, Major Simon P. Ambraz. If the name was reminiscent of Simon Legree, it was misplaced. He was temperate, thoughtful and evenhanded with his authority. To further soften his handling of power, our new CO was clearly dazzled by being assigned to Irving Berlin and his company of performer-soldiers.

As his assistant, Phillipson assigned First Lieutenant James Fuller, Supply Officer. He also had no experience with show business. He was trim and young, very pleasant and pleased to be in our glamorous world. Ambraz gave Fuller all of the boring detail work so that he could spend most of his time being sure that Mr. B. and the show had what was needed from the Army.

To further glamorize assignment to our detachment, our official Army headquarters was in the Broadway Theatre, in New York City's theatrical district. Conveniently, the theater had offices one flight up the elegant marble stairway, above the theater lobby. This became company headquarters for the officers and for the administrative cadre.

To afford Mr. B. a place to work with relative quiet for concentration, the Buick was put in a large anteroom in the mezzanine next to the ladies' room (quiet except when our leader was at the keyboard).

We needed four rehearsal locations. First, the stage of the Broadway Theatre, where we rehearsed all the ensemble numbers, and ultimately where the show would be performed. Bob did all the ensemble direction: the Opening, the Navy Number, the Closing, plus "Ladies of the Chorus." Bob and Eddie Barclift split up most of the choreographic work. Barclift did "That Russian Winter," "I'm Getting Tired So I Can Sleep" and "A Soldier's Dream." Fred Kelly, brother of Hollywood star, Gene Kelly, did "Mandy" with Bob Sidney. "What the Well-Dressed Man in Harlem Will Wear" was done by Pete Nugent initially and then by Pete and Bob Sidney working together. Gradually, with Mr. B.'s blessing, Bob took over supervision of all staging except for Barclift's numbers.

Second, in the lounge of the Broadway were the soloists, the sketches and the specialty acts with Ezra, Rosie and usually Mr. B. Third, in the National Theater on 41st Street the pit was used for orchestra rehearsals with Rosie and often Mr. B. Fourth, the stage of the Ritz Theater on West 46th Street was used for choral rehearsals with Lynn Murray, our only civilian director.

I had a stage manager present at each of the rehearsals to make sure that everyone showed up on time at the right place and to coordinate with Ezra for the overall direction of the show.

There was one almost fatal breakdown in communication between Army and show business in our progression from Upton to Broadway.

At 3:30 p.m., the day before rehearsals were to begin, the men were busy getting settled with places to live and were due for a meeting at the theater at 4:00 p.m. Ezra, Rosie and I were in the Broadway Theater lounge discussing the daily schedule. We had just agreed we would start rehearsals at 10 a.m. each day. Mr. B. would come in at noon, his favorite hour to start work. At that point, Major Ambraz appeared hurriedly.

"I'm glad you're all here. I've just been on the phone with Upton this morning and we've worked out a daily schedule." He held up two sheets of paper.

"We'll announce this at the four o'clock company meeting." He read it to us.

> "'MONDAY THROUGH FRIDAY, THE DETACHMENT WILL FALL-IN PROMPTLY AT 7:00 A.M. IN FRONT OF THE THEATER AND MARCH TO OUR OPEN PLAYGROUND AREA ON 54TH STREET AND TENTH AVENUE, WHERE TRAINING AND DRILLING WILL BE CONDUCTED UNTIL 11:15 A.M., WHEN COMPANY WILL RETURN TO THE THEATER, ARRIVING AT 11:30 TO BEGIN REHEARSALS.'" HE LOOKED UP AT US. "THAT LEAVES YOU THE REST OF THE DAY FOR REHEARSALS."

Rosie and I looked at Ezra. The ball was in his court. "Major, if I may, the show opens on July 4th. We only have four weeks to rehearse the show involving over three hundred men. I don't think Mr. Berlin was planning on doing anything for those four weeks but rehearse."

"Can't put it off, Sergeant. I just received this letter from Colonel Supplee. The letter explicitly points out that Mr. Berlin wants the men to be fully trained soldiers."

"Yes, sir. We'll have time everyday to work on that—after the opening."

"Here's what Mr. Berlin told the Colonel. It's in his letter." He waved the paper at us and then started to read.

> "I don't want the men viewed by the public as pampered actors wearing Army uniforms. I want them to look like a company of well-trained soldiers who happened to be professional entertainers."

He looked up at Ezra and smiled. "That's gonna take a little work, Sergeant."

"But, sir—"

"Sergeant, I can't afford to disobey an order. The colonel is just following Mr. Berlin's wishes." He waved the letter again and headed for the bulletin board. Ezra picked up the only telephone in the lounge and I put the phone list in front of him that I carried with me day and night. He tried Berlin's office. He had been there and had left an hour ago. He called Ellin Berlin. She hadn't heard from him since he left for the office. General Phillipson was on his way back from Washington. Captain Rankin didn't think he should try to overrule the Colonel. It was 3:55. We went into the theater for the meeting. The Major read the schedule from his piece of paper. They all stared.

The next morning, the company formed at 7 a.m. and marched to the parade ground—otherwise known as an empty lot—and went through a rugged training schedule. We then marched back to the theater and after a ten minute break for a drink of water, began rehearsals. Bob started work on "Ladies of the Chorus." Ezra and Rosie decided to work on solos. They started with Earl Oxford.

Mr. Berlin arrived at the theater promptly at noon, looking forward to an afternoon and evening of rehearsal. Berlin first watched Bob Sidney working on "Ladies of the Chorus." The performers were staggering around, trying to respond to Bob's pleas to put some life into it. Berlin looked unhappy. The number wasn't working. He went to the lounge where Morty Kahn was accompanying Earl Oxford in the song, "I Left My Heart at the Stage Door Canteen." Earl's voice sounded as though he'd left it in the outhouse. Our song pluggers had been assuring Berlin that this one was a sure hit.

Berlin turned to Ezra and Rosie, "What's wrong with everyone today? They act as though they'd been up all night!"

"They might as well have. They've been on the drill field since 7 a.m."

"They've what?" Berlin said.

"We've all been up since 6 a.m. with your training program."

"My training program?" asked Mr. B., who still found it difficult to believe that anyone rose at that hour on purpose.

"Drilling," said Ezra. "You told Colonel Supplee you wanted them to look like real soldiers."

"Drilling? They're not supposed to do anything but rehearse the show from now until the opening!"

"Mr. Berlin," Ezra said, plaintively, "Major Ambraz told us it was all your idea!"

"What? 7 a.m. training? My idea?"

"He was reading a letter from you—"

"Get him in here! Right now!" Berlin said.

"Mr. Berlin, the Major read us a letter he got from the Colonel."

"Just get someone in here who can straighten this out. I don't care what somebody said in a letter!"

"Alan, get the Major, will you?"

I phoned the Orderly Room on the second floor. Corporal Emil Skarda, my company clerk, answered.

"Where's Ambraz, Emil? Berlin wants him on the double."

"He had to go home. His wife was sick." I hung up and gave them all the message.

Berlin yanked his jacket off and pulled his tie loose.

"Sir," I said, trying to calm everything down, "why don't we walk up to the Orderly Room where there are three phones and we can get hold of someone?"

Earl Oxford met us on the stairs. "I'm sorry, Mr. Berlin. I'm just tired. We had a hell of a workout this morning. I hope we don't have to do that every day!"

Mr. B. said, "You're never going to have to do that again, Earl. Go on home and have a good night's sleep. I'm going to send everybody home. I'll see you at ten tomorrow, after a good rest."

"The drill's canceled for tomorrow?"

"It's canceled until after the opening, Earl. It never should have happened."

"Thank you, sir. Shall I tell everyone I see?"

"Yes, thank you, Earl." Earl dragged down to the lobby.

"Alan, get the word to everybody: Rehearsals are canceled until tomorrow at ten."

"Yes, sir."

"Now, let's get on the phone, quick." We went up to the Orderly Room. Skarda and the rest of the cadre had all gone to lunch. Our phone calls revealed that Colonel Supplee and his wife were taking a long weekend. I dialed Major Ambraz's number. The Major answered. "Ambraz here," came the gruff reply. "The Major, sir." I hastily shoved the phone in Berlin's hand. We listened.

"Major, this is Irving Berlin. I just tried to reach the Colonel. . . . Yeah, Supplee. . . . I was going to tell him he's sabotaging my show. . . . That's right, getting all these guys up at dawn when they have to rehearse for ten hours after you're through running them around in circles. Major, I want you to cancel everything immediately except my rehearsals until the show opens—or there's not going to be a show. The first call for these guys is going to be 10 a.m. for rehearsals from now until opening night. . . . You can't what? Look, Major, if you can't authorize, you'd better look for another assignment because the first call I'm going to make when I hang up is going to be to Washington. . . . That's right, General Marshall, the Chief of Staff, so you'd better authorize. . . . It'll get you in trouble? Major, you're already in trouble."

"Sir, Mr. Berlin," Ezra was urgent. "Mr. Berlin, I've got Mrs. Phillipson. She's getting her husband."

Berlin looked at the phone in his hand which held a waiting Major Ambraz. He shoved it in my hand.

"Get rid of him, Alan." he said.

I took the phone and gently hung up, saying nothing. Better to blame it on a bad connection. As I did so, I heard Ezra say into the other phone, "He's right here, Flossie."

Ezra handed the phone to Mr. B. with a sigh of relief.

"Hello? Mrs. Phillipson? This is Irving Berlin. . . . Thank you." He was calm now, waiting. "Good afternoon, General. . . . There's no need to apologize, but we've lost a full day of rehearsal and we need every minute we can get." He listened, looking off, nodding.

"Thank, you very much, General." He hung up, looking at Ezra and Rosie and me.

"Let's go have a martini."

We all agreed. It was the first martini the boss had had with us since we left Yaphank.

☆ ☆ ☆ ☆ ☆ ☆ ☆ ☆ ☆ ☆ ☆

The next day everything went beautifully. Earl sang like a dream. The so-called "ladies of the chorus" were funny. The orchestra was magnificent. The dancers didn't miss a beat. The sketches got all the laughs. Everyone was excited.

It was Monday afternoon, June 22. Two more weeks to go. Mr. B. and I were in the back of the National Theater. Mr. B. started pacing back and forth listening to the orchestra. All of a sudden he wanted a phone. I took him out to the front lobby where there was a booth and gave him some change. He left the booth open and got the operator and made a collect call to someone in Hollywood. I heard him ask, "Is Frank Tours there? . . . I'll wait." I knew Tours was an old friend of his, a well-known conductor/arranger/musician that he'd worked with on several shows.

"Frank, you're not working are you?... That's great. Listen, please fly in here tomorrow. I want you to hear the band."

Evidently, Tours tried to argue his way out of it. But Berlin wouldn't give an inch. Tours arrived the next day and came right to the theater. Following Mr. B.'s orders, I took him up to the balcony of the National Theater, where he could listen to the band without being seen by anyone. Rosie was finishing up a rehearsal of the overture. Then he rehearsed the second act ballet number. Berlin kept watching Tours, who listened to the ballet music and then "What the Well-Dressed Man in Harlem Will Wear" twice. Tours grabbed Berlin's arm and walked him out to the lobby.

"The kid is great, Irving! He handles those guys like silk. And he knows that music like you'd written it just for him. It's beautiful."

"You're sure?"

"I'm sure. God, there's nobody who could do better than that kid. What's his name?"

"Rosenstock."

"Well, don't lose him. He's superb. Rosenstock knows that music better than I ever could!"

Tours went back to Hollywood. I never said anything to Rosie — or anyone but my wife.

Two days later, Berlin was watching the sketches in rehearsal. All of a sudden he got up and walked out.

The next day, Mr. B. called me into his office. "Alan, you know Josh Logan, don't you?"

"Yes, sir."

"Well, he's coming in this afternoon. I want you to take him to each of the rehearsals with me so he can see how we're doing."

Berlin discovered that Joshua Logan had enlisted in Army military intelligence somewhere in Virginia. He got someone in Marshall's office to spring Josh, and twenty-four hours later my old friend was with us. I had known Josh since 1938 when he was directing summer stock and I was stage managing for him as an apprentice.

I got cabs for them and took Josh and Mr. B. from one theater to another. Josh heard the chorus, he heard the orchestra, he watched the dance numbers, he watched the sketches.

"Are they funny, Josh?" Berlin asked.

"Irving, they're great. But I do have a couple of thoughts."

Berlin listened eagerly.

"Get rid of all the costume-uniforms and use real ones. Costumes are okay for anything else, but when they're supposed to be soldiers, they should be soldiers. Change the order of the first act and put some music behind the acrobats that helps to dramatize what they're doing." Josh stayed with us for a week. He gave Ezra some timing notes for the sketches. Ezra was grateful. They were good ideas. And then Josh found Berlin. "Irving, I have to go. You've got a great show. It'll run forever."

"We've got less than two weeks," said Berlin.

"I'll bet when this show opens, the reviews will be so great they won't let you close."

☆ ☆ ☆ ☆ ☆ ☆ ☆ ☆ ☆ ☆ ☆

Josh was right about everything, but we didn't know it until later. In the meantime, he went back to Virginia to become a spy and I went to our 47th Street apartment with Pete and decided we should all celebrate by going out for dinner. It was Saturday night, June 27th. We opened in one week! I reminded Nancy of this when we were getting ready to go out to a restaurant.

"It might be time for a celebration. Guess what?" she said, grinning at me. I looked at her for a moment and I had a feeling she was blushing.

"You're not!" I said.

She did a kind of half shrug, half grin. I put my arms around her. "It's too soon to be sure," she said. "Okay," I said. "Mum's the word. Oops, there I go." She gave me a good punch and we went to dinner.

☆ ☆ ☆ ☆ ☆ ☆ ☆ ☆ ☆ ☆ ☆

Two days later, Monday, June 29, five days before the opening, at 9:30 a.m., I was headed for the theater entrance when a taxi door opened in front of me and an officer who looked somehow familiar climbed out.

"I'll be a son of a bitch! It's Marc!" Like me, Marc Daniels had been a stage manager; he had taught at the American Academy for Dramatic Arts when Ezra was also teaching there. He had been recommended to Phillipson for the Theater Section and had spent a few days with us just after I joined. But he had applied for Officer Candidate School at Fort Benning and when his acceptance came through the day after he joined us, he decided he should go.

"Excuse me, *Lieutenant* Daniels!" I said, giving him a quick salute.

"Hi, Top Kick," he returned the salute and grinned at me, reaching for my hand.

I was puzzled. "What are you doing here?"

"I'm reporting for duty," he said. "Phillipson had me assigned here as soon as I graduated."

"I hope you learned a lot," I said. "We're going to need some training for these guys as soon as we open and we've got the time."

I explained that Berlin was worried about the company not looking like a snappy Army outfit and I told him about the debacle when Ambraz tried to start a training schedule at 7 a.m. every day before rehearsals.

"You mean you started training at seven in the morning and rehearsed until 10 p.m.?" Marc was incredulous.

"It never happened," I said. "When Berlin saw the dancers staggering through a number, he found out why and Phillipson chewed out Ambraz."

"Jesus! That's crazy. We can do something after the opening, but not before."

"Right! Boy, am I glad you're here."

"Me, too. I'd better go check in with the Major. I still have to find a place to live. I'll see you later," Marc said.

I went off to rehearsals, but I was puzzled. Why did Berlin change his philosophy? Why did he want to mix up show business and officers? Maybe it would be okay. Marc knew show business. He had been a stage manager. After all, they were sensible types.

☆ ☆ ☆ ☆ ☆ ☆ ☆ ☆ ☆ ☆ ☆

We did our first complete run-through at the Broadway Theatre on Tuesday night. As we expected, it was a long one. A show of that size, involving such a large number of people, was bound to be lengthy and exhausting. The virtue of the suffering is that all the problems of moving smoothly and promptly from moment to moment, from scene to scene through a whole two-hour entertainment involving a huge number of participants, are encountered and either solved or noted for a later solution. We finished at 1:00 a.m. and came in at noon on Wednesday to spend an hour on notes so we'd be prepared for the full dress rehearsal on Wednesday night.

Our first dress rehearsal on Wednesday was pretty smooth, considering all the costume changes and lighting cues that were brand new. Henry Jones was beautiful in "This Is the Army, Mister Jones," singing his verse of the song, querulous, cynical: "This is the Army, Mr. Brown,/You and your baby went to town/She had you worried, but this is war/And she won't worry you anymore!" Rosie and the orchestra were flawless. Earl Oxford supported Mr. B.'s confidence in "I Left My Heart at the Stage Door Canteen." It should be a big hit. And Mr. B. with the old timers from *Yip! Yip! Yaphank* were charming. It was the first time we'd heard Mr. B. do a full performance of his solo on "Oh! How I Hate to Get Up in the Morning." Everybody was in the wings to see and hear. The suffering and bitterness in the words he had written in 1918 had lost none of their heartfelt resentment. He *still* hated to get up in the morning.

We had a small audience for the final dress rehearsal on Friday. Mr. B. had invited a few trusted friends and his wife, Ellin Berlin, came with their oldest daughter, Mary Ellin. This was a tiny audience, but of course an especially responsive one, because they were all connected with the show in some way and responded to every moment from the first to the very last. The love from this intimate audience gave us a great feeling of confidence.

☆ ☆ ☆ ☆ ☆ ☆ ☆ ☆ ☆ ☆ ☆

Opening night our hearts were pounding. Now we were faced with the real test of all that had been prepared just for this first show. As curtain-time approached, I accomplished one of the pleasant duties of the stage manager: going through the side door into the auditorium for a brief check on how quickly the audience was filling the house. It was truly a radiant sight — a rare combination of civilians and armed forces personnel, a splendor of beribboned, handsome uniforms of the Army, Navy, Air Force and Marine Corps, and a sea of beautiful bare shoulders, sparkling, lush evening gowns, black ties, gleaming white dress shirts; people waving, chattering, beaming with expectation. The house was filled to the brim.

I went back on stage, waiting, then ready. Warning light to conductor. Audience settling. House lights dim halfway. Audience sounds down to a hush. Cue the overture and wham! — the opening music, every face riveted to lighted curtain and *the music*. Rosie and his glorious orchestra inspired. Everyone backstage was on their own starting line. The overture ends. Applause. Curtain up. Opening chorus and we're off! The show is on!

When the curtain opened on the next to closing number — Mr. B. sitting all by himself on an Army cot, with puttees wrapped around his legs — the audience was a sea of adoration, vocal cheers, and vigorous hand clapping that went on and on. It seemed they would never let him get into his ardent, wholehearted complaint — "Oh! How I Hate to Get Up in the Morning" — a passionate statement of the universal pain which tugs deep at the heart of every soldier impassively torn from the tranquility of sleep.

The reviews the next day were uniformly ecstatic. It was proclaimed to be not only the best show of the year, but several critics used the most glowing words in their pens or their typewriters: *One of the best shows ever produced.* Kate Smith had bought a box for the opening performance for ten thousand dollars and Josh Logan was there to see that his prediction was *on the nose:* the run was extended from four weeks to twelve, sold every seat, and drew an offer from Warner Brothers for the movie rights.

When news about *This Is the Army* spread across the pages of every paper and found the attention of the First Lady, she saw the show immediately, came backstage and greeted Mr. B. and the cast. She then called the President and insisted that he ought to see the show. He agreed, and as a consequence, in the planning of a road tour, Washington, D.C. was to be the first stop.

In the meantime, our Broadway run was stretched to twelve weeks. During those weeks on Broadway members of the cast, to some extent, settled into their professional lives. They had all been facing service in the Army in a world war, going through the uncertainty of the weeks in camp not knowing what was to come. Suddenly they were out of the war for a few weeks, doing a show, going back to their life's work. And then the show was a hit and was going on a few weeks longer. So they found friends, relaxed into this familiar life, almost forgetting at times that it was temporary. Of course, there were differences when they were off stage in their Army uniforms. They were drilling, training, saluting officers and taking a big cut in salary!

Once our New York run was extended, Lieutenant Marc Daniels convinced the Major that he should organize and run a regular training schedule and that we no longer needed a cadre because we had plenty of guys in the outfit that could conduct the administration and training. Marc set us up with two platoons divided into eight squads with two acting first sergeants, Chet O'Brien and me, and eight acting sergeants to head up the squads. The problem of getting a Table of Organization and real ratings for the whole detachment still had to be faced.

For our training, we continued to use the empty lot at 54th Street and Tenth Avenue that the City had loaned us. We assembled at 2 p.m. and took the roll every Monday, Tuesday, Thursday and Friday, and drilled for two hours. We skipped training on all weekend and matinee days, Wednesday and Saturday. After two weeks of that we were a snappy-looking bunch in spite of the differences in age, height, weight, girth and physical abilities. We hid the clumsy ones in the middle, put the sharp ones at the edges and with Rosie's band whipping up our spirits, we looked mighty good.

This Is the Army Detachment was unique! *TITA*, with its platoon of black singer-dancer-comedians *was the only racially integrated military organization* in the United States in World War II and was to retain that unique position throughout the war. What's more, that platoon was the sharpest-looking in the detachment, to the credit of Sergeants Clyde Turner and Jack Brodnax. These two expert entertainers had earned their stripes in infantry outfits before they joined us.

The biggest star of all of our black guys was an incredible comic dancer, Sergeant James A. Cross, known in the vaudeville world as "Stump Cross."

The truth is, when *TITA* marched down the streets of America, there was enough ham actor and showmanship in our guys to make them look like ten-year veterans. Admittedly, there were several who were far from perfect examples of the rugged fighting man, but they knew how to *act* it. We got cheers and applause every day when we marched back and forth between the theater and the playground.

In addition to the training, we assigned traditional Army work details. I posted a duty roster on the stage door bulletin board each week. It made for some unusual contrasts.

One morning, I was just going into the theater when a limousine pulled up in front of the marquee. The chauffeur jumped out and opened the door. Private First Class Burl Ives climbed out of the car wearing his fatigue uniform. Burl, a very well-known folk singer, had been drafted and ended up in the show with nothing to do but sing in the chorus, except when there was a party or some special appearance when he might do some entertaining. But on this particular day, he knew from the company duty roster, he was right on time for his 9:00 a.m. latrine duty.

BUY U.S. WAR SAVINGS BONDS

UNITED WE STAND

THIS IS THE ARMY
☆ THE BROADWAY THEATRE ☆

Chapter 6

THE WAR

—*Jun 23, 1942: Rommel pushes east, crossing into Egypt.*

—*Jun 25, 1942: Fifty-one year-old Dwight D. Eisenhower, who served as MacArthur's Chief of Staff, appointed to command American land forces in Europe.*

—*Jul 1, 1942: The first heavy bomber from the 8th Army Air Force, a B-17 Flying Fortress, lands at Prestwick, Scotland.*

—*Jul 4, 1942: At Sebastopol the Germans take more than 90,000 prisoners. An even greater number of Russians are killed.*

—*Aug 19, 1942: Disastrous attempt to land at Dieppe. 3,350 men killed or captured. Failure of the mission due mostly to German intelligence intercepting Allied communications.*

"Now I know why you're springing for dinner at Sardi's, Anderson!" Pete raised his glass of wine. "Here's to the first baby in *This Is the Army!*" We all clinked.

Dr. Ralph Hurd had confirmed Nancy's suspicions.

"Well, we thought you deserved to be the first to know, since you were involved."

"Wait a minute!" said Pete. "Involved!?"

"We never would have found the apartment without Katie's help!" Nancy explained.

Pete turned to Katie. "That's a new one. They're going to blame it on the apartment!"

"Actually, I don't think we would have had the guts without you two," I said.

Katie went around the table and gave Nancy a kiss.

Pete growled. "Don't encourage them! We'll end up having to sit with the kids while they go out." Pete's consistent belligerence I regarded as a sure sign of his affection. Nancy wanted to know what was good for babies.

"You won't find it on *this* menu," Pete warned her.

"Don't let Vincent Sardi hear you say that!" I said. "Italy is full of healthy babies."

☆ ☆ ☆ ☆ ☆ ☆ ☆ ☆ ☆ ☆ ☆

When we got to the theater, Mr. B. was already there. He didn't usually show up until curtain time. He greeted us with a big smile.

"Ladies, I've got news I think you'll like. Your husbands are going to be in New York for a while longer. We've booked the Broadway Theatre until September 26. And then we go on the road for four or five months."

"Thank you for telling us, Mr. Berlin," Katie said. "It's probably selfish of us with the war going on but Nancy and I love hearing it."

Berlin leaned closer to the girls, and spoke confidentially. "Don't tell them but we're finally going to get some ratings for all the boys. Alan, why not tell everyone to stay after the show tonight so I can tell them the news. I think they'll be happy."

"That's great news!" I said. "I'll have Jus and Hayden tell them to stay for an announcement."

Mr. B. waved to us all and headed for his dressing room. Katie and Nancy kissed us and left.

I went to find Jus and Hayden.

Jus Addiss and Hayden Rorke had lived and worked together in the theater for several years before the war. They'd started producing their own shows out of town. Jus had done some directing and a great deal of stage managing. Hayden was a very good character actor. When Jus received his draft notice, Hayden had volunteered immediately so that they reported for duty at Camp Upton at the same time. Ezra had pulled them into his Opry House group immediately. Jus was older than I by a couple of years; Hayden by another two or three.

Jus and Hayden had done as asked. Everyone gathered on stage behind the curtain after the show. Mr. B. started out with the plans for a road tour and then said, "We're going to start with Washington because the President has requested that he see the show." There was a roar of delight. "We'll finish the road tour on the Coast and then we'll make a movie at Warner Brothers." Another happy roar. "But one more thing: before we leave Washington, we've been promised ratings for the whole outfit." That got the biggest roar of all.

"I'm really glad you guys are finally going to get some recognition you can put in your pockets. The show is a big hit and I've got Ezra and all of you to thank for that." Hayden applauded and everybody joined in.

"I don't know what will happen after the movie but it sounds like we'll be busy until next summer. So get a good sleep and keep doing great shows." With a wave, Mr. B. left one big bunch of really happy guys.

We played eight shows, Monday through Saturday, and now added training for four afternoons every week. I already knew how to be a Stage Manager so I decided to put in some time being sure I knew how to be a good first sergeant. Even so, the show was our prime concern. The show was going well—selling out for every performance. We had made very few changes. After the second week, we did drop a song and dance number called "Aryans Under the Skin." It attempted to portray the Japanese and the Germans in a satiric routine. With the seriousness of the war, Mr. B. decided it was just a little too coy. Nobody argued.

In spite of the smooth running show, there was one disturbing change in the atmosphere: the question of "credits"—who should get credit for the success of the show. Such credit was usually registered by news stories that reflected successful aspects of the performance. Columnists are always looking for stories about the Broadway shows and they often approach performers to help them get such stories. Until the ratings actually came through, we had no way to reward soloists, important parts, and exceptional performances with higher ranking and pay.

Mr. B. issued a rule through his press representative, Sergeant Ben Washer. The following notice on the bulletin board brought the problem to a head. It read in part:

YOU ARE REMINDED THAT NO ONE IS TO TALK TO THE PRESS ABOUT THE SHOW OR THEIR OWN PERFORMANCE. IF YOU ARE APPROACHED BY THE PRESS, REFER THEM TO ME IN ALL CASES. DO NOT GIVE OUT OR DISCUSS STORIES ABOUT THE SHOW OR ABOUT YOURSELF OR ANY PERFORMANCE. SIGNED, SERGEANT BEN WASHER.

To some of our cast who were experienced professionals, this seemed unfair. However, it seemed unlikely that anyone wanted to disobey the policy. We wanted to be in the show and there was no question that we had Mr. B. to thank for our being there.

But one prominent person could not contain his displeasure—Ezra. Not long after we opened, Ezra started to gripe about the lack of credits to individuals in the show who deserved more. "You'd think the whole damned show happened by itself. Nobody did anything but the guy with the piano."

"Ez," said Rosie, "isn't it better to be doing this show than lying in the mud afraid to stick your head up?"

"That's not the point. Someday the war will end and he will get credit for This Is the Army. When we go back to the theater after the war, shouldn't we also get credit for what we did to make this show a hit?"

"It says 'director' right there in the program."

"Rosie, you know what I mean. When there's an interview or an article about the show, my name never shows up. Larry Weeks gets more press for throwing three balls in the air."

It was true that Ezra had been an especially important factor in organizing the show. Mr. B.'s choice of Ezra for director, was based on his directing experience certainly, but also on his experience gained in putting on shows at Camp Upton, a role created out of his own initiative. However, Mr. B. followed an instinct he had from his years in Tin

Pan Alley, on Broadway and in Hollywood. He picked Ezra in part because he was not an officer or a star. He would not let Ezra or anyone else in the show become stars. The program credited Ezra as the director. That was as far as Mr. B. would go. I realized, as did those who were aware of the history of *Yip! Yip! Yaphank*, that Berlin's name was the only one that stood out in that show.

Another problem arose of much less importance. There is a special privilege for hit shows called "house seats." It is customary for the authors, stars and directors of a show to have a few pairs of seats reserved for his or her use at every performance. It meant that they could promise especially good seats to friends or relatives who could then pick up and pay for the seats when they came to the show or any time before. However, if your house seats aren't used, you get charged for them unless you remember to cancel them before the show date.

By the end of July, when Mr. B had made it clear that the show was going on and on, he called Ezra into his dressing room. Pete and I were waiting for him because we were supposed to have a quick dinner together. About ten minutes later, when Ezra hurried out, we walked over to Eighth Avenue to one of our inexpensive restaurants—Italian or Chinese or nondescript—something we could afford.

"Well, what was all that about?" Pete asked Ezra.

"He said he had heard that I still wasn't reserving any house seats and I told him that was true because I didn't want them. They were a nuisance. And he kept insisting that I would need them and I could have all I needed."

"Ez," I said, "maybe he was just trying to do something nice, a peace offering."

"Yeah, well, you could be right, because when I turned down the offer, he said, 'I gather you're unhappy about not getting more credit for the show.' I said something like, 'It would seem as though no one assisted you in getting this show on stage.' And he said, 'You're credited with being the director and you're credited for your performance.'

He also said, 'This is the way the Army wants it. There are no prima donnas in the show. It's just the Army show. Period. My name's the only name they want up there with the name of the show.' So I said, 'Okay, you're the boss and there's no way we can change that, but I don't want any house seats because they're a damn nuisance to keep track of and to remember to cancel.' So he said, 'You're just being a sorehead.' And then I said, 'It's dinner time and I'm getting hungry. Do you have anything else you wanted me for?' He said, 'If you change your mind, let me know.' I said, 'Thanks,' and left."

"Well, that's it, babe. You might as well forget it," Pete said.

"You know, Pete, if we live through the war, a lot of us are going to need work when it's over so it wouldn't hurt if our names were not entirely ignored until Armistice Day. It wouldn't hurt the show. In fact, the more people hear about the show, the more tickets we sell. Publicity for what *we* do doesn't take anything away from *him*."

"Our names are in the program," Pete said. "He gives us credit for working on the show. He just doesn't want the newspaper columns to pick out individuals for credit."

"Why the hell not?"

"Ez," I said, "Ben tells me the Army wants it to be an Army show, not a regular Broadway show, and they also want it to be Irving Berlin's gift to the war effort."

"What about what we're giving to the war effort?"

"We're in the Army. With us it's not a gift. We have no choice."

"The hell we don't!"

Pete responded, "You'd rather be doing something else?"

Ezra didn't answer, but by the look on his face, I wasn't sure what he might be thinking.

He started to jump on that one, but our food came.

Ezra and Mr. B. just stopped talking to each other completely. Since they were never on stage at the same time except for the curtain calls, the audiences were unaware of anything being amiss. But we were fearful of it getting its own publicity! In the meantime, Mr. B. leaned on Bob Sidney and Rosie and me for discussions of performance problems and general operation of the show.

Thursday night, September 17, as the curtain calls ended and the band was putting away their instruments, Marc came to me and said, "Get Rosie and Ezra and Pete and Chet and the platoon leaders and meet me in the lounge."

Fifteen minutes later we were all together. "I think I've got a great idea," Marc said. "This could take care of Mr. B.'s desire that we look like a first-rate outfit, it would be great PR for the show, and it could set a pattern for us wherever the show goes!" We all looked at him. It was hard to see any excitement in Ezra's face. "Our arrival in Washington, D.C.," said Marc, "gives us a glorious opportunity to have the whole outfit march into the nation's capital like a crackerjack outfit, led by the world's greatest soldier-band with Rosie leading 'em with his baton, trumpets blaring and drums booming, playing 'This Is the Army, Mister Jones!' and some other rousing marches, all the way from the railroad station to the National Theater! We'll alert the press ahead of time and get people in the streets and knock the town dead!"

"Yeah! Yeah," said Rosie. "Fantastic! I love it! I love it! Wait'll I tell the guys!"

We all took in Rosie's reaction with pleasure. Even Ezra came along. "It's great, Marc. Nothing would do more to keep up the guys' self-esteem," —he ended with a bitter jab, "while they wait to get some stripes on the arm."

"Come on, Ez," said Rosie, giving him a gentle sock on the shoulder, "The ratings will get here."

"Just one thing," Marc added, "I've got to get Ambraz to go along."

"We've got some insurance there," I said. "If Ambraz hesitates, we can get Mr. B. to tell him he wants it."

"Okay," Marc said. "I'll get him first thing in the morning."

Ambraz thought it was great. Berlin loved it. Ambraz loved Marc. Almost everybody was happy. We still had nine days before the New York closing to work on the details.

Rosie picked the musicians who played band instruments and rehearsed them in three marches to start with. He also managed to avoid the overweight or flat-footed. The main number was our show theme, "This Is the Army, Mister Jones," for which Willard Jones and Joe Lipman did a brass arrangement. The others were Sousa military marches that everybody in the country knew.

Two dancers, Gene Nelson and Paul Draper, would lead off ahead of the band, one carrying an American flag and the other a show flag. The show flag was designed and painted by Al Rubens, using the show title in red and a yellow background echoing the theater curtain that Al had designed. Next was Bandleader Rosenstock, flourishing his baton as only one could who had earned a degree with honors in conducting from Juilliard. And then came the whole company in platoons.

We rehearsed the march routine between the theater and the Tenth Avenue playground several times that week. With the band music playing, the company seemed to want to look as good as the band sounded. Sergeants Jack Brodnax and Clyde Turner requested that the detachment's black members be allowed to form their own platoon rather than be scattered through the company where they could not demonstrate *their* ability. It was a great success. They were so good that the competition they gave the other platoons raised the level of the entire company.

We developed a regular audience going across town in both directions, that came out every day once they heard us going by. The kids ran alongside shouting. People put flags in their windows and there were signs saying "Go Get 'Em!" and other expressions of patriotic fervor. Everybody was grateful to Marc for his initiative. The newspapers picked up on the excitement Berlin's show was causing in the theater district.

The twelve weeks in New York was almost over and there was never an empty seat right through the hottest days of August, the least popular theater month for people to be in the city. The Broadway run ended with its ninety-seventh performance on Saturday,

September 26, 1942. We were to begin our road tour with two weeks in Washington followed by a week in Pittsburgh, a week's furlough, and two weeks in Philadelphia. The rest of the tour to the West Coast was still being booked.

Broadway had been wonderful, but our excitement reached a new peak with the prospect of marching into town and playing the National Theater in Washington, including a command performance for our Commander-in-Chief.

We worked out a travel plan that meant almost the whole outfit could get off the train and march to the theater without carrying anything but their backpack and rifles. All their barracks bags traveled with the scenery on trucks, which meant Pete and his stage crew had to miss the march to make sure everything got packed and shipped.

The march to the National Theater from the train was a triumph. Ben Washer had alerted the papers and they played it up. The police had put barriers along our route and a police car escort front and back. It looked like the Fourth of July had hit town all over again.

We had arranged for the whole company to stay at the Red Cross, with the exception of those who wanted to pay for hotels themselves. Our march ended at the Red Cross facilities. The trucks brought the baggage. Marc and I went to the desk. The lobby quickly filled behind us with forty or fifty men including the black platoon led by their leader, Sergeant Jack Brodnax.

The Red Cross manager, identified by a nameplate on the desk as Philip Bronson, an elderly gentleman, balding, on the chubby side, neatly dressed but somewhat nervous faced with such a large group, welcomed us politely and then, with equal politeness, said that our black members would be welcomed at their own Red Cross which was in a slightly different part of town.

"I'll give you that address," he said and started to write.

I glanced at Marc. He glanced at me and then turned to our host. "That won't be necessary, Mr. Bronson," Marc said politely, "unless the other Red Cross facility is large enough to accommodate all of us. You see, Mr. Bronson," Marc explained quietly and firmly, "We travel together, we work together and we *live* together!"

"I see. We were told that there would be more than two hundred men. The, uh, other Red Cross could not accommodate that many."

"We were told," said Marc, "that you had room for as many as three hundred men here."

"Oh, yes, we do," and then he gestured toward the mass of men who were sitting, standing, chatting quietly. "I wasn't told that you were not all. . . . That is—"

"White?" asked Marc pleasantly.

The manager nodded and smiled, grateful that Marc understood his predicament.

Marc leaned closer to Bronson with the pleasantness gone from his voice. "In that case," said Marc, "if you will show me where there is a phone, I will call the newspapers, and in the meantime, we will wait here in the lobby."

"The newspapers?" The manager looked past us at the sea of khaki that filled the lobby.

I called out to the waiting men. "Take the load off, guys. We'll have a short wait. Jack, would you pass the word to the guys outside?"

"Okay, Sarge." Jack was Sergeant Jack Brodnax.

"You're going to wait here?" Mr. Bronson asked. We nodded. "The whole company?" he asked unhappily.

"That's General Marshall's orders."

"I see. Uh, General Marshall. That would be—"

"General George C. Marshall. Yes," Marc replied, "the Chief of Staff."

There was an infinitesimal pause before Mr. Bronson replied.

"I'll be right back," disappearing into the office.

He returned in about five minutes. I timed him.

"Just have your men register, Lieutenant."

"All of them?" Marc asked.

Bronson nodded. He couldn't bring himself to speak. Marc turned to me. I handed him the alphabetical and numbered roster of the entire company which had been signed by each of the men who had chosen to stay at the Red Cross.

"This will serve as our registration, Mr. Bronson. I will sign the register for the company. As you will find, two hundred forty-three men have already signed."

"Two hundred forty-three," he said rhetorically, looking at the roster. "Fine."

"By the way," I said, "there is no designation of race on the roster."

"I understand, Lieutenant," he said.

As soon as all the guys were checked in at the Red Cross, Marc, Pete and I cut out for our hotels. Katie and Nancy had spent a day moving us out of the 47th Street apartments before joining us in a modest theatrical hotel that I knew of from playing Washington before the war. I called Ben Washer from the hotel so that he and Mr. B. would be aware of the evening's events.

The morning paper carried a colorful story about our parading into town. Nothing about the Red Cross. The evening paper repeated much of the earlier story and then quoted a proud announcement by Mr. Bronson that the Red Cross was accommodating two hundred fifty men from Irving Berlin's wonderful Army show, including the talented Negro singers and dancers."

When I saw Ben at rehearsal he said, "Good work. I think you guys made some history."

We opened in Washington on Tuesday night, giving us extra time for our first setup on the tour. Once again we suffered the nervous excitement of an opening night.

As in New York, it was a very glamorous audience, with jewels sparkling, dress uniforms, black ties, and evening dresses filling most of the house. We were heavy on generals and admirals.

I delayed the opening since the audience was still not seated by curtain time. Many of them knew each other and there was talk and waving and looking around to see who was there. Finally they settled down. I signaled Johnny to dim the house lights. At 8:40 I gave Rosie his signal, he raised his baton, the audience fell silent and the overture filled the theater with music and expectation.

The show was as good as ever it had been in New York, and the reception for Mr. B.'s appearance was so tremendous that he had to sit down on his cot again and mimic tying his shoe. When they quieted down, they were breathlessly *silent*. And he began, "Oh! How I hate to get up . . ." When he finished, his applause went on and on. He took a couple of bows but they wouldn't stop until Rosie began the intro to the finale. At the final curtain, with the full company on stage, the applause was tumultuous. Then Mr. B. entered from audience left to join Ezra and the rest of them for several curtain calls.

We played Wednesday and Saturday matinees as usual. On Tuesday afternoon of the second week, our drill and calisthenics in the nearby park were cut short when Mr. B. appeared and asked the company to hear some good news.

"The Pentagon has finally got their act together and we're going to get you guys some ratings — *before we leave town!* See you tonight. Keep up the great shows!" He waved and hopped into his limo.

The next morning my company clerk, Emil Skarda, and I were asked to meet in Major Ambraz's office. We were introduced to General Marshall's aide, Colonel Frank McCarthy. I realized it was a name I'd heard several times from both Mr. B. and Ben. Marshall had assigned McCarthy in the very beginning to make sure that Irving Berlin had everything he needed for the show. The colonel handed me a letter addressed to a major in the Personnel Division in the Pentagon and said with a smile, "Let me know if they don't take good care of you."

Thirty minutes later, Skarda and I were shown into the office of Major Ledyard Hopkins. Hopkins looked up from some paper work. I saluted and handed him the envelope without comment.

He looked at the envelope, opened it, read it quickly, and looked up with a smile. "I've been expecting this." He pulled a three-ring binder off a shelf and opened it up.

"The Colonel informed me you've got about three hundred ten men in the show. I figure a couple of TO's would do the job, give you a few more sergeants on the average." Skarda and I had talked about the possibility that we might run into an Army bureaucrat who looked upon us as a bunch of goldbricks, looking for a soft berth. So we had done a little rehearsing.

"That sounds wonderful in terms of the numbers, sir," Skarda said smoothly and with great respect in his elegant Polish accent. "We would have thought that was the answer, too. But Colonel McCarthy warned us that we should not think of those three hundred plus men as a single unit even though they are working together in one show."

I chimed in. "You see, sir, there are a great number of highly specialized talents involved in such a group and the Colonel suggested, sir, that in choosing the appropriate Table of Organization we think in terms of, for instance, a highly technical antiaircraft unit, say, or a headquarters unit. The orchestra, for instance, is composed of highly trained experts. They've been star players with the Dorsey Brothers, with Guy Lombardo, and other groups you will know well. The singers, many are soloists, from big shows on Broadway, Radio City Music Hall, and the Metropolitan Opera. The stage technicians have been in the key jobs with prestigious shows on Broadway, some with motion picture jobs. I could go on with this example of why this case seems to require an unusual approach."

Skarda took over, "As Mr. Berlin put it, 'Be sure to remind the Pentagon that you are a group of many specialists.' You see, sir, Irving Berlin personally selected every one of the men who are to be functioning in this show for their extraordinary background and talent in their particular specialty." Skarda paused to see where we were.

"Well, gentlemen, that's a pretty eloquent presentation. I see what you're gettin' at, gentlemen. The Colonel's obviously picked you for a specialty in bullshit. But I admire that ability. And I know that this request is coming from the Chief himself so we'll go all out on this. What we could do would be to give you one infantry company and one headquarters company. That'd give you a high percentage of four stripes and up."

Skarda cleared his throat and tried again, "Would you think we might extend that slightly, sir, with, say, two headquarters companies?"

"No, goddamn it! Christ's sake, you wouldn't have nothin' but stripes from wall to wall! Wouldn't be anybody to give orders to." He chuckled, "Well, lemme see. Maybe we can kind of sneak some extras staffs and sergeants into the infantry outfit. That's as far as I can stretch it."

"Thank you, sir," I said firmly. "That's very thoughtful of you. Is it possible you could give us a list of the ratings we could show to Colonel McCarthy and Mr. Berlin?"

"Why sure," he said, pushing a buzzer that brought an attractive young WAC.

"Janice, would you write up this list for these . . . gentlemen, with a carbon for me?"

I pulled myself up to an attitude of military attention and Corporal Skarda joined me.

"Thank you very much, Major. I know Mr. Berlin will be very grateful for your support."

"You're very welcome, Sergeant—and you, too, Corporal." He shook our hands. And to further his relationship with Mr. B. he added, "Also, be sure to tell Mr. Berlin my wife and I loved the show."

"He'll be very pleased to hear that, sir. He has the greatest respect for the military."

We gave him a snappy salute to which he replied with a nonchalant response. We waited in the outer room while Janice readied our bounty. We took our package of ratings back to Major Ambraz and Mr. B. The Major was stunned; Mr. B. was happy. I told them that if there were special medals for superb, smooth talking bullshit, Emil and I would be pleased to accept them.

The next day, in a meeting between Mr. B., Major Ambraz, Marc, Ezra, Rosie, Pete, and myself, we decided who would wear what stripes on their sleeves. Divvying up the Pentagon spoils, Mr. B. said that as the production stage manager. I should be the top first sergeant. I said that in that case, I felt strongly that Chet O'Brien should be the other first sergeant, because he had already earned that rank when he came to us and his training background would be invaluable. Marc agreed. The master sergeants went to Ezra, Rosie, Pete and Bob Sidney. Carl Fisher and Eddie Barclift were techs. The rest of the techs, staffs, sergeants, corporals and pfcs, were balanced between Army and theatrical responsibilities.

The show ran routinely through the Wednesday night performance. Before anyone left the theater they were ordered to be in at one o'clock sharp on Thursday. When we arrived, Mr. B. announced that we were giving a special matinee at 2:30 for an all-soldier audience, except for a couple who would be sitting in the first box on the right side of the audience, our Commander-in-Chief and Mrs. Roosevelt. Then we were briefed by the chief Secret Service man, who having watched one performance, instigated some precautions: we were to remove the bolts from our Springfield rifles, rendering them harmless except as clubs. Comedian Hank Henry, six feet tall, two hundred fifty pounds, had to substitute something for the twelve-inch carving knife in the "Kitchen Police" sketch. Someone suggested a turkey drumstick. Everyone laughed. Hank Henry said, "Great idea!" And the decision was made. The laughs were better than at any other show, so Hank never went back to the knife.

Mr. B. then spoke to us very seriously. "Boys," he said, "play the show as usual. Don't play to the box. Play directly to the audience as usual—and *that's an order!*" His final, fierce emphasis made us aware of his nervousness about the show. His passionate patriotism for the country that had saved him and his family was personified by that man. Among our company of three hundred men, there were various levels of truly understanding who and what he was in our lives. Awe, deep respect, huge admiration, nervous humorous responses in a pretense of blasé nonchalance. We answered with our own serious response, "Yes, sir!" Looking around at the faces of the men, some uttered oaths of awe, cussing just to bury their own nervousness. The fact that we were going to have *that* man in our audience made the pulse quicken, the eyes pop, the face break into foolish grins. We'd come a long way from Camp Upton and Dixie French.

Then our father figure had another piece of news. "One more thing, boys. We're all invited to have supper Friday night, at the White House with the President and the First Lady. Cheers went up. "We were first invited for Saturday night," Mr. B. said. "But when I said a lot of you would be busy taking down the show, the First Lady changed it to Friday."

The unusual atmosphere backstage continued. There were jokes, laughter, and there was more preparation than usual—running scales, tuning violins, dancer's limbering. Costumes were being checked with care seldom shown before. Cooper and I checked every light bulb. Al Gorta checked his follow-spots in the booth earlier than usual. The sound man checked all his microphones. Jus and Hayden reported to me that, for some reason, everyone was ready half an hour early.

It was a great performance, without a glitch. When we came to the final curtain after a rousing and splendid closing chorus, the band struck up the music for the curtain calls. I signaled for curtain up and had to swallow. It was a moving moment. The curtain opened. The entire company was looking straight front, carefully avoiding the box. Routine from that moment was as follows: with the whole company on stage, Mr. B., lighted by one of Al Gorta's powerful arc light follow-spots, enters from stage right, walks to his mark to join the company for his curtain call, then faces front and acknowledges the applause. Ezra, who is in the front row center of the cast, turns to his right and salutes Mr. B., who returns the salute. Then they both turn front for the following calls as the applause continues.

My mouth fell open when Ezra defied Mr. B.'s clear and emphatic order. Instead of turning to Mr. B. and saluting him, Ezra turned to the left and saluted the President. When Mr. B. turned to receive and acknowledge Ezra's salute, Ezra's back was facing him which forced him to direct his salute to the President also. President Roosevelt reacted in a normal fashion and lifted his hand to his brow toward the performers.

The applause continued, but those in the audience who had not been aware of the President's attendance now were. Fortunately, Al Gorta did not compound Ezra's folly by swinging an arc spot on the President. When the President dropped his hand, I quickly signaled for curtain close and because the applause continued, immediately opened them again. Ezra and Mr. B. now bowed to the audience with the rest of the company for the remaining curtain calls. As the applause finally started to fade, I signaled curtain close and house lights fade up.

Mr. B. exited briskly and as he passed me, paused long enough to say, "Tell Stone I want to see him right now," and continued to his dressing room. I went straight to Ezra's dressing room door, which was open, stuck my head in and said, "Ez?" He looked around and before I could speak he said, "Yeah, I know—he wants to see me now." "Right," I said, went back to my desk, picked up my script and headed for the stage door. I was stopped there, as was everyone else. The Secret Service guy at the door just said quietly, "As soon as the Chief pulls away we can all go home." I saw Ezra, heading for Mr. B.'s dressing room. I thought he might fire Ezra from the show. Or he might simply give him hell. We didn't hear loud voices.

Pete and I went for coffee. Ezra joined us ten minutes later.

"When I walked into his room, before he could speak, I said 'I'm sorry, sir, but I was so aware of that presence and all he meant to me, it was an involuntary response. I was simply compelled to acknowledge him.' Naturally, he looked like he wanted to kill me. All he said was, 'I will never trust you again. Get out of here.' Cold as ice. So I got out."

"Jesus Christ, Ez," Pete said.

"Hey, guys, I'm sorry. I probably shouldn't have done it. He had refused to do what I suggested to him when I first heard the President would be there. I said I thought the whole company should turn to the box once and then back to the audience. I still think I was right."

The whole dramatic incident was discussed over and over throughout the company. When we all discussed the incident among ourselves, some thought Ezra was right, wondering whether it might not have been better to have planned to have the whole company acknowledge the President. After all, there was no way to hide the fact that the President was there. On the other hand, it was argued that it would have caused the whole audience to follow the same impulse to stand and acknowledge the President. Perhaps Secret Service had made some ruling about it of which none of us were aware.

The glacial silence between Mr. B. and Ezra dropped by several degrees. Very few of us were aware of how serious the matter was to Mr. B.

Our impending dinner with the President and the First Lady had most of us too excited to dwell on the incident. Each member of the company received a white card, slightly larger than a business card, printed in gold, admitting us to the White House by the East Entrance.[1] Our rank and name were scripted in a beautiful hand, the message continued in print, "will present this card at The White House" and then the scripted date, "October 9, 1942 at 11:45 o'clock p.m." Below this, in block print, the words "Not Transferable" were underlined.The wording was superimposed on a golden image of the White House, surrounded by trees.

After the curtain closed on our Friday evening show, there was a general rush to get out of costume, take off the makeup, put on the freshly pressed uniform and get into one of the busses that were lining up outside of the theater to make the short trip to the fabled East Entrance.

Marc and I preceded the company by cab in order to stand at the East Entrance with Secret Service men and identify each man who came to the door. The agents watched us both for a special signal that

1. A photo of my card is on page 90.

would cast doubt on the identification of the individual.

As we entered, we found ourselves in a reception hall with doorways to a dining room at the far side. We were directed alphabetically to the appropriate door, where we received a seating card indicating the room and table number to which we were assigned. We passed into a waiting room where Mrs. Roosevelt was standing nearest to us; the President was seated beyond her. We gave our name and rank to a Secret Service man, who then turned and gave it to the First Lady. She held out her hand and greeted us. A few steps more took us to the President, who greeted us as we shook his hand.

"Good evening, Sergeant Anderson. Glad to have you," was what I remember him saying to me. Later when we discussed it all with our friends, we agreed that the words differed slightly from man to man. The First Lady's manner was warm and direct, with an easy smile. She sometimes said something personal. To Earl Oxford, who was just ahead of me, she said, "I enjoyed your singing so much." The President's grip was firm on my hand—one had no sense of physical weakness—and his words were spoken with a relaxed and genial ease, as though you were the only guest. Even so, I turned to jelly, but made myself answer as firmly as I could muster, "Good evening, sir. Thank you for having us."

Although it was late, there was no hurried rush. Everyone waited quietly and patiently in the receiving line, so pleased to be there and to be allowed this incredible meeting. As we moved away from our host and hostess, many seemed almost stunned, but as the men proceeded further toward their tables, their excited voices were comparing what had happened, talking about it already as an extraordinary, lifetime experience. Eventually, we all found our room and our table and started gabbing as soon as we were seated. Three rooms were needed to accommodate us all—ten tables in two of them, eleven in the third. The White House had asked us to prepare table lists ahead of time, and Ambraz gave this task to Marc and me the day before. We aimed at compatibility as much as possible.

We ate our meal in a daze, so much so that I don't remember what we ate. What we all remembered was that Mrs. Roosevelt came and sat in turn at each table and chatted with us about the show, about us, about the war. She was incredible. She took in everything; she responded to everything and to every one of us. The President vanished after our first greeting. I was glad to see that. It was incredible that he had given us so much attention at that time in history.

After dessert and coffee or tea, the waitresses and the maitre d' took over the hosting very gracefully, making us feel welcome to the end of the evening and our return to the buses.

For days afterward we would talk to each other about the sensations we had had in meeting those two individuals. Some said they could not even remember the President's face, because as soon as they looked at his eyes, they somehow had to look away or down.

We went to bed Friday night, looking forward to our last and perhaps busiest day in Washington: two shows to give, strike the show, and load trucks. Well, at least we could relax a little. A week in Pittsburgh seemed an easy challenge.

A Z

EAST ENTRANCE

Sgt. Alan Anderson

will please present this card at

The White House

October 9, 1942

at 11; 45 o'clock p. m.

NOT TRANSFERABLE

Chapter 7

THE WAR
— Oct 7, 1942: On Guadalcanal the US 1st Marine Division breaks out
from the beachhead to try to create a larger safety zone around the
airstrip.
— Oct 10, 1942: Kesselring orders an aerial offensive against Malta. Two
hundred seventy flights of Italian and German aircraft are sortied
daily.
— Oct 12, 1942: A British Coastal Command Liberator sinks German
U597; first success by single aircraft from this section of Royal Air
Force.

Pittsburgh was a letdown. It was hard to match the three months in
New York City and dinner with the President and First Lady in
Washington, D.C. The adrenaline is not pumping as hard. You are used
to the audience. You're even used to applause. You know your lines.
You remember the lyrics and you could do the dances in your sleep.
You expect the laughs, even the quiet intensity of an audience that is
moved, emotionally rapt. What happens? The comedians start to
broaden the jokes, the singers play around with the tempo and the
phrasing, the dancers get careless or they add some movements,
turns, taps.

Stage managers are trained to worry about the performance level. Is
the show being played the way the director left it? In our case, the
director, the dance directors, the musical director, were all in the show,
and so was our producer, Mr. B. This was unusual and it helped to
keep the performance "up."

At the same time, as the performance of the show began to take less
of our attention, the news of the war took more. Suddenly, in these
few months, American forces were at war around the world. The disastrous losses suffered in August at the landing in Dieppe hung over us
still. It was a first attempt of the Allies to get a foothold on the conti-

nent—a costly and almost total disaster. Those of us who read the papers and listened to the radio, were aware of what our men and women were involved in around the world. Our hopes were up since the flashy Montgomery was chasing the Desert Fox in Africa. We also knew that we were doing what we had been told to do, yet we couldn't help feeling both lucky and guilty. I said as much to my good friend, Pete Feller, because I knew we shared the feeling. Pete, of course, didn't believe in showing his emotions. "Anderson, are you so anxious to get your ass shot off?" he said.

"No," I said, "the idea is not appealing at all."

"Well, don't worry about it. You may get your chance before this is over. For the moment, just start focusing. We've got a show to do tonight!"

Maybe *This Is the Army* had sent the word out to all the Red Cross chapters. They welcomed the whole company without batting an eye.

We skipped the drill and calisthenics on Monday. It rained on Tuesday. The boys had only two days of exercise. Of course, the dancers and the acrobats got plenty in the show anyway. Besides, most stage professionals exercise to keep in shape, with some notable, fleshy exceptions. Musicians, sitting in an orchestra pit don't have a chance to move around much.

The Nixon Theater in Pittsburgh was a venerable and elegant old building, inside and out, its interior dominated by red velvet and ornate white sculptured decor. With the magnificent chandeliers alight, the effect was perhaps more suitable for a living room drama by Philip Barry than a rambunctious musical variety show. But once the house lights dimmed and the overture began, it was just the audience and the performance for another triumphant eight shows and rave reviews. The Army Emergency Relief Fund was growing fast.

After taking down the show Saturday night, the crew loaded it into trucks for the trip to Philadelphia, our next booking. The trucks went to Philly Sunday night and Pete went with them to oversee the load-in at the Mastbaum Theater Monday morning. Only then could he get a train to New York and begin his one-week furlough. The rest of the company had left for New York at 9:00 a.m. Sunday morning. Mr. B. and all of us would have a relaxed, restful week.

Nancy and I spent the furlough in the country seeing the whole family. We discussed suitable names. Alan Junior looked like a winner unless my mother's name, Margaret, was more appropriate. This was in the days before medical science had eliminated the need to be ready with names both male and female.

On October 26, 1942, we resumed our road tour, opening at the big Mastbaum in Philadelphia. The furlough had been a useful rest. We continued to draw cheering sidewalk crowds in our energetic marches from the railroad station to the theater in every city. On several occasions these marches were augmented by local Army installations who added military rolling stock to the parade. These varied from jeeps to half tracks, to tanks, to field guns. The performances were full of spirit, greeted with applause, laughter and many curtain calls.

The rest of our Eastern tour continued to produce big headlines in the entertainment pages of every newspaper. The show filled every seat for each performance. Theater publicist and author, Private First Class Max Wilk, was responsible for snaring this extra excitement by contacting the Army brass when we were approaching each city. He let them know how grateful Mr. B. would be for the added, colorful military hardware.

After two weeks in the Mastbaum Theater and a week in the Baltimore Opera House, we headed to Boston for two weeks in the opera house. Even Boston's much-feared and formidable theater critic, Ashton Stevens, gave us a rave review.

The Fellers and the Andersons had an especially pleasant time in Boston; we splurged at the Palmer House with a diet that included a lot of New England sea food. Nancy and Katie decided they'd better leave us when we left Boston—Nancy to check in with Dr. Hurd and settle on a place to live; Katie to get back to work and earn a little money. We put them on a train Saturday morning. We were very good and nobody cried at all—until the train had rumbled slowly out of sight.

The company received an invitation for a closing night after-theater party at the extremely popular Coconut Grove nightclub. The owners apparently wanted us to enjoy all their food and drink in the hope that we'd remember it whenever we came to Boston. A great number of our cast read the invitation on the backstage bulletin board and at least half of them rushed to take off their makeup. I joined my regular associates for a nightcap at a recommended nearby pub. Sunday would be an early and busy day. Pete needed six or seven hours to strike and load the show on trucks. Rosie, Carl and I were back at our hotel by 12:30 a.m.

I turned on the radio in my room to listen to Beethoven's "Violin Concerto." Sometime after it ended, I drifted off to sleep. Suddenly I was awake, hearing strange voices that cut across the usual undertones of the music host. The news announcer was almost hysterical. And then I heard the word "fire," and then "Coconut Grove," and I was wide awake. The radio clock said 3:15 a.m.

> *"Smoke—fire—dense chemical smells—Kitchen fire spread into dining area. Doors swing inward—blocked by bodies—dense, choking smoke—trampling bodies of those who were blinded in smoke. And darkness. No lights—no exit signs—hysteria, chaos—no way to assess the horror."*

In my half sleep, the continuity of words was lost in my own panic. I looked for the phone and tried to think who to call.

Barclift—call Barclift and see if he's home. He had been going to the club—a bunch of them had.

The radio announcer again, with facts:

> *"Poisonous, acrid smoke from the burning plastic furniture and curtains—"*

"Eddie? Hi, you're there. Thank God."

"Alan?"

"Yeah! God! The Coconut Grove—what's happened?"

"It's okay," he said.

"What do you mean? How do you know?"

"I mean I know why you're calling, but by a miracle we all left."

"You all left? My God, that *is* a miracle!"

"The bastards had promised a lot of free drinks. They weren't giving us anything. Nothing was free, so we all left. We had one drink, told the owner to go fuck himself, and we left."

"Oh, God! That's incredible. I'd better call people and tell them you're okay!"

Eddie went on. He felt so good that he was alive—that they were all alive. "I told the guy I was going to have him put out of business! I said I knew the Mayor and everyone in the city government; I'd take away his liquor license and every union would blackball him and sue his balls off. I scared the shit out of him. And then we marched out. Everyone went with me. Do you want me to make some calls?"

"Call Rosie, and Bob. They're both staying here."

"Okay."

"I'll call Jus, Marc, the Major." We hung up.

I got Marc. He had heard the radio, too, and had called the police and the hospitals with the news. "We'll have to check with a roll call in the morning—to be sure."

"Okay. We can check everyone on the station platform at nine o'clock. I kept thinking we could have been somewhere fighting, winning the fucking war instead of dying in a nightclub fire! Thank God, whoever he is!"

We hung up and I called the Major. He hadn't heard. I gave him a full report of what I knew.

"Good work, Alan. We'll find out how we stand on the railroad platform."

"Yes, sir. Goodnight." I hung up.

I didn't dare call Nancy at that hour. She was staying with her mother and stepfather, Bernie, at the Park Avenue apartment. They had stayed there instead of going down to the Carolina farm in the fall because her mother had wanted to be with her expectant daughter. I called them at 7 a.m. to tell them that all was well. And then I called Lexington Avenue to be sure her father knew I was okay. The papers and the radio would be full of the calamity that our men barely missed.

At the 9 a.m. roll call at the railroad station, the story of the fire was still circulating. Some of the men had been among those who had walked out, but hadn't they heard of the fire until the roll call.

Except for Pete Feller's stage crew—and we knew where they all were—the roll call turned up one missing man. Where was violinist Abner Silverstein?

"Okay, let's get aboard, fellows. We'll put a tracer on Abner."

Just as we were starting to board our assigned cars, little Abner came rushing down the platform, hugging his precious violin case, which was almost as big as he was. He spluttered, Sergeant! Sergeant!" He was a tremendous musician, but his speech had none of the clarity of his bowing, especially when he was excited. Of course, he knew nothing about the fire.

"I couldn't help being late! I couldn't find my violin! I went to a party—they wanted me to play. There were a bunch of us—and I guess I had a couple of drinks. When I was leaving, I couldn't find my violin. Another guy had taken mine and left his! It was junk! So I had to find him. The host told me where he lived and it took hours riding around in taxis, carrying his instrument, until I finally found him." He held up his instrument proudly, smiling, "And I found this!" He held his case over his head and kissed it.

The fire made huge headlines in the morning papers. Over one hundred people lost their lives and many others were injured. I couldn't help wondering if our luck would always be as good.

On Sunday, the company took a morning train from Boston to Cleveland. The setup crew worked through Sunday night; we finished set-up and lighting on Monday. We raised the curtain at 8:30 p.m. on Monday for one week in the Public Music Hall.

Ben posted our schedule backstage from there on: one week in the Auditorium, Cincinnati; a week at the St. Louis Municipal Auditorium; and then for Christmas and New Year's, a two-week run at the Shrine Auditorium in Detroit.

The parades were triumphant, the shows were a smash hit, and the reviews were raves. There were articles in the papers about the acrobats, the juggler, the magician, the dancing, and of course, a lot about Berlin's wonderful music and lyrics. There was *nothing* about Ezra Stone, the director.

And then we were in St. Louis. "If I don't get mentioned in the paper here, I've had it," Ezra said.

"What are you going to do? Turn in your uniform?" Pete said.

The program credits didn't change, but press releases never talked about him. And Mr. B. discussed production matters with everyone *except* Ezra, the director.

Before the Wednesday matinee in St. Louis, we had a staff meeting with all the department heads, including Ezra, to discuss our next move. Berlin sat in with us. Although it wasn't really the subject of the meeting, Mr. B. remarked that he thought we had "dead wood" in the show. Ezra asked him what he meant. Where was the dead wood? Mr. B. said he thought there were a lot of guys who didn't do anything but sit on the minstrel stand and pretend they were singing. Ezra replied that there wasn't anyone on the stage who didn't do what he was supposed to do. Berlin turned to the rest of us.

"Keep your eyes open." And he left us. Ezra was fuming.

After the matinee, I was in Ezra's dressing room with my first assistants, Jus and Hayden, talking about the general morale of the company. Mr. B. walked by, saw us and came in to listen. Jus remarked that he felt a little "let down" in the energy generally. I asked if anyone else felt the same. Mr. B. broke in where he'd left off in the morning meeting with a remark about "dead wood."

"We've got a lot of Ezra's Jewish cronies who aren't doing anything. They sit up there in the stand mouthing the words — if they even know them." None of us could handle that one. Ezra turned to Berlin.

"Speaking of dead wood, take a look at all the kikes in the music division." Ezra's animus had been building week by week for months. All his unexpressed anger vomited up that word. It hung in the air, venomous and repulsive, stunning us all. The room was silent and still for a long moment. Then in one motion, Mr. B. turned and was gone. Ezra sat down at his dressing table. I walked out. Jus and Hayden followed me.

We stood together for a few moments. We had known we were living with a powder keg in the relationship between these two men who had worked together so closely for months to put the show together and now were enemies. Hayden looked straight at me and said, "That was a beauty. Okay, now what do we do?"

I had to think. There was nothing we could do. There was only one boss. "What made him bring up the music division," I said. They both shook their heads.

"What do we do? Nothing," I said. "We act like it didn't happen. We work hard, keep our eyes open and our mouths shut. The only one who *can* do anything is Mr. B." We stood there digesting it all. Jus spoke up brightly.

"I know one thing we can do."

We looked at him hopefully.

"Have a drink and eat a steak," he said with a goofy smile.

"Good plan!" Hayden said, and I nodded agreement.

The show went on. The schedule, the full houses, the reviews, the applause, the speeches, gave us so much momentum we just went with the tide. Jus, Hayden and I kept a sharp eye on every performance to make sure there were no signs of trouble. We also kept an eye out for dead wood!

Chapter 8

THE WAR

—*Dec 17, 1942: The Russian winter aids home forces when the Volga freezes over making it easier for supplies to reach their troops. German airlift to their army destroyed by bad weather.*

—*Dec 18, 1942: Australians winning the battle in New Guinea with fresh tank support.*

—*Dec 28, 1942: British forces in Burma repelled by Japanese.*

—*Dec 31, 1942: Defeated Japanese forced to evacuate Guadalcanal.*

When Mr. Berlin checked into his hotel in Detroit before Christmas, he was prepared to spend a lonely evening living his own song, "All Alone by the Telephone." The assistant manager took him up to his room. He opened the door and found himself in an enormous suite, grinning into the smiling faces of his lovely wife, Ellin and daughters Mary Ellin, Linda and Elizabeth. Beyond them he saw a partially decorated Christmas tree and a crackling fire in the fireplace.

Mr. B.'s surprise became the subject of a front page story and family photograph in the morning edition of the *Detroit Free Press* arranged by Ellin with Ben Washer's assistance.

We were at breakfast in our more modest Detroiter Hotel—"we" being Rosie, Pete, Carl and me, with two notable additions: Katie and Lil, Rosie's wife, who, like Nancy, was "expecting" (only their expectation was for March, a month later than ours). Carl's wife, Betty, was working in New York, and Nancy was with her mother in the Park Avenue apartment.

"You remember what I told you," Rosie said, looking up from the front page, which we had been passing around. "That guy has two completely separate lives: business and family. Just look at his face, at how proud he is. And when he's with us working on the show, you'd never know the family existed." Certainly there was nothing in Mr. B.'s expression to tell you that the ugly St. Louis confrontation had ever happened.

I looked at the picture again. Then I looked at Katie and Peter, then at Lil and Rosie and made up my mind. I put down the paper and said, "Excuse me, folks. I've got to make a phone call."

"Hello, Mr. B.?" I'm sorry to bother you. . . . No, nothing's wrong. I have a favor to ask you. Would you mind if I let Jus take over for a few days while I went to New York? . . . Thank you very much, sir. I'll see if I can get Swampy to give me a five-day pass!"

I sat up all night in coach. When I got to Park Avenue and put my arms around her, Nancy and I both sobbed for a moment; it was such an unexpected present. We spent the day with Gulia and Bernie and then we were in the country for Christmas with all my family, including my little sister, Hesper, her eyes full of wonder, with her hands on Nancy's beautiful tummy.

With the magic that was about to come into our lives, being together left us both dazed.

Suddenly it was over, but we knew that it was not for long.

My train got into Detroit Monday, December 28, at 4 p.m. Jus filled me in on some problems: Dick Bernie was ad-libbing, which threw the pace of his act off; Bob reported "Ladies of the Chorus" was sloppy; and there were some further complaints from Mr. B. about the dead wood in the chorus. We did some rehearsing on Tuesday morning. Ezra was not invited. I chewed out Dick Bernie for improvising; Bob ran several big numbers over and over to tighten them up; and Mr. B. felt much better. The show played well through Saturday. The audience was overly responsive on New Year's Eve. Oddly enough, they behaved as though they had been drinking.

☆ ☆ ☆ ☆ ☆ ☆ ☆ ☆ ☆ ☆ ☆

Sunday, January 3, we pulled into Chicago. I'd forgotten what it was like to be really cold until I felt the wind off Lake Michigan once more.

My frozen face and fingers are what I remember about the march from the station to the theater. It helped a little that there were actually stouthearted natives smiling and waving when we went by. The seats were filled for our two-week run, and on Sunday morning, January 17, 1943, we eagerly climbed on board our troop train for sunny Los Angeles.

As a child, I had made this same journey with my father and mother on the Santa Fe Super Chief, so I knew it could be done in three days. On the troop train, the bunks stacked three high, it took five days, and the Chicago temperature lingered in the drafty train for three of them.

We worked like hell for a night and a day to be ready for our Friday opening in the Los Angeles Philharmonic Auditorium. We filled every seat for the next twelve performances, and were dazzled by the dozens of Hollywood faces in our audiences. It was familiar territory for much of our company. Many were LA natives, and quite a few of our New Yorkers had been in LA for jobs — or the hope of jobs. I had been there on a few occasions when I was lucky enough to stage manage Broadway shows that made cross-country tours.

We went north to the San Francisco War Memorial Opera House to play our final two weeks of *This Is the Army*, thus completing the tour. It was a good place to finish. They were bright, appreciative audiences, and the critics and the closing night speeches made us feel it was still a great show. Then back on the train to Los Angeles and the excitement of actually being in a Hollywood movie!

☆ ☆ ☆ ☆ ☆ ☆ ☆ ☆ ☆ ☆ ☆

In true Hollywood fashion, Warner Brothers Studios' set builders and prop department had created an Army tent city in their Burbank back lot, complete with parade ground and obstacle course, all laid out to Army specifications. This would give us a place to live and keep the guys busy on days when they weren't on the movie set. There was no

Army kitchen, though. We would eat in the Warner Brothers commissary. We had separate tents for the Orderly Room, the officers and Mr. B. Detachment members could live in the tents, or "off camp," as long as they appeared for a daily formation at 9:00 a.m., Monday through Friday. With the lure of Hollywood and the knowledge that we would be here for at least three months, those who could afford to live "off camp" did so.

Pete and crew stored the stage production in a Los Angeles warehouse. No one knew when, or whether, it would be used again.

Marc and I posted a notice about tent assignments, meal times, mail calls and daily activities for those not involved in filming.

Our commanding officer, Major Simon P. Ambraz, seemed to see this as his chance for stardom. After a week in *TITA* Tent City, he appeared at our formation in a brand-new uniform, including a handsome leather crop and boots designed for cavalry. His freshly polished golden oak leaves gleamed on his shoulders. His hair was trimmed clean around the ears. When his hand came up to return my salute, his nail polish glistened. He was probably comfortably resigned that he would never be a general — except, perhaps, in movies! His movements were brisk. His chin was up and his shoulders back. He would certainly be snapped up by the first passing talent agent.

Transportation was not a problem for the Major; he sported an olive drab Army sedan. The rest of us either bought secondhand cars or cadged a ride with those who had. There were two company jeeps available for Army business, and we had an Army bus that made daily roundtrips between Hollywood and Vine and our tent city. Soldiers could also count on hitchhiking if need be. The daily commute came to be known as the Battle of Cahuenga Pass, Cahuenga Boulevard being the route over the mountain.

Rosie and I moved into a two-room suite in the economical Hollywood Hotel and kept in touch with our expectant wives from there. Lil Rosenstock had gone home to New York when we went to

San Francisco. The Rosenstock heir was expected soon, and Nancy was expecting any day! The doctor projected something close to Washington's birthday. We became what is known as an "item" in Walter Winchell's column in the New York *Daily News*. It read in part:

> Playwright Maxwell Anderson's Army sergeant son and his
> bride are expecting—probable name George Washington
> Anderson, date February 22.

A journalist's gamble as to date, name and gender. When Mr. B. saw the column, he mystified me by saying, "That gives me an idea."

Since furlough's were only twelve days long, I planned to leave when Nancy was about to leave the hospital. That would give me maximum time to be useful in the postnatal days.

Expectant fathers in the detachment received unexpected good news from General Phillipson, who informed Mr. B. that the Army Emergency Relief Fund would cover the cost of all infant deliveries in *This Is the Army* Detachment!

On February 21, Nancy's mother called. "Nancy is in labor and we're on the way to the hospital." Her next call came at 1:30 a.m., on February 22, George Washington's birthday, confirming Winchell's gamble as to gender and date, missing only in the name of Alan Haskett Anderson, Junior.

Rosie had a chilled bottle of champagne sent up to our room, popped the cork and proposed a toast to the wondrous miracle for both of us. I responded in kind and we continued to create new toasts, one after another. When he raised his glass for the last one, I pointed out that the bottle was empty. He stared at it for a moment and dropped off to sleep. I decided to wait for my telephone calls but fell asleep before any came. My mother-in-law called each morning.

Major Ambraz was able to get me on an Army transport flight on March 1st, to be sure I would be in New York before Nancy and the

baby were discharged. He also surprised me by handing me a furlough letter for twenty-four days instead of twelve. I thanked him
heartily.

I was on the phone a lot that week. The morning I left, I received an
envelope in our Orderly Room company mail. On the back was printed the return address:

> Irving Berlin, Warner Bros. Pictures, Inc., Hollywood,
> California.

There were two pages. The first page bore letterhead printed with
"Irving Berlin." The message was typed by Mr. B. on his Remington, in
his usual style, with my name misspelled. He had dated it, March 1,
1943, and it read:

> Sergeant Allan (Mr. B.'s spelling) Anderson, "This Is the Army"
> Inc., Warner Bros. Studio, Burbank, California. Dear Allan, Here
> is the chorus lyric of the new song. Please give it to your wife
> and tell her I hope the song becomes as popular as that baby is.
> Best to you both and a kiss for the kid. Sincerely, Irving Berlin.

The second page, also typed by him, read:

> "What Does He Look Like (That Boy of Mine)?" Words and
> Music by Irving Berlin,
>
> CHORUS
> What does he look like,
> That boy of mine?
> Since the news came, I can't get him off my mind.
> Does he resemble
> His homely dad?
> Does he look like the girl that I left behind?

Bring on the Germans
And bring on the Japs,
Bring on the first two you can find.
One for the rascal
I haven't seen
And one for the girl that I left behind.

I read the letter and put both sheets back in the envelope. I didn't read the lyric until I was on the plane. It was undoubtedly the most generous gift a songwriter can offer. Reading it now, with the war a part of history, the tenderness of the music and the mixture of tenderness followed by violence in the lyrics seems shocking given the background of the nightclub scene in the film. Despite that, I was moved by having that incredible man write a song which was inspired by our first child.

With both the envelope from Mr. B. and a twenty-four-day furlough in my pocket, I taxied from the airport to Women's Hospital on West 110th Street. After spending several precious minutes with Nancy and Gulia, I showed them the letter and the lyrics from Mr. B. Nancy couldn't get over it and kept looking at them in great excitement. I left them to have another visit with my newborn son through the nursery window.

Nancy and young Alan were not released for two more days. By then I had picked up our Plymouth '38. We thanked Nancy's mother, loaded up the car and headed for the Red Barn on South Mountain Road, right across the road from my brother Quentin and his wife Meg. We settled into our new home, with a baby to take care of, no nurse, no grandmother and a not-very-warm house. But we were so excited and so young we knew that we could do anything! Nancy decided that in a drafty barn Alan Jr. needed extra food, so she added some formula to his meals. We turned on an electric heater in his room and kept the door closed, then I gave him his first warm bath. He loved being in the warm water and we knew everything was going to be great!

We had family and friends coming in and out admiring the baby, helping with various chores, bringing us things to eat. Meg was there several times with my one year-old niece, Martha, and Hesper, of course, was there over and over, fascinated by her young nephew, wanting to hold him.

Naturally, we worried about whether he was losing too much weight and then when he started to gain, whether it was enough. In those days, schedules for babies were strict: you fed them at feeding time, not when they were hungry. But he survived it, and we survived the 2 a.m. and 6 a.m. feedings. And when Nancy was worried, we phoned his pediatrician in Manhattan.

Twenty-four days went by in a flash. By then we were feeling confident that he was strong and healthy in spite of our inexperience, and I went back to Tent City to wait for the day when my small family could make the train trip to California.

I showed a picture of my son to Mr. B. and thanked him again for letting me be there. He spent some time looking at the picture. I didn't know that he had lost a son in infancy; later I understood better his special interest in our son and the fatherly attitude he showed many of us.

We started shooting the movie early in April, about ten days after my return. As was usual in those days, when Hollywood took over a Broadway creation, everything was oversized, over costumed, and cosmetically, unbelievably perfect. The basic story Warner's writers had built was of the two Army shows in the two great wars, with the older generation producing *Yip! Yip! Yaphank* and their youngsters doing *This Is the Army*. The story was obvious and sentimental; the acting was routine. The music and Mr. B. were great.

Some of the guys in the stage show who had made important contributions to its success were assured that the film would propel them to stardom. Julie Oshins, who was the most prominent comedian in the original show, was given little to do in the movie version but to play straight man to a colorless Warner Brothers contract comedian.

The performance credits were divided between civilians and those in uniform. Of the screen credits, among the civilians were George Murphy, who played Ronald Reagan's father; Joan Leslie, who played Reagan's girl friend; Frances Langford, who sang the song dedicated to our son; and Kate Smith, who sang "God Bless America." The credits listed for those in uniform were (in order): Lieutenant Ronald Reagan and Sergeants Joe Louis, Alan Anderson, Ezra Stone, Alan Manson and Earl Oxford. Fourteen other members of *TITA* were given credit listing, including the comedian who was also given promises, promises—Julie Oshins. Julie and Ezra were both in the original production, but when it was screened everyone agreed that the numbers they had in the opening scenes didn't work and so they were taken out, which left them with very little. Ezra Stone only appears in one shot, where he is being told to report to the set. He replies, "Yes, sir," in his Henry Aldrich falsetto, and is never seen or heard from again.

Michael Curtiz has the sole director credit. Bob Sidney and Milt Rosenstock were importantly involved in the film: Bob shared the credit for the choreography with Warner's stable offering, which read,

> Production numbers staged by LeRoy Prinz and Master
> Sergeant Robert Sidney.

To the shame of those responsible, in every shot of the orchestra Rosie was on camera conducting, but for some inexplicable reason, which can only have been an incredible oversight, his name never appears in any credits!

In the stage version of *This Is the Army*, we had a chorus of one hundred seventy-one—nine rows of nineteen men. The sound was impressive. It was also impressive visually.

For the movie, Warner Brothers rounded up another one hundred twenty-nine volunteers from local Army posts, for a total of three hundred men. It didn't improve the singing because they didn't bother to get good voices. They weren't even up to our so-called dead wood.

Of course, the set was huge. There was room for Bob and LeRoy to add drama to the lyrics for "This Time" by putting fixed bayonets on the rifles, having the men perform a stabbing motion in their choreographed marching in "Dressed Up to Kill." It was a stirring number, a rousing finale and the lyrics conveyed the story of the two great world wars: the second war being dedicated to finish the job that was begun in the war that ended in 1918. It was a message that Berlin felt deeply. His anger at the threat to the civilized world moved him to use the word "kill," but in rehearsal the word offended many people, including religious leaders who regularly monitored the work of the big studios. Under pressure and with deference to these opinions, Mr. B. softened the violence of the title, changing "Dressed Up to Kill" to "Dressed Up to Win," thus satisfying everyone without sacrificing the objective of the song.

Perhaps the strongest contribution the stage version gave to the film version was the inclusion of the entire Stage Door Canteen number just as it had been done on stage. Alan Manson did a glowing Jane Cowl; James McColl was very successful in his parodies of Alfred Lunt, Charles Boyer and other stars who are remembered by few today; and Earl Oxford's singing of "I Left My Heart at the Stage Door Canteen" was a strong emotional presentation.

Major contributions from our cast elsewhere in the film were made by the soloists. The songs remembered today in addition to the title song, "This Is the Army, Mister Jones," are Jimmy Burrell's "I'm Getting Tired So I Can Sleep," and, of course, Mr. B's sincere complaint, "Oh! How I Hate to Get Up in the Morning," which will never go out of date. There were several chorus numbers that were kept in the film version. None of the sketches were included, except for a rather old-fashioned vaudeville turn by Dick Bernie and Alan Manson. The songs in the movie that were not in either of the Army productions were "God Bless America," sung by Kate Smith, and Frances Langford's "What Does He Look Like."

A notable missing element in the film was Ezra Stone's "The Army's

Made a Man Out of Me," which he sang in the stage show before we went overseas.

Ronald Reagan, the male lead from the Warner Brothers stable, starred in the show. He played me, the stage manager, and very briefly I played his assistant. In one scene that I played by myself, I said, "Come on, let's go! Curtain's going up!" But having established my character as a decisive assistant stage manager, I then played a two-line scene with Reagan in which I exhibited a dismaying uncertainty for one with my responsibilities. Reagan, my boss, said, "Anderson, is everything all set for the Stage Door Canteen number—props and everything?" My response after glancing at my clipboard was, "Yeah, I think so." Think so! Then, without showing any concern, I handed him a telegram, said, "This just came for you," and abruptly left the star (our President-to-be) and yelled at the cast, "All right, get on stage, you prima donnas! Let's go! Get on for Stage Door Canteen!" Without further concern for the canteen number, Reagan opened the envelope and yelled, "Hey, fellas, get a load of this wire! We're goin' on tour!" These scenes could only occur in the shooting of movies, where there is no public audience present.

Hollywood's knowledge of backstage Broadway was comical at best. Don't they know you never yell backstage when the show is on—even if you're going to be President some day!

✮ ✮ ✮ ✮ ✮ ✮ ✮ ✮ ✮ ✮ ✮

Nancy and our three-month-old son, Alan Jr., arrived in Los Angeles by train on May 3rd. Katie, who had joined Pete in March, helped me find rooms to rent in Hollywood. She had a hard time finding a rental that would take a baby, but a sweet widow, Helen Waggoner, finally relented. She fell in love with mother and child and shared her small house with us just a block from Hollywood and Vine.

At 8:15 a.m. sharp, six days a week, I was summoned curbside by the friendly roar of Pete Feller: "Hey, Blub-*ber!*" It carried for blocks!

It's true I was a bit rounder than he, but I thought him seriously skinny. My self-image wounded, I ran for the car so he wouldn't have time to repeat the affront.

For a while, the movie kept us all in suspended animation. Nancy and I reveled in being together with our son. We even had some freed time to see a few movies and eat a meal now and then in places like Hollywood's famous Brown Derby restaurant. I was involved in the movie only occasionally for my brief scenes, and I spent most of the time in the Orderly Room in my administrative role. The studio gave me a bicycle so I could shuttle back and forth between the Orderly Room and the studio.

Roughcuts were shown to Mr. B. regularly so that he had a good sense of how the show was being treated.

We finished shooting the movie early in July. The studio was in a rush to make a July 28 world premiere. The film would then be a contender for "the fastest completed movie in Hollywood history." No matter how high it ranked among movies, it made a very real contribution to the war effort by raising over ten million dollars for the Army Emergency Relief Fund, in addition to the funds raised by performances to the public and the purchase of Mr. B.'s wonderful songs.

Chapter 9

THE WAR
—*July 1, 1943: Discord in Axis. Mussolini fears invasion by US troops. Afraid to raise issue with Hitler.*
—*July 2, 1943: In New Guinea, Australian forces link up with US troops and additional US forces land unopposed at Zanana in New Georgia.*
—*July 4, 1943: General Sikorski, the Polish leader, is killed in an air crash. A loss to the Allies.*

It was July 4, 1943, just one year since the show had opened in New York. The cross-country tour had ended, the movie was finished, our job was done.

Pete and the gang dropped me off at Argyle Street. Nancy was nursing our son, the heir. I kissed them both.

"Daddy seems a little jumpy," she said to Alan Jr. "I wonder what's going on."

"Is this a three-way conversation? We've finished shooting the last foot of film."

"Ask him what's going to happen next."

His eyes were closed. He stopped nursing. "He's bored," I said. "You're going to have to talk to me. I don't think anyone knows yet."

"Well, that's pretty dumb. They must have some idea what they're going to do with three hundred fifty soldiers sitting around in the Warner Brothers back lot." I laughed. She was right.

"There are only three hundred ten." The correction produced a scowl. My wife enjoyed dramatizing by exaggeration and couldn't understand my need to be exact. She lifted our son into his crib. He was sound asleep.

She was all business. "Who decides?"

"Washington, I guess.General Marshall's office."

"Doesn't Ben know anything?"

"He probably does. We're going to have a meeting tomorrow at 2:00 p.m. in Berlin's tent. That will probably tell us everything."

"Who's in the meeting?"

"Bob, Rosie, Pete, Marc, Johnny Koenig, me and Ben.

Ben Washer, who had started out as our publicity man from the Broadway opening, had gradually taken on a role as Mr. B.'s right hand-man and confidante. He and I had become good friends. Ben dropped me a hint that Washington wanted us to go to England as a goodwill gesture to our Allies. "We're going to have a meeting about it tomorrow," Ben had said, "but don't say anything to anyone. Don't tell Nancy, because it may not happen. Wait until tomorrow when we'll have a better idea."

Nancy was looking at me. "You know something."

"What?" How the hell did she know? "Ben said not to tell you because we won't really know until tomorrow."

"I'm a big girl. Okay, don't tell me. Just tell your son."

"Yeah. Okay." I directed it to the crib. "Washington may want us to take the show to England as a goodwill gesture to our Allies."

She didn't say anything; she just came over and put her arms around me. I was going to be in the war zone. It scared her.

☆ ☆ ☆ ☆ ☆ ☆ ☆ ☆ ☆ ☆ ☆

The next day, Monday, July 5, Ben informed everyone of the meeting and we met in Mr. B.'s tent at 2 p.m. as planned. Marc had arranged to have the other first sergeant, Chet O'Brien take the rest of the company out in the field for an hour of drilling so no one knew there was a meeting being held.

Mr. B. was smiling when he started to talk. "From now on," he said, "this group is called the committee. We're all equal members, each with one vote, and when I'm not around, you'll make all the show decisions. We're starting off with a big decision." I realized that what he had done by forming "the committee" was to be sure that all show decisions would be made by the department heads of the show, not by Army rank.

Berlin continued. "General Marshall—and you all know who he is—decided that if I agreed to go, he wants us to take the show to London to strengthen our friendship with our British allies. I hope you're all happy with my decision, because I said yes this morning."

We looked at each other and then broke into smiles and cheers, and finally, we all applauded.

Then Pete and I exchanged a look, both of us realizing who this decision was going to affect in our lives.

The boss continued. "Marshall has assigned one of his closest aides to work with us on everything we do. Whenever we need help, we call him. His name is Frank McCarthy. He's a colonel, an old Broadway theater man. McCarthy called me yesterday. First of all, he said we all had to keep our mouths shut. Not a word to anyone. Explain why, will you Ben?"

"When you think of the reason, it's really pretty obvious," Ben said. "If the show is going to London, we immediately become a big security risk, not just for ourselves, but for everyone who goes across the ocean with us. There are still a lot of German submarines looking for targets, and Frank reminded us that there's nothing Axis Sally would rather broadcast to the world than 'We just sunk the Irving Berlin show on their way to cheer up the British.' "

"Who the hell is Axis Sally?" Rosie wanted to know.

"Axis Sally is a sexy-voiced German actress who sends broadcasts out to our troops by radio everywhere, trying to damage the morale of all the Allies. And, by the way, Japan has their own version of sexy Sally, called Tokyo Rose." Ben paused for a moment and then turned to Mr. B. "Shall I tell them the rest?"

"Tell them," said the boss.

"Well," Ben went on, "Colonel McCarthy said that it would be difficult and dangerous to send a show to combat zones with more than about one hundred fifty men. He had an idea that we could split into two companies and send Mr. Berlin to London with one and Ezra with another one to Africa. Mr. Berlin, as you can imagine, vetoed that idea right away. He said he was very excited to have the show go to London but that he couldn't allow the show to go anywhere without him."

Berlin interrupted, "You fellows might as well know, Ezra is not going to be with the show wherever we go. And so McCarthy agreed that there will be just one show, with a maximum of one hundred fifty guys." Mr. B. looked around at us after saying that and then went on.

"I know you guys were all friends and I want you to understand, Ezra did a great job in the beginning. It would have been far more difficult to do it without him. I'm sorry to tell you, though, I can't work with Ezra anymore."

Rosie broke in, "Mr. B., I don't think any of us are surprised to hear that."

Berlin looked around at us.

Pete said, "I'll miss the bastard, but Rosie's right."

We all nodded and murmured agreement.

Bob Sidney went further. "Actually," he said, smiling, "I know he did a lot in getting the show organized, but I think his attitude would be poisonous to have with us."

We could feel Mr. Berlin relax.

"Thank you, fellows," he said, and after a moment, "Cutting down to one hundred fifty guys is going to be tough and after we do that, we've got to do some rewriting—make changes, new songs, new sketches. We're going to play for soldier audiences in war zones. It's a different audience—even the emotions will be different. First of all, each of you make a list in your department of the guys you can't do without, and give me all the lists."

Ben added, "One more thing: Frank McCarthy said that when you think of who should go with us, keep in mind it's going to be rugged a lot of the time. We need healthy guys."

"I'm going to write a special song for the British," Berlin added. "Remember, we'll need to look at the whole show from the point of view of being in combat zones: playing for men and women—civilians—who are in the war. We've got a lot of work to do right now." He paused for a few moments and looked at Ben, and then went on. "McCarthy wants us to make a test. He wants us to do some shows right here in California for an all-service audience—men and women who are scheduled to go overseas—to see how they react. And he wants us to have a sample show ready to open in seven days."

"Holy shit!" Rosie said with his usual direct economy. Everyone laughed helplessly.Pete was shaking his head. "Buddy, you sure have a way with words." Even Mr. B. laughed, and then gave Rosie a smile and a slap on the shoulder, and the first committee meeting was adjourned.

We couldn't talk about the plan to go to England. But of course, Pete and I decided Katie and Nancy could be trusted—for our sakes.

"Oh, my God!" Katie said. "I knew it. You're going overseas."

"Katie, dear," Nancy reassured her. "They're going to London to do the show."

Pete gave her a hug. "Don't worry, Babe. It could be a lot worse."

"They'll be as safe as all the British civilians," Nancy said.

"That's what I mean," Katie said. "I hear those mournful, wailing sirens for the air raids every night. Even Edward R. Murrow is scary: 'This is London!'" She did a pretty good imitation. We all laughed.

"Is there a schedule yet?" Nancy asked.

"Well," I said, "we go back to Camp Upton; Berlin works on new songs; we get some new sketch material; Pete and Johnny Koenig revise some of the scenery to make it easier to travel; we rehearse everything. That's just the show part of it. The Army's going to put us through some special training stuff before we go.

"How long will all that take?"

"Probably two to three months."

"Really?" She was smiling. "I can write you overseas send you some pictures."

"Yep. You'd better buy a camera. Get someone to show you how to take lots of pictures."

"At least you won't be in trenches."

"Yeah," I said.

☆ ☆ ☆ ☆ ☆ ☆ ☆ ☆ ☆ ☆ ☆

Once we had lists from each of the department heads, Mr. B. called me into his tent. Ben was with him. Mr. B. explained.

"I thought it would be easier not to have the whole committee work this out. You've been with all these guys from the beginning, Alan, and they've come to you when they've had problems. I want your opinion about the final list."

Ben broke in. "We have one temporary exception."

Berlin took over. "We have to ask Ezra to do his opening number, just for these trial shows. We don't have time to substitute another number."

It was ironic. Ezra would be doing "The Army Made a Man Out of Me." It didn't even work in the movie but it would work on stage. We added up the lists and it came to one hundred seventy. We took out five, then gradually another ten. We decided to start with one hundred fifty-five. We would have to lose four more, plus Ezra, before we finished rehearsing. We showed the new list to the committee. The committee okayed it. Ben called McCarthy and told him we had done our cutting. Before we posted the list, we had a meeting of the whole detachment and Mr. B. had to break the news.

He opened on a friendly note. "Boys, Washington has told me that we will probably go overseas. We don't know where yet, but we were told that we could only take half of the company so we've had to make a lot of difficult decisions. When you see the list of those who are going and those who aren't, I want you to know that you've all done a wonderful job and I wish that we could all stay together, but it isn't possible. I just have to thank you from the bottom of my heart for all the work you've done."

Berlin showed the list to Ambraz and then asked him to sign it and post it. It took some of the heat off us—but they came after us anyway. Quite a few of those who were not on the list wanted to get on. Very few of those we picked were unhappy.

About forty-five of the wives were with us in Hollywood and we decided to entrust them with the plans for England.

Marc Daniels's wife, Meg Mundy, had an appointment for a job interview in New York and she offered to help Nancy with the baby if they could take the same train. Nancy and I jumped at the offer. Despite having to say good-bye so suddenly it was too good to miss. Marc and I made reservations for two bedrooms on the Super Chief, departing July 12, the day before we had to leave for Santa Anita.

Helen Waggoner and Nancy were both in tears when we were loading up Marc's rented car. Alan Jr. gave Mrs. Waggoner a big smile, which helped considerably, and then the two Daniels and the three Andersons drove to Union Station, where there were more tears. Then Marc and I were standing on the platform, waving at the faces we could see through the double wall of window glass, until suddenly the windows were moving, the faces were sliding silently, drawing us along for a few steps, and then they were out of sight. We dropped our hands and stood for a few moments while the long train picked up speed, rumbled steadily faster, and disappeared from our view.

"Let's go get a drink and something to eat," Marc said.

"I especially like your first idea," I said.

☆ ☆ ☆ ☆ ☆ ☆ ☆ ☆ ☆ ☆ ☆

Camp Santa Anita, a short distance east of Los Angeles, was picked for the tryout week for all-service audiences—no civilians. Pete got the production out of storage and loaded the trucks for the camp.

We were booked for five shows. It was a big amphitheater normally used for movies. The Army regiment, Air Force, Seabees, Nurses, Red Cross, and other services in the region were enough to fill the little amphitheater for every show.

We spent four days rehearsing and setting up. In spite of their deep enmity, Mr. B. asked Ezra to do his number to help the show, explaining that there wasn't time to develop another comedy number. Ezra agreed. He was still in the Army and he knew it would make it easier for all his friends on the show. We had cut most of the ballet dancing. We kept all the specialty acts, the comedy and the love songs. Mr. B. did his song without the Old Timers. In rehearsal the orchestra of twenty-four men (instead of forty-six) and the chorus of sixty men (instead of one hundred seventy-one), seemed not to lose any of their effectiveness.

After our dress rehearsal, Carl said, "It's a piece of cake. McCarthy will love it!" But we were all nervous about how it would go. Only the committee members were aware of how much hung in the balance.

Our first performance was on July 17. The audience was in place right on time. I gave the cue to dim house lights and for Rosie's cue to start. Rosie and the boys charged into the overture with gusto; the twenty-four men sounded like fifty. The overture got us an enthusiastic reception. The opening number produced a wildly cheering, stamping audience. The whole show went that way. The reactions were bigger than any of the civilian audiences. These guys were hungry for us.

"Why the hell wasn't McCarthy here tonight?" Pete said after the show.

We kept watching for him every day. Before the curtain went up on the fourth show, Mr. B. asked me to keep everyone on stage after the show. No sign of McCarthy. It was another great audience response. After the final curtain, Mr. B. surprised us by walking on stage leading a colonel.

"Boys, I'd like you to meet Colonel Frank McCarthy from General

Marshall's office."

McCarthy walked to center stage and spoke very briefly. "Absolutely great show, gentlemen. It's going to be a hit wherever you play it. Thank you for your hard work." With those brief but welcome words, McCarthy and Mr. B. left us. Pete, Rosie, Carl and I went into town for a drink. "Where the hell did he come from? Did he actually see the show?" Rosie asked. None of us knew.

The committee met with Mr. B. and the Colonel the next morning. McCarthy smiled at us and made a confession. "I didn't want you to get nervous about my appearance so I slipped into a side seat after the show started. In case you're wondering, Mr. Berlin and I have been talking about your plans from here on. I'll just say this much. You're great. Give 'em hell in London!"

We all cheered.

"Holy shit!" said our infallible Rosie. The Colonel couldn't restrain a laugh.

"I take it you like the idea," he said to Rosie. "But please remember—it's still a military secret."

Rosie, somewhat chastened, but happy said, "Yes, sir."

"What can we tell the boys, Frank?" Mr. B. asked.

"Tell them they're doing a great job and that the show is going to keep going." Then he relented a little. "Actually, you could tell them they're going back to Camp Upton to work on new material in the show before they start playing—somewhere."

☆ ☆ ☆ ☆ ☆ ☆ ☆ ☆ ☆ ☆

When we returned to Burbank, most of the company was still in Camp *TITA*. Very few transfers had occurred thus far. There was little to do but wait eleven days for the troop train departure. We maintained a regular three-hour drill schedule on weekdays for the company.

Rosie, Pete, Carl and I gave Ezra a farewell dinner at the Brown Derby.

"Have you got anything on the fire yet, Ez?" Rosie asked.

"I kinda knew this was coming. I talked to Phillipson some time ago. I'm supposed to meet with him next week. And I'm making notes for a book."

"Be sure you spell my name right," Pete said.

We drank to each other and to our wives and talked about some of the things they all remembered about Camp Upton and the Opry House days. I hadn't been there so I listened.

We promised to keep in touch with Ezra and to let him know where we were. And we managed to keep laughing a lot.

We didn't talk about Mr. B. I was glad Ezra didn't bring him up.

Private First Class Alan Lowell, basso, mail-carrier, came to me with a letter. Alan never quite lost a German accent. "Sergeant, I guess this will be the last mail we'll have in Hollywood. We switch to Upton from here on."

I had one from the Red Barn. "I think he said daddy." Wow! I stuck it in my pocket.Major Ambraz couldn't bear to leave Hollywood. He arranged what he called a Thank You Party for the Warner Brothers on the Sunday afternoon before we were to leave for Camp Upton. He had the Orderly Room staff mail out invitations to the entire cast and crew from the movie, and with help from the Warner Brothers production office, to a few stars they thought were in town—Bette Davis, Joan Crawford, John Garfield, Humphrey Bogart, Errol Flynn, and a half dozen others. The invitation read:

> 4:00 p.m. to dark, in honor of the Warner Brothers, champagne picnic and entertainment in Irving Berlin's *This Is the Army* tent area.

Rosie had a small band prepared to provide music. The prop department had installed a modest dance floor in front of the band.

The sound department had provided microphones for both speech-making and singing. Several of our guys volunteered to do some singing and dancing. Mendes the Magician was going to do his stuff. The result was that most of the detachment showed. Free champagne, after all, wasn't available every day.

Regrets were received from Ronald Reagan, Michael Curtiz, LeRoy Prinz and our own Mr. B. who had flown east for a weekend with his family. Joan Leslie, who played Reagan's girlfriend, appeared graciously, as did Charlie Butterworth, the bugler in the movie. Conspicuously absent and without regrets was everyone else, including the guests of honor, the Warner Brothers.

Major Ambraz, looking somewhat bewildered by Hollywood's careless treatment of his grandeur, drank several glasses. And, of course, most of the detachment took advantage of the lavish quantities of alcoholic liquids available.

Private Louis de Milhau, an intelligent young man from a well-to-do Boston family, whose only contribution to the show was to sing in the chorus, loosened his tongue with champagne and climbed to the top of the jungle gym in the obstacle course. Teetering above us, he spoke in clear, precise Bostonian, utilizing his theatrical speech training.

"We are honored to present this festive occasion in the majestic confines of this Hollywood acreage. In the world of klieg light and sound boom, we'd hoped to be amidst the glamour of contract players and names that light the marquees of a thousand cinema houses. We raise a glass, our hearts aflutter, searching in vain to find ourselves ignored. For sad to say, there is not among this gathered throng one *single, solitary Warner Brother!*"

Louis, his arms raised, supplicating some unseen Gods of Filmdom, lost his balance, slipped from his perch and tumbled into a welcoming sawdust pit, from which he was plucked by some of our gallant lot, who lifted him to their shoulders and carried him safely to his tent. Rosie, whose band was silent during Louis's performance, played a farewell coda. Major Ambraz thanked Joan Leslie for coming. She kissed him on the cheek, everyone applauded her gesture and the Hollywood careers of Simon Ambraz and Louis de Milhau came to an end.

Chapter 10

THE WAR
—July 10, 1943: US and British forces make successful landings in Sicily against poorly equipped defenses.
—July 16, 1943: Churchill and Roosevelt call on the Italians to surrender.
—July 22, 1943: Patton's US 7th Army enters Palermo, Italy.
—July 25, 1943: King Victor Emmanuel III relieves Mussolini of his office.

This Is the Army, the movie, had its world premiere at the Warner Brothers Theater on Sunset Boulevard. To no one's surprise, it got very good reviews. The Hollywood press was not going to let the stage show top the motion picture version.

We ourselves were disappointed in the film. In spite of the hoopla and the elaborate production, it lacked the vitality and immediacy of our show. However, our boys did well and Mr. B.'s songs and his performance were superb.

It was fun to have been involved with the movie, even playing tiny scenes, and wonderful to have had so much time with my wife and son. I knew I would be missing that soon.

Leaving the world of Hollywood and coming down to earth, we could not help being aware of the sobering war news that was everywhere. During the months of making the movie, the Allies had been fighting bloody battles in North Africa, on the Russian front, in the Balkans, and all over the islands of the Pacific. Our Navy and Air forces were trying desperately to gain control of the Atlantic so that we could supply our Allies without the loss of so many ships and men to German submarine attacks. We and our allies were gradually winning ground on most fronts, but necessarily at a great cost of lives.

In Poland, following a desperate uprising of many thousands of Jews held prisoners, came heartbreaking news:

THE WARSAW UPRISING IS BRUTALLY CRUSHED. GERMANY BLOWS UP
SYNAGOGUES. 14,000 HAVE BEEN KILLED AND ALMOST THREE TIMES
THAT NUMBER SENT TO THE TREBLINKA EXTERMINATION CAMP.

Our troop train moved east through San Bernardino, heading
toward the east and Camp Upton, leaving the world of Hollywood
behind and rumbling slowly through the low rent suburbs toward San
Bernardino. From the elevated train windows you could almost touch
the tenement buildings — all brick, little apartments, flags in some windows for sons and husbands away at war.

"Hey, let's get out of this town," Rosie said. "This is depressing."

At that moment, Danny Longo, on duty to distribute K-rations,
dropped one in Rosie's lap.

"Maybe lunch will cheer you up," said Pete.

Rosie lifted a packet of nourishment like a trophy. "Yeah! Who needs
the Brown Derby? I'm sick of all that rich food!"

"Well," said Pete, "maybe you and Blubber will slim down on this
ride."

We made a lot of stops, dropping cars off, hitching others on.
Occasionally we'd stop long enough to take an exercise break. I stood
up and tapped Rosie on the shoulder.

"Before you open all those goodies, how about a little exercise?
We're about to have forty-five minutes in Laramee, Wyoming. I'll bet
you've never even been there."

My suggestion spread through the cars like wild fire. I ended up
leading a large group for a jog. When we rounded the block we passed
a huge, hospitable-looking saloon. On impulse, I made a left turn,
leading the guys through the swinging doors. I set an example by
ordering a boiler-maker — a shot of bourbon with a beer chaser — plus
pretzels. Finally, it was time to start back to the train. Even Rosie was
smiling when we got back. A lot of guys picked that moment to dig
into the K-rations.

In Chicago, we had a three-hour wait while they shifted our cars to a Pennsylvania Railroad engine. I got Nancy on the phone in the red barn and asked about their trip.

"He adored Meg," she said, "so it was actually restful. It's Daddy, Punk." Silence. "Talk to Daddy." Silence. So I talked to him. No reply. "He can hear you and he's looking into the phone, trying to see where you are." Her voice sounded so good.

Arriving at Camp Upton, we settled into the Army routine for three weeks of training, orientation lectures and instructive films in the same CCC barracks we had left fourteen months earlier. No Buick this time. Mr. B. worked on new songs in New York. We were on our own from Friday afternoon until Monday morning for reveille. I spent several glorious weekends in the Red Barn, which I reached by train and ferry. I saw everyone, swam in the pool and had lots of time with Nancy and Kett, a new nickname everyone was using. Our son and I shared my mother's maiden name, Haskett, as our middle name, hence, Kett!

We finished up our training films with how to behave in a foreign country and what to do if you are taken prisoner. Mr. B. appeared during our last week and the committee spent an afternoon with him discussing rehearsal plans and changes in the show. On September 19 we took a train into Penn Station, found our own quarters, and rehearsed daily at the Labor Stage Theater on 32nd Street and Sixth Avenue for three weeks and three days.

We decided everything had to be new and shining for the London opening. Bob Sidney rehearsed the staging; Jus Addiss and I worked with the sketches and the variety numbers. Pete Feller and crew completely rebuilt, painted and stained the scenery, actually making it easier to travel. Costumes were either new or renewed; props remade. Everything was new and shiny, ready for the great Palladium. .

We did a dress rehearsal for a small, invited audience to make sure everything worked before packing up the show. We got a wonderful response from wives, family members, people from Mr.B.'s office. Nancy got a sitter and came with Byron and Betty.

We all said good-bye to Mr. B. The Army was flying him to London. We would see him next in London, before the opening. "Don't be late!" he said, little knowing how relevant his warning would be. Huge, deep-voiced, uncouth strip-show comedian Sergeant Hank Henry replied on our behalf, "Don't worry, Boss! I'll promise the captain a Piccadilly chick if he docks on time."

Pete and his crew struck the show, ready to load trucks in the morning. Nancy and I left the theater at midnight and went to Byron and Betty's apartment. We all had a nightcap and talked for an hour before turning in.

I set the alarm for 7:00. After breakfast, Byron and Betty came down with us in the elevator. Byron had called the doorman, who had a cab waiting. I said good-bye and thanked them for all the times they had given us a home in the past year and a half. And then Nancy and I kissed and I slipped quickly into the cab.

When we turned left at 69th Street, she was still standing under the awning waving. Her father had his arm around her. And then the buildings cut us off and I was staring at limestone.

Once again we were apart, never knowing how long it would be.

✩ ✩ ✩ ✩ ✩ ✩ ✩ ✩ ✩ ✩ ✩

We assumed that it must have been at Mr. B.'s request to change CO's and leave Ambraz behind. Ambraz had been assigned as Assistant Provost Marshall at Camp Shanks, which was our embarkation point. In addition to Marc, we had Lieutenant John Koenig, our scene designer. Two lieutenants! Not much clout with the Army bureaucracy. I felt sure Mr. B. would request a CO with higher rank before long.

At 1:30 p.m. on Wednesday, October 13, 1943, the Detachment left the Labor Stage Theater in a truck convoy, with all our baggage and equipment and made the two-hour drive uptown through Manhattan to the George Washington Bridge, and then north through the eastern edge of New Jersey, into the southern edge of New York state to our staging area, Camp Shanks. And there he was again, our ex-CO, Major Ambraz, assigned by the camp to meet us.

It was completely familiar country to me, paralleling my route when I lived in the country and drove to my theater stage-managing jobs on Broadway. I kept staring off to see the familiar outline of "High Tor," the mountain peak above South Mountain Road. I came back to earth when we jumped out of the trucks in front of the three barracks buildings we had been assigned—fifteen miles from Nancy and Kett. This huge overseas staging area had been built at the beginning of the war in Orangeburg, New York, right next to the West Shore Railroad. The site was chosen because it was just a half hour train ride from the Hudson River piers from which the ships left to cross the Atlantic.

We assigned the men to our three barracks and I set up our orderly room with my two clerks, Sergeant Dave Supple and Corporal Arnold Bachner. We assembled in the day room and Marc read off the security regulations. *TITA* was under particular orders not to let anyone in the camp know our identity. We were known only as Detachment 0665-A, *period*. We were allowed to make phone calls and write letters from the camp, but we were not to let anyone know our whereabouts. Carrying rifles, wearing helmets, in uniform we looked like every other outfit—almost. One hundred forty-nine of us were white; the other sixteen were black. That was not only unusual but unique in the United States Armed Forces. I couldn't help noticing when I looked around that racial integration wasn't the only red flag. Show folks betrayed characteristic abnormalities of behavior that unquestionably separated them from the average Joe. Some were too handsome or too agile or too prone to make jokes in accents or with facial exaggerations or do things with their feet or their hands that were too big, somehow—a sort of habitual flamboyance.

Pete, Rosie, Carl and I slept next to the Orderly Room. We were busy making up our bunks when Rosie brought up the subject of our anonymity.

"What'll you bet before we've been here two days, they'll be asking us to do a show!"

"I'll take that bet. I say three days—unless you guys blab!"

Pete could never resist a gamble. "Twenty-four hours for five bucks from each of you! Put up or shut up!"

"Let me remind you of one thing: It's not worth fifteen bucks to get our boat sunk!" I said. "So we'd better hope we're all wrong."

☆ ☆ ☆ ☆ ☆ ☆ ☆ ☆ ☆ ☆ ☆

We had a typical GI Army schedule. Mr. B. would have loved our routine. Reveille 5:20 a.m., formation 5:45, breakfast 6:00, dinner 11:15 a.m., supper 4:30! And then they kept throwing things at us. The first day we had dental inspection right after dinner. The next day, we were issued impregnated clothing to keep the germs away. There were lectures on behavior in foreign countries, on secrecy, on making a good impression, on cleanliness, punctuality, on how we would be able to write V-Mail home wherever we were.

We made it through two days. Pete lost. On the third day, a first sergeant walked up to me, saw my stripes and said, "Hi ya, Sarge. Where you from? Where you going?" I realized we all should have had answers ready for questions like that.

"Uh, actually, I don't know," I said, avoiding eye contact. "They've changed our orders a couple of times."

"We're headed for Italy," he said. "Actually, I'm looking forward to it. I'm half Italian." "Hey, that's great!" I said, and then I saw Marc down the hall and decided to use him. "Excuse me, I have to catch my lieutenant." So I got past that one. Half an hour later, I was talking to Sergeant Stump Cross and joking about how we loved being out in the country—all free meals and a place to sleep—when a young lieutenant came up to Stump. We both saluted.

"At ease, guys. Excuse me, Sergeant, but I wonder if you would consider doing a little entertaining while you're here?" Boom. Just like that. Stump smiled his characteristic wide grin, all teeth, and a jolly crinkle around his eyes. He looked at me and didn't know what to say. Stump's broad grin was no help at all.

"Sir," I said, "Would it be possible for you to approach our CO, Lieutenant Daniels, about this? He would be in a better position to give you a reply. I think he's in our Orderly Room. I'll take you there, if you like." Boy was I being secure.

The result was that Marc agreed we could do a little entertainment as long as it was understood that our only identification was 0665-A. The lieutenant, who turned out to be the Special Services officer of Shanks, understood, but it was the same old story: he was desperate to give the troops some distraction. He and Marc talked to Ambraz, who brought in the Shanks CO, a Colonel Lambert. The Colonel was delighted.

A formation was called for 6:00 p.m. and the detachment was marched to Theater Number Three. The sign on the door said there was to be a lecture. Title: "Personal Services." That was us. Promptly at 6 p.m., our guys proceeded to give about an hour and fifteen minutes of song, dance and jokes to an audience of about one thousand men and women, all in service. We had done such impromptu shows so often for so many gatherings, large and small, that it was no problem. The audience loved it. Our comedians threw in some ad-lib gags about Shanks that drew special appreciation. Hank Henry added a bit of censurable filth, which also found a grateful audience, even among the several nurses and WACs present. After the show, the audience was warned not to talk about it to anyone outside of Shanks. And, of course, they wouldn't, except maybe to their wives or girlfriends or parents or lifetime buddies.

"I guess as long as that's the end of it we'll be all right," Marc said.

☆ ☆ ☆ ☆ ☆ ☆ ☆ ☆ ☆ ☆ ☆

The next day we turned in our Springfield rifles, actually World War I weapons, and were told they would be replaced by .30 caliber carbines before leaving Shanks.

"What the hell is a 'car-bean'?" Rosie asked.

"It's a gun! Act like you know," I said. "I think it's just easier to carry around."

After breakfast, Marc took me aside where no one could hear us talking. "I took the liberty of having Meg call Nancy to see if she could pick us both up and drive up to your place tonight for one last visit. We may ship out the next day so it would be our last chance. Was that okay?"

"Was that okay!" I said, my grin completely transparent. Marc was able to get passes from Colonel Lambert, who was happy to show his gratitude for the entertainment.

At 8:10 p.m. we showed our passes to the MPs, met Meg out at the gate and drove to the Red Barn. We couldn't believe we were together. She and Meg had a little supper for us. We had a good chat and once Kett was asleep, we all retired.

Having not even hoped for such an opportunity, we were both filled with the most enormous, relaxed joy. It seemed like a miracle visit. After breakfast the next morning we said good-bye again. Nancy gave Marc a big hug for making it all possible. Kett put on Marc's cap and made us all laugh. I kissed them both and got in the car. Meg drove us back to the Shanks gate. The MPs checked our passes. We waved to Meg as she drove away. We were back inside Camp Shanks by 8:00 a.m.

☆ ☆ ☆ ☆ ☆ ☆ ☆ ☆ ☆ ☆ ☆ ☆

There was a formation called at noon. We were informed that we were now on alert for departure. All passes were canceled and we were strictly limited to Shanks. We all had typhus shots and once again fell into the old Army routine: hurry up and wait. We went to bed Saturday night with no idea when we would leave. On Sunday we had to practice packing our rolls properly. Every man's equipment was checked and once again we went to bed without knowing anything. Monday after breakfast we had a medical examination of every member, followed by a lecture on the .30 caliber carbine rifle, which was then issued to each member except to master and first sergeants: we were assigned .45 caliber revolvers and had separate instructions on their operation. After we had all broken down and reassembled our pieces, we learned that we would learn how to fire them the next day.

Tuesday morning, we boarded trucks at 6:15 and drove to Camp Smith in Peekskill, New York. We were all on the firing range with our new carbines and side-arms until 4:15 p.m. when we returned to Shanks. Once more we were told that we must be prepared to move out at any moment, day or night. Then, instead of a bedtime story, we had another security lecture, with special emphasis on how critical it was to hide the identity of our outfit. Finally, on Wednesday, October 20, 1943, we were awake for reveille at 5:30 a.m. and told to pack all our gear for departure. Port Authority officials inspected us at 8:30 a.m. and once more we waited. Dinner was served at 11:15 a.m., and finally, at 1:30 p.m. we put on our packs, picked up our arms, marched to the Orangeburg Railroad Station and stood at ease waiting for the train to arrive. Major Ambraz arrived by jeep and climbed out, took our salute and wished us all a fond farewell.

The men looked great. Our anonymity was the best we could do. You couldn't tell a dancer from an infantryman. I guess you could tell black from white. Maybe no one would notice.

Suddenly, as the train slid into the station and stopped, and we were lined up to board, the Camp Shanks post band appeared and with great gusto started to play "This Is the Army, Mister Jones." Our instinct was to be invisible. We didn't know whether to laugh or get angry. Marc signaled us to climb on board as rapidly as possible. Johnny Koenig hurried over to the bandleader waving his arms at him, shaking his head. There weren't many civilians around to hear the music, but then it would only take one. The band began to falter a few at a time as they got the signal from the leader, and finally fizzled into silence, looking very confused. They milled around, not knowing what was expected of them next. The leader tried frantically to find a substitute song. By the time they broke into a rough rendition of "Anchors Aweigh," the last of the company was boarding the train and the conductor was calling "All Aboa—rd!" The activity and the new music struck a rather unusual mix.

Once I was in the old West Shore Railroad car, it reminded me of all the familiar neighbors in Rockland County, who commuted to work from Haverstraw and Congers to Manhattan by way of this train and the ancient Weehawken ferry, which we would board in half an hour or so.

When we debarked from the ferry, we marched to Pier 50 and faced quite a large ocean liner. Again there was a military band on the pier. It was not playing when we arrived, but as we marched along the pier toward the gangplank, they broke into a lusty rendition of—guess what?—"This Is the Army, Mister Jones!"

It seemed an absolute certainty that if there were any spies anywhere within twenty blocks, they would have to be deaf, dumb and blind by now to be unaware that the *This Is the Army* Detachment was at this very moment, on the 20th of October, 1943, boarding a ship bound for Liverpool, England, and according to the newspapers, would play the Palladium Theater in London, England. Now they knew how and when we were traveling.

If it were possible for men to put their tails between their legs, a hundred and sixty-five mortified, indignant, embarrassed soldiers did just that as they trudged slowly up the crowded gangplank. In spite of wearing winter uniforms and bearing the weight of combat equipment and heavy field packs, we felt absolutely naked.

Chapter 11

THE WAR
— Oct 13, 1943: In Italy US 5th Army has begun its push at the Volturno River. Italy declares war on Germany.
— Oct 15, 1943: The Allies breach German line on Volturno. The Germans make a fighting withdrawal.
— Oct 22, 1943: An RAF raid by 486 bombers made on German aircraft factory.

My first thought when I stepped off the gangplank and onto deck of the ship was, did everyone see or hear that debacle, that disclosure of our identity, with the band playing us aboard? But the guy asking me for my berthing card was all routine, businesslike — no sign that I was one of the jerks who had blown the security of the whole ship. Nothing. He just read my card, "Starboard Writing Room. That'll be on B deck, mate, forward, starboard side. You're on C deck."

I said thanks and told him the guys behind me were going to the same place. I moved to one side, they stuck their cards out, and he sent them on with me. We all started up to B deck.

"Nobody seems to have heard what was going on," I said to Pete as we went.

"They're all too busy to notice what happened," Pete said. "Only a spy would pay any attention!"

"Oh, great!" I said.

We were surrounded by hundreds of men and some women — nurses, WACs, Red Cross — a wide variety of uniforms, all searching for their berths. Every square foot of the ship seemed to be occupied by either tiers of bunks or sleeping mats. There was a runty little crewman just outside the Starboard Writing Room. He glanced at Rosie's card which was in his free hand.

"You lucky blokes are right in here."

"Lucky?" said Rosie. "Is this a lucky ship?"

"Nice quiet room. She's a good ship. I was on her years ago when she was just a cruise ship. You know her name? *Monarch of Bermuda.* British Navy brought me back. Used to carry twelve hundred, New York to Bermuda. You wouldn't know it. She carries five thousand Yanks now, layin' all over, everywhere." He shook his head, hated to see her this way.

He stayed in the doorway, wanting to gab. "We'll try to treat her well," I said. I looked around, the desks and chairs were gone. Five tiers of bunks, three in each tier. We slid our bags under the bottom bunks. I grabbed a bottom bunk, Pete was above me, Carl on top, Rosie next tier.

"She's twenty-three thousand tons, 580-foot. Luxury ship. Not no more. You won't like the mess. I'm glad I don't have to eat it."

"Thanks for warning us," Pete said. "You couldn't slip us a little of your food, could you? Make it worth your trouble."

"You won't mind much. You only get two meals a day—there's no time for three. Maybe that's for the best!" He laughed heartily. "I'll see if I can slip you something." And he disappeared.

"I guess we can be sure of one thing," Carl said. "The food must be *lousy.*"

More of our guys showed up for the other eleven bunks including Bob Sidney.

"I thought this was the Ladies Writing Room," Bob said seeing us. "What are you all doing in here?"

"We didn't want you to be alone, Bob," Pete said.

"Well, you'd better not snore. I need my beauty sleep." At that moment, Lieutenant Marc Daniels appeared at the door.

"Oh, here you are. Good." We all greeted him. "We have to make some plans, fellows. It seems Frank McCarthy made a deal with the American troop commander, Colonel Green. They want us to give two shows a day in the main dining area. In exchange for that, he would give the show priority treatment including permanent bunk assignments." He handed me a list. "Alan, that's a diagram of where all our guys are berthed. Could you get your stage managers to help you round everyone up for a meeting in the dining room on C deck as soon as everyone gets settled—let's say in one hour, okay?"

"Fine," I said.

Lieutenant Koenig appeared at the door. "Hooray! I've been all over the ship looking for you guys."

Marc explained his discussion with the troop commander. "They have trouble keeping up any reasonable morale level on these long, slow convoys, because there's very little room to move around and very little to do and, according to him, not very good food. Having a show like ours on board is a godsend. By the way, Rosie, all the musical instruments are available."

"Good thinking!" was Rosie's response. "It'll give our guys something to do."

"I suggested to the Colonel," Marc continued, "that in addition to doing two shows a day we have a variety unit that goes around the ship." The suggestion was met with a moment of silence and then Bob Sidney spoke up. His tone was somewhat condescending.

"Thank you for the suggestion, Lieutenant, but I think actually we ought to have several small units with a variety of performers, just as we've done hundreds of times."

Marc's reply was dismissive. "I've already presented the idea to the Colonel and he liked it."

"Forgive my saying so, sir," said Bob, "but the colonel knows nothing about our show or our capabilities—and we do. And as a matter fact, as long as we're planning shows, I think you ought to let the show people do the planning."

"Just a minute, Sergeant, I've already made an agreement with the Colonel—"

Bob interrupted, "The Colonel only expected two shows. He's certainly not going to object to our covering the whole ship—"

"I don't want to change things."

"Marc, sir, we're not changing anything. We hadn't decided anything!"

"I had!"

"Well, it wasn't your business—"

"Sergeant! You're out of order!"

Johnny Koenig jumped in with an amiable smile and a good, loud voice. "*Gentlemen*, this is clearly a committee matter and so it should be decided according to committee procedures. It isn't something you and Bob should decide without the committee."

Marc was silent for a moment. We could feel his officer's bars steaming. He attempted to take back some of his control. "I don't want to hold up the decision by taking the time for a committee meeting."

"The committee is all here," John said looking around the room. "Let's settle it this minute. I think I agree with Bob, Marc." The rest of us said, "Agreed."

There was a frigid moment of silence. Then Marc spoke. "Give me the time to go back to the Colonel and tell him we'd like to improve the plan by changing it to several show units and see if he has any objections."

"Fine," said John enthusiastically. He looked at the rest of us.

"I agree," said Rosie. Pete and I said "Fine," and the question was settled.

"I'll be right back," Marc said and then he stopped.

"By the way, the Colonel told me in confidence that in exchange for our entertainment we get our own bunks around the clock—no hot bunks.

"What the hell is a hot bunk?" asked Pete.

"When the bunks are shared," Marc said, "one occupant gets twelve hours then another one takes over. That's a hot bunk."

"That doesn't sound bad at all," Bob said. Everyone laughed and the crisis passed. Marc smiled in spite of himself and left us.

"Holy shit!" Rosie said.

"Thanks, John," I said. "That was close. Marc doesn't like Berlin's committee."

"But you tease him, Bob."

"Honestly, she's so square."

"But you know that. Just try to avoid arguments."

Marc came back looking cheerful. "The guy almost kissed me!" he said.

"I knew I should have gone with you!" said Bob.

"Next time, Bob," Marc said.

"I'll get Jus and Hayden and we'll print up a schedule," I said to Marc.

"Thanks," he said and left us.

We all looked at each other. John gave a forced chuckle.

"Thanks," I said. We breathed a sigh of relief and went to work on the scheduling.

When I returned, I met Carl at the rail, watching the crew. The gang-plank had been stowed away but we were still tied up to the dock.

"Maybe they're waiting for the bangers and the Brussels sprouts." I said.

"Not the caviar?" Carl said.

Finally our dinner bell rang and we had our first meal aboard. Both the bangers and the sprouts were in ample supply. There was no caviar.

The bangers were ninety percent bread. There were some seriously overcooked green beans, something white and mashed which could once have been potato.

Our breakfast next morning did nothing to raise our hopes about the food. We were still tied up to the dock. Rosie moaned. "If Mr. B. could see us sitting here while he's pacing around London, he'd cut somebody's balls off!"

At 1:15 p.m. we felt a shudder, voices shouting commands. We went out on deck. A tug was alongside taking a line. Pete joined us and Rosie gave him a whack on the back. "Here we go, Pete!"

Pete responded with a smile and then, "I wonder when we join our convoy."

The rails were covered with uniformed men and here and there again, nurses, WACs, Red Cross. I tried to think of what it would be like for me if Nancy were one of them, wearing a uniform, going to the war fronts.

I suddenly remembered when I was only fifteen, my father putting me at the wheel of our family boat, in this same water, keeping clear of huge ships like the *Monarch*.

The buildings of lower Manhattan were slipping away. We were moving faster, the buildings further from us, the lower harbor widening ahead. Pete and I looked at each other, smiling, sharing the sense that our adventure had started. Nancy and the Red Barn was a world away. The ocean stretched out—on and on.

"Man, does that guy have any idea what he started!"

"Mr. B.?"

"I'll bet he never thought he was going to be in command of his own Army outfit heading for London!" Carl said.

"He's been in England before. The British are crazy about him!" Rosie said.

New York looked like a tiny model sitting on the horizon—tinier and tinier.

"Here they come, Pete!" Out in open water, suddenly we were not alone. Pete came over and stood next to me. "Look at 'em!" Our convoy was forming—one, two, three ships at a time—with a long double line of freighters and troop carriers of which we were the largest; and then a half mile or so on each side of us, another line—destroyer escorts plowing along, small and gray, low in the water, competent and businesslike. And every so often, huge impressive battleships and aircraft carriers cutting the water with authority.

Rosie was next to us. He said quietly, almost to himself, "Will you look at those big bastards!"

"Yeah," I said. "Could submarines get past all that?"

The convoy was moving slowly, almost languidly, an easy target. What was the convoy rule? Oh, yes: Convoys could travel no faster than the slowest member. How long would it take to reach Liverpool, our assumed port, at the speed of our slowest ship?

We heard that the British were so anxious to get the show on in London that they considered putting us on the *Queen Mary*, which could make the crossing in half the time and outrun any u-boat as long as no one knew her route or schedule. However, judging by our experience at the railroad station and dockside, it would have been hard to sneak us aboard the *Queen*.

I looked out at the four lines of ships—stretching from horizon to horizon. Thousands of men and women, thousands of tons of materiel, freight, food, arms, people, all going to war.

On the second day out, we started giving two evening shows and several small daytime shows in different sections of the ship. Shows of any length—whatever we did, they gathered around and clapped and laughed and cheered. We gave them everything: tap dancers, acrobats, a juggler, a magician, comedians, soloists with and without choral background, jazz combos, a string quartet, a brass band, and a special: Max Showalter playing piano and singing pop solos in the dining room.

Could Mr. B., flying, look down and see us four or five miles below, singing and dancing his songs as we plowed through the Atlantic waves?

I gave Marc a copy of the show schedules. I was glad to see he didn't seem to be upset about having the committee override him.

Johnny Koenig joined us at the rail on the third day. "Hey, kiddies! Have you heard? The other ships in the convoy are calling us 'The Showboat.' They want us to send them some entertainment."

"Where'd you hear that?" Rosie asked.

"Ship's officer," he said. "The Captain replied, 'Not on your life!' The subs would love a situation like that. Small boats going from ship to ship in the open ocean would be a disaster."

☆ ☆ ☆ ☆ ☆ ☆ ☆ ☆ ☆ ☆ ☆

The food didn't help morale. It was uniformly tasteless. Boredom drove some of our intrepid members to look for an answer. They talked to the cooks, offered bribes, scrounged around the storage rooms.

TITA's champion scrounger was Private First Class Danny Longo. Danny was listed as a singer on our duty roster. He was an okay singer. As an "operator" he was number one. When we needed something and there was no wholly legal way to get it, we called upon Danny. Another characteristic of Danny's was his tendency to curry favor with authority. He buttered up the boss or "kissed ass," as his comrades put it. The result was that when Danny discovered where there were several cases of C-rations, otherwise known as canned corned beef hash, he brought a case to the Starboard Writing Room, together with a can opener. The case slid nicely under my bunk. We shared it cautiously with our Writing Room mates. Everyone agreed that C-rations were a culinary masterpiece next to the *Monarch*'s kitchen.

The weather provided some variety. Our first day was sunny and beautiful with a smooth ocean. Our second brought sheets of rain and high waves and some seasickness. A PX[1] opened on day two, selling chocolate candies and cookies which were devoured rapidly. We all received a routine medical check. In addition, nurses worked their way through the ship giving typhus shots.

On day three, Rosie put together a small group to play dance music on the upper deck in the afternoons. Nurses, USO and Red Cross girls volunteered their time for that.

Poor weather continued through the fourth day. I cheered myself up by writing a V-Mail letter to Nancy. The censor's black ink prevented me from telling her much that she didn't already know. I could tell her that today several of the guys were seasick, but I could not report on how anxious we were to hear the bells ringing in Westminster Abbey.

The fifth day was rainy and even rougher. The sixth was cloudy but memorable because the crew said we were halfway across. Days seven

1. An Army, Navy or Air Force store carrying all sorts of supplies to eat or use.

and eight were beautiful, and then as we approached the coast of Ireland on day nine, we ran into heavy fog. So far, there was no behavior from our escort vessels which indicated submarine activity.

Rosie invited the three of us to join him for a little party in our room. He had acquired several bottles of 3.2 beer and two attractive Red Cross girls who had approached him during the afternoon dancing party. Rosie decided Carl's bunk was the ideal choice. We climbed up to the top bunk, where we could hang our legs over the edge or sit Buddha-like and cheer ourselves up with chatter and beer. We shared tales of how we all got there, told some jokes and discussed the world in general and this voyage in particular. The subject of how we missed our wives and how pleasant it was to enjoy mixed company arose somehow with a further observation from Rosie.

He could be counted on for bluntly addressing any subject. "You spend enough time with nobody but your own sex and you begin to wish you were a fag," he said, and roared with uninhibited laughter.

"I wouldn't go that far," Pete said. "They must have to pick and choose."

The brunette spoke up, "Rosie's got a point, though. We have some ladies on board who have the same advantage."

"No matter where we go, they've got us beat," said Rosie.

"There's gotta be a better answer," said Carl.

"Doesn't everybody play around?" the blonde wanted to know.

"Yes and no," said Pete.

"Yeah, but a fag doesn't have to feel guilty."

As Rosie finished that statement, we were interrupted.

Clearly we did not have the room to ourselves. Cassie Jaeger rose from a lower bunk near the door and marched out of the room without saying a word or looking at us. There was a stunned silence. Why did it have to be Cassie? A very nice guy and always a gentleman. He was gay but was he was quiet and retiring—never flamboyant.

"Oh, shit," said Rosie. "Me and my big mouth. How long has he been there?"

"He must have been asleep when we came in," Carl said.

"Oh, dear. You mean he's a fag?" the blonde asked innocently.

"That's the general supposition," said Pete.

"Shit," Rosie repeated. "He's a fag all right, but he's also one of the nicest guys in the outfit."

Carl tried to reassure him, "It's probably happened to him before, Rosie. He'll get over it."

"What'll I say?" Rosie was mortified.

"Nothing right now," said Pete. "Wait'll he cools down a little. He's probably telling Miss Sidney about you right now. He'll tell you off!"

Cassie was one of the dancers who had been in several Broadway shows with choreographer Bob Sidney. They were good friends. The whole outfit was generally friendly—gays, straights, blacks, whites. Nobody in the outfit cared. But there was a difference between Bob and Cassie. If it had been Bob who had heard our conversation he would have verbally ripped our guts out. Cassie was too gentle and sensitive to fire back.

The subject changed. Nobody wanted to talk about that for the time being. The sea was still rough. It was raining. There was no place to go. We kept sipping beer

"I wonder what we're having for dinner," Carl said. "Perhaps a beautiful scaloppini of veal—in a light creamy sauce, just a touch of lemon." The brunette said, "How about a Caesar salad? Pete suggested a filet mignon, rare. I opted for a three-pound steamed lobster with lots of melted butter. It did no harm to dream. We helped the girls climb down.

"Keep doing the shows," they said. "Maybe we'll get a chance to see you at the Palladium."

After they left, Rosie climbed down, too. "Sorry, guys. I think I'll do some letter writing."

I went up on deck, thinking about Cassie. Morale is a primary concern of first sergeants and also of stage managers. I filled a double parental role with these guys. I tracked Cassie down in the dining area

Kate Smith, the singer who introduced Berlin's "God Bless America" to the world, wrote a $10,000 check for opening night seats in New York as Irving Berlin and several *TITA* members looked on.

A beaming Eleanor Roosevelt visiting backstage at the Broadway Theatre in New York. *Foreground, left to right:* Irving Berlin, Eleanor Roosevelt, Mrs. James Roosevelt and in profile, in a white Navy uniform, Lt. James Roosevelt. Between Mr. B. and Eleanor is Sgt. John Cooper, our head electrician. Between Eleanor and her daughter-in-law are Sgts. Alan Anderson and Carl Fisher.

In Boston, *left to right:* Alan Anderson, his wife, Nancy, Murray Deutsch, Peter Feller and Pete's wife, Katie.

Pathetic draftees opening the show, dressed in their long underwear and staggering under the weight of the barracks bag, sing "This Is the Army, Mister Jones."

Zinn Arthur singing "Russian Winter" with members of the chorus. This number was dropped after New York.

Mr. B. talks to the Royal Family, visiting backstage after the opening.

Opening night at the Palladium in London brought together Mr. B., Lady Mountbatten, two generals and several members of the show.

A special filming of Mr. B. singing "My British Buddy"
with our chorus was filmed in London for inclusion
in the UK release of the film.

General Dwight D. Eisenhower addressing our cast in glowing terms
after seeing the performance which he requested be given.

Palace in Naples—the dwelling for French and Polish troupes and the *TITA* Detachment, in spite of the bombed out portions of almost every room.

The washing area Pete Feller constructed in the Royal Palace in the open air of the third floor.

When playing in Santa Maria, Italy, we received an enormous cake in appreciation from the Fifth Army. *Left to right:* Peter Feller, Milton Rosenstock and with knife, Alan Anderson.

Left to right: Anderson, Fisher, Feller and Rosenstock on the approach road to Monte Cassino, Italy.

Santa Maria, Italy, playing most of the show in the town square because of a bomb threat in the opera house.

ECCEZIONALE SPETTACOLO
DI BENEFICENZA
al TEATRO REALE DELL'OPERA

Mercoledì 28 Giugno · ore 18.30

PER CORDIALE CONCESSIONE DELL'ESERCITO DEGLI S.U.
IL PUBBLICO ITALIANO
POTRA ASSISTERE ALL'UNICA RAPPRESENTAZIONE
DELLA CELEBRE RIVISTA

THIS IS THE ARMY
di IRVING BERLIN
ESCLUSIVAMENTE ESEGUITA
DAGLI ELEMENTI DELLE FORZE ARMATE AMERICANA

SOTTO IL PATRONATO DEL SINDACO DI ROMA
LO SPETTACOLO SARA A TOTALE BENEFICIO
DELLE ISTITUZIONI SCOLASTICHE DELLA CAPITALE

Mr. B. in uniform in Rome, Italy, in front of show poster.

Our soldiers, dressing and applying makeup suitable for "Ladies of the Chorus," the comedy number in Act One.

Hank Henry being readied to play First Sergeant and mother-in-law in a sketch.

"Stump" Cross and others doing some entertaining in a hospital.

and took him aside. "That was about as crude as it could be, Cassie."

"It's okay, Sergeant. I've had worse things said."

"Well, Rosie couldn't feel worse. You're one of the most intelligent, dependable and likable guys in the whole outfit—and a hell of a good dancer."

"Thanks," he said. "I shouldn't be so sensitive."

"And we should behave like intelligent adults, especially in our position." I thought I'd better leave it there. "I hope you'll forgive us someday."

I started to go, without acting as though there should be a reply. He spoke before I'd finished turning away.

"I suppose I will."

He stopped there. We both smiled and I left.

☆ ☆ ☆ ☆ ☆ ☆ ☆ ☆ ☆ ☆ ☆

We kept our end of the bargain with the Colonel. A lot of the guys were working hard every day and every night even without the benefit of a good meal. After the evening shows, Rosie always had to play encores and special requests. The one request we couldn't grant was for someone to sing "Oh! How I Hate to Get Up in the Morning." Mr. B. had issued an order, "I reserve the right to sing that song for the boys myself."

It was okay. Actually, it helped to sustain our faith in his return.

We woke on Saturday to continuing rough seas. The breakfast bell was exciting only because we expected to hear it just once more. We were due in Liverpool on Monday. Pete and I looked for the coast of Ireland north and east of us. Nothing visible so far. We could see nothing but a few of the nearest ships, plunging into the high waves.

Pete kept staring. "The waves are so high our destroyers seem to disappear into them. I wonder how many submarines are out there trying to get through to our convoy."

"Come on, Feller," I said, "let's eat before all the French toast is gone!"

He turned and we started do go. Suddenly I heard a boom. Pete turned back. "Did you hear something?"

"Sounds like it!" I said. And then another boom.

"Look," Pete said. "There's a geyser!"

"Depth charges!" We peered at the destroyers northeast of us.

There was another boom. "Jesus Christ, another one!"

"They're right in our path to Liverpool." The PA came alive. "All passengers, report to berthing areas. Repeat, report to berthing areas, and wait for further instructions."

We went below. We'd had boat drills several times but this was no drill. Everyone was moving quickly, slipping on life jackets, headed below. The depth charges continued northeast of us.

And then we waited. No further command. My watch said 10:15. Our engines had slowed. The minutes passed. With the tension, the tendency was to make cracks—playing against the concern. Half an hour. At about 10:45, the PA came on again. "Retain life jackets. Resume normal activities. Resume serving breakfast. Repeat, resume normal activities." We headed for the dining room and the chatter began again.

"Would you consider eating this food a normal activity?" Carl asked as we lined up for oatmeal. Marc appeared.

"What the hell are you doing down here?" Pete asked. "You could be eating!"

Marc smiled. "I don't want to deprive you. I won't stay. I just wanted to tell you what I heard on the bridge."

"Did they get a submarine?"

"They think there were at least two and they've either sunk them or chased them away. The captain said that they reported seeing an oil slick and some debris surfacing. So, who knows?"

"Thanks for telling us. We could see depth charges going off but without binoculars you couldn't tell much."

"I'd better get out of here," Marc said, watching me take a bite. "You're making me hungry."

"You're right. If you're hungry, you'd better get out of here," Pete said. "Blubber will eat anything."

Marc laughed and left us—and I ignored my friend.

☆ ☆ ☆ ☆ ☆ ☆ ☆ ☆ ☆ ☆ ☆

I woke early Sunday morning. It was to be our last full day at sea. We were due in Liverpool the next morning. After breakfast, the four of us went to the upper deck and peered out at a calm sea and a drizzle. Somebody yelled out. "It's Ireland! I can see bloody Ireland, off to the west!"

Rosie yelled at the voice. "O'Rourke, you drunken Irishman! Who wants Ireland! We're looking for Liverpool!" Gangly Private First Class O'Rourke stumbled over to the rail on the port side.

"It looks beautiful," he said. "Let's skip Liverpool and head for Dublin. It's only a stone's throw."

All the ships were moving slowly, almost stopped. Everyone who was on deck went to the port rail to watch the Irish coast slide by. "The bugger's right, Rosie, even if he's crocked. You can't see anything to the East where we belong."

Marc appeared and saw Pete, Rosie and me. "They're going to have to anchor for the night. Liverpool is jammed and there's no place to dock even if we could see it in the fog."

O'Rourke leans over the rail, stretching out his arms. "I've come home at last!"

We ate our last dinner and turned in that night with some excitement. Tomorrow we could all put a smile on Mr. B.'s face when he saw us get off the train.

Monday morning, December 1, we finished breakfast and hurried up on deck. Colonel Green approached us in the drizzle. "I was just on my way to your quarters. I gave Lieutenant Daniels a letter of thanks but I want to thank you fellows in person for the great entertainment on this whole long trip—although it doesn't seem to be over yet!"

"To tell you the truth, sir," I said, "I think our guys would have gone crazy if they hadn't been able to do the shows." The Colonel shook hands with us and then went off toward the bridge. We kept staring to the East, waiting for Liverpool to appear.

I was wrong about making Mr. B. smile. We sat in the fog the whole day, ate the C-rations for dinner that night and rose the next morning still in the fog. A little supply ship came alongside and delivered some emergency rations.

We put up a notice which read:

NO SHOW TONIGHT. YOU'VE HEARD ALL OUR JOKES!

Tuesday morning came and went, and by six in the evening, the fog hadn't moved. We spent the day writing letters, playing cards, losing money to Pete Feller in poker.

Wednesday morning, Rosie let out a yell. "The fog is gone! Have a look, before it comes back. There's actually land over there!" We could see the masts of sunken ships in the Liverpool harbor, and beyond them, what was left of the docks.

"Unfortunately," said a voice over the P.A., "there's ships ahead of us that have been waiting to dock. By then the tide will be too low for us to go into the dock area. We will remain here until high tide at approximately 0700 hours tomorrow morning."

The anchor went down once more, within sight of our Liverpool dock. We'd never make the opening date. Three whole days lost in the fog. Mr. B. must be going crazy.

Chapter 12

THE WAR

—*Oct 23, 1943: The British lose two ships in the English Channel,*
attacked by German air squadron while attempting to stop blockade
runner, the HMS Charbydis, cruiser, and HMS Limbourne, destroyer.

I woke suddenly, startled by daylight streaming in the portholes. And something else, the thrum of the engines and men's voices calling commands. I swung my legs out of the bunk, reached up and gave Pete a shake.

"Wake up, skinny! We made it!"

Pete said something rude as he sat up, so I knew he was feeling good. Carl climbed down the ladder from his high perch, padded to a porthole and gave a report.

"We're headed for the dock! And the sun is practically out! I mean, you can see!"

☆ ☆ ☆ ☆ ☆ ☆ ☆ ☆ ☆ ☆ ☆

Two hours later, after fifteen nights on the *Monarch of Bermuda*, we wobbled on sea legs down the gangplank, loaded with our full field packs and equipment into the stark destruction of Liverpool. We marched the few blocks to the Mersey Railway Station, past bombed-out buildings—chimneys sticking up forlorn, a baby-carriage, a kitchen stove, piles of rubbish from which all identity has been picked away, a bare lot from which all had been cleared, a crater from a direct hit—twisted metal and scattered raw violence. The area near the docks must have been a prime target. But then the people, the men who were working on the docks, were smiling at us, calling out, "Hey, Yanks!" with a wave. We all waved back. Their energy and friendliness in the midst of the devastation was contagious. That they were so glad to be alive in what was left of their city lifted our spirits, too.

Our mere presence continued to produce this warm reception from everyone we passed. The sight of Yanks seemed to buoy their hopes.

We climbed onto the train with our heavy loads. Abner Silverstein started to fall backward with the weight of his duffle bag and Geno Erbisti reached out and with one hand lifted Abner and his load into the train. Abner could make a strong man cry with his violin, but he didn't weigh more than one hundred ten pounds soaking wet and he was proportionally muscled. Geno was the under-stander of the acrobatic team. He weighed about two hundred twenty, all muscle, and he could lift twice his own weight. I watched Geno's protective act and realized how close I had come to loving the outfit. And I thought of how Mr. B. must be worried about his boys.

When we docked, we were informed that some of the show had been put aboard other ships in the convoy. Poor Pete. He, Marc Daniels and Jus Addiss were picked to stay behind. Those three guys had to locate all the scenery, the lighting equipment, the costume trunks, the baggage, and get it loaded on another train. Already three days behind schedule, we faced more problems.

Arriving at London's Kings Cross station at 8:45 p.m., I climbed down the steps and the first face I saw belonged to our very worried and impatient boss. Ben pointed at me and Mr. B. started to smile. Once we were on the platform, he gave us a happy welcome. "I can't tell you how good it is to see you all here! I'd love to march to dinner with you, but I don't want to slow you down, so I'll meet you in the dining room in a few minutes."

He and Ben went for their car. We got into formation with our packs and equipment on our backs, and began our march to Club Foyer Suisse, an American Red Cross facility. Most of the Londoners we passed were carrying their torches,[1] which were masked down to a slit of light. When they caught glimpses of us, we heard surprise and some excitement in their voices and the word Yanks on their lips.

1. British for flashlights.

We hadn't gone more than two blocks when the air-raid sirens began their mournful wail. There it was again! The ominous sound familiar to us from the Edward R. Murrow radio broadcasts we heard back home. We continued to march. Some of the Londoners seemed to disappear into shelters. Suddenly the pounding of antiaircraft guns began nearby. None of us had heard that before.

We found out later that the antiaircraft battery we heard was in Hyde Park, a few blocks away, and that it was under the command of Lieutenant Mary Churchill, daughter of the prime minister, who was a member of the Auxiliary Territorial Service (ATS) — the equivalent of our WACs.

Carl mumbled to me, "Sally missed us with the submarines so she's trying again!"

"I wouldn't take it personally. I'll bet she does it every night."

It felt good to make jokes.

We were in luck again. We heard no bombs. They must have been headed for targets a long way from us. Just as we reached the Foyer Suisse building, the all-clear moaned steadily.

Johnny Koenig was waiting for us. He had gone ahead in a Jeep. When Rosie saw him, he let out a desperate roar, "When do we eat?"

Johnny replied, "As soon as you drop your stuff in your rooms and climb in the trucks, we eat!"

Within half an hour we were in the MP Headquarters mess hall. Ben and Mr. B. were waiting for us. As the boys held out their plates, cafeteria style and saw the food being piled on by the Red Cross women, they were already roaring like wolves. It seemed—after the food in Camp Shanks, topped by the unhappy experience of the ship's mess — like the greatest food we had ever eaten. It was simple enough, but beautifully cooked and seasoned and hot: meatloaf, carrots, green beans and mashed potatoes. This was followed by apple pie and ice cream! We devoured it all!

☆ ☆ ☆ ☆ ☆ ☆ ☆ ☆ ☆ ☆ ☆

Sleep would have been good, but we had a social obligation. We were invited into the auditorium so that we could be officially welcomed to the European theater of operations by a brigadier general. As soon as he concluded, Mr. B. assumed a fatherly role. He thanked the General for his words and for the great meal, and then ended the evening abruptly by saying, "And now, I know the General will understand if I tell you guys to go straight to bed, including me! We've got a hell of a lot of work to do in the next four days!"

Only General Irving Berlin could do that to a general who wanted to chat with show people-soldiers and pal around with the great American composer!

☆ ☆ ☆ ☆ ☆ ☆ ☆ ☆ ☆ ☆ ☆

I managed to get a V-Mail letter off to Nancy, worded to avoid the censor's black ink. All I wrote was,

> It was a jolt for everyone to come close to the war. But our first
> reaction was a profound respect for the spirit of these people
> who are enormously hospitable.

At 6:30 a.m., I woke Hayden Rorke and our third assistant stage manager, Corporal Joe Bush—Jus, of course, was still in Liverpool— and the three of us banged on all the doors. After last night's dinner, it wasn't hard to get them to the breakfast table. Private First Class Alan Lowell, in his usual basso, announced our first mail call, which had beaten us to London by air. Pete, Rosie and I were still without any mail from home. Carl had two letters from Betty. Boy, did we hate Carl! In addition to the Palladium Theater, where we would open the show, they gave us the nearby Scala Theater for rehearsals. Our short drive gave us our first view of the city in daylight. Londoners were walking briskly to work or duty through the devastation. It seemed to me their faces said to the enemy: nothing you do will stop us. They also said to me: the show had better be good. Ben Washer appeared and read a message from Mr. B. for Rosie, Bob and me.

"Start rehearsals and I will join you in a couple of hours with a big surprise—a good one. In the meantime, Bob, start with the Navy number at the Scala Theater. Rosie, in the pit at the Palladium."

"What about the new sketch?" Bob asked.

"He'll tell us about that when he gets here. He wants the cast of the sketch to be at the Palladium at eleven o'clock." Ben looked at me when he said that.

At 8:30, Bob and Rosie started rehearsing. I went to the Palladium with Johnny Koenig and Ben so we could get ready for the sketch rehearsal in the lounge. I asked Hayden to get the cast together for the sketch. At eleven o'clock sharp, Mr. B. arrived with company— Lieutenant Joshua Logan! Mr. B. had done it again—spirited Josh away from his Military Intelligence duties. We had a warm greeting.

"Josh! What are you doing here?"

"I don't know," he said, grinning. "Ask the boss. I was over here on duty and all of a sudden, once again I got orders to report to General Berlin. So here I am!"

Berlin explained, "Well, to paraphrase Alan's father in 'September Song,' the days were dwindling down to a precious few while I waited for you guys, so I made a call to our friends in Washington and asked them to find Josh and send him here. I thought he could work on the new sketch while Bob worked on everything else. And here it is, scripts of 'Daddy's Furlough,'" he said, handing them to Josh.

"And the cast will be ready for you in the ladies lounge," I said.

"Tell them Josh will be there in a few minutes," said Mr. B.

"Sure." I looked at Hayden and he jumped up.

"They'll be ready in two shakes!" Hayden left us.

"Before you go, Josh," Mr. B. said, pulling out the piano stool, "I've got something I want you all to hear." Without script or score, he played and sang "My British Buddy." We gave him a big hand. It was a sentimental winner. With emotions running high, it was sure to wring tears from the London audiences.

The rehearsals went without a hitch. Josh reported that the new sketch—the only new number, except for Mr. B.'s "My British Buddy"—was going to be great.

On Sunday, November 7, Pete, Jus and Marc arrived with a loaded train, two days from dress rehearsal, three days from opening. Once everything was hauled to the theater, while rehearsals continued, Pete, crew, Johnny Cooper and I worked through the night on scenery and lights, being fed lunch, dinner, and various snacks by the trusty Red Cross volunteers.

At 9:00 a.m., Monday the 8th, we began a technical rehearsal which worked through the day and the night and finished at 6:00 a.m. on Tuesday morning. The Red Cross kept appearing with food. The one who had the least trouble rehearsing through the night was Mr. B. himself. Those were his favorite working hours!

We lay down backstage from 6 a.m. to 1:00 p.m., when Mr. B. and Marc came in with a young captain we'd never seen before.

"Boys, I'd like you to meet your new Commanding Officer"—he looked at a card in his hand—"Captain Donald G. Bentley."

I was standing close enough to Bentley to see the infantry hardware on his lapel. He was close to six feet, trim, rigid, athletic looking. He smiled rather uncertainly as he responded to his introduction.

"Good afternoon, men. I know you have a heavy schedule for the rest of the day and the evening so I won't take any of your time now. Good luck with the show."

Feeling sure he would expect it, I threw him a salute and said crisply, "Thank you, sir. Welcome aboard." Bentley saluted with a pleasant smile and went offstage toward the lobby with Marc. He didn't appear to have any show business connection. My first thought was, maybe Mr. B. felt we should have an officer of higher rank than Johnny or Marc—a CO with no show business connection. Leave it to the committee.

After our new CO left, Bob and Rosie had notes. We rehearsed various scenes and numbers and checked out technical changes including light cues, curtain cues and sound problems. Everybody made remarks about the new CO. Bob said he didn't want him in any dance numbers. Someone suggested he could take tickets at the door. It was 4:15 p.m. when we broke and told everyone to be back in one hour to get dressed for the 6:00 dress rehearsal with an invited audience of service men and women.

The big concern was the new sketch. We knew everything else worked.

☆ ☆ ☆ ☆ ☆ ☆ ☆ ☆ ☆ ☆ ☆

We roared through act one, ending with a tremendous hand for the closing Navy number. Act two, from the "Stage Door Canteen" through the Air Force number, kept them riveted every moment; and then the new sketch, "Daddy's Furlough," which rolled them in the aisles from start to finish. Then Mr. B. brought the house down with his "Oh! How I Hate to Get Up in the Morning" and waves of emotion with his new song, "My British Buddy." The finale was followed by unending curtain calls. Berlin's instincts about what to give the soldier audiences couldn't have been better. The exuberant, energetic audience, mostly young, clapped, shouted, whistled, and roared with laughter. We forgot all about being tired and we had no doubt we were a hit again, bigger than ever.

Opening Night! We made it in spite of spending three days in the fog! At 6:10 p.m., Wednesday, November 10, 1943, I gave the cue for the overture and Rosie brought his baton down to begin what turned out to be the best performance of the show we'd ever given. Everyone knew it. What made this show in particular a triumph was the dazzling audience to go with the dazzle of the show—added to which was the response of sophisticated, theatre-wise Londoners and the genuinely warm, loving friendship of the British for the American soldier. Mr. B., after a standing ovation for "Oh! How I Hate to Get Up in the Morning," sang "My British Buddy" and then had the audience sing it with him. It was an emotional moment for the audience, with applause and "bravos"—and tears.

For all our thirty-two shows in London the audiences included luminous stars on the level of Noel Coward and Beatrice Lillie, as well as high-ranking service people and members of the diplomatic corps, rich, famous, and esteemed men and women from Britain and the United States, together with representatives of our many Allies. It was an unbelievable two weeks with those special audiences seeing the show and visiting us backstage and then inviting many of us to parties and all sorts of social engagements.

A few special moments stood out.

Lady Mountbatten addressed the audience before the opening night curtain went up on behalf of the British Service Charities Committee, to which all the profits from the performances in the British Isles would be donated.

We played a special show in Hyde Park for Lieutenant Mary Churchill and her antiaircraft battery, "manned" entirely by women in uniform. Some of those who saw the show and came backstage were not often seen in London: the Russian ambassador, commanding generals of Czechoslovakia, the Netherlands, Belgium, the Free French and Luxembourg.

The topper, however, especially for Mr. B. and for me, was the Tuesday matinee, November 16, when the King and Queen and the two princesses not only came to the show, but afterwards came to meet Mr. Berlin and the cast. We were told this was a rare occasion. Mr. B. met them in the corridor between the auditorium and the stage entrance, at which point I enjoyed a special role.

What I had not known until that day was that it is the custom in England for the stage director, the British term for the stage manager, to greet monarchs at the entrance and invite them onstage. I described the visit the next day in my V-Mail to Nancy:

The royal family came to see the show yesterday afternoon and for the first time in about twenty years, they came backstage, and I had lines! They were met first by Mr. B. who then introduced them to me. I shook them each by the hand as naturally as I could and then said — (my prepared script) — "Your Majesties, may I lead you on stage?" Her Majesty very graciously gave me the right answer and I led. They went about the stage with the princesses and spoke to a few of the boys, the most salient remark being that of Her Majesty to Big Hank Henry, who played the mother-in-law in "Daddy's Furlough." "You gave us a bit of a laugh," she said. Hank thanked her, blushing through all his great bulk.

We missed having Thanksgiving dinner so Mr. B. made that up to us by giving the whole detachment a turkey dinner at Claridge's Hotel after the show on Friday evening. Beatrice Lillie, more formally Lady Peel, saw the show again, joined us for dinner, and then entertained us afterwards. Finally, our boys sang a medley of Berlin songs and we presented Mr. B. with a testimonial letter which Marc and I had written. It read in part:

Nothing in our lives could have prepared us for the privilege we felt to be part of the show here in London. What led up to these moments — the New York opening, the tour of the country, playing for the President, making the movie — were great experiences, but to be chosen by Mr. Berlin to play overseas for our Allied forces had been beyond anything we had imagined and we owe it all entirely to you.

He was very moved and said that he would always cherish the letter. He was described in the official record as having had "tear-dimmed eyes." I think many of us could have been similarly described.

There was good reason to have our party on Friday night. When the curtain fell on our final London performance, Saturday night, we had about six and a half hours to take down the whole show, grab a quick supper at the mess hall, load everything in trucks and catch a 2:40 a.m. train to Glasgow, Scotland.

Chapter 13

THE WAR

—Nov 26, 1943: *Germans sink British troopship in Mediterranean with 1000 men.*

—Nov 28, 1943: *The US 8th Army crosses the Sangro River, Italy, with a tank brigade.*

—Dec 3, 1943: *German planes attack the port of Bari, Italy. The explosion of a munitions ship sinks 18 transport ships.*

We had our own ten-car train for the trip from London to Glasgow: one engine, five freight cars, four coaches and a sleeper—not just for the officers, but also for the top three grades. This was unfortunate. Giving special privilege to four-stripers could only add to the resentment felt by corporals and sergeants who were featured players. Ordinarily, the whole company shared the same facilities—which was far better for our working relationship.

"Let's not ever do this again, Marc," I said when I heard about the sleeper. "I'd rather we all get the same deal wherever we go." Adding to the problem was the fact that quite a few of the guys deserved higher grades, considering their contribution to the success of the show. Mr. B. knew this and had requested that we get some promotions. Unfortunately, Washington hadn't obliged. The guys knew that he had tried. So as long as we avoided having special privileges for anyone, we got along well.

The special privileges that officers had was another matter. We all knew, including Mr. B., that we had to have officers in order to function within the Army structure. So in their case the privilege of a sleeping car was accepted. What officers had to learn when they were assigned to *This Is the Army* was that they were there purely for administration and for obtaining from the Army what Mr. B. or the committee (if he was not present) needed to operate the show.

It was a problem, of course, to find officers whose personalities made them comfortable, first of all, with the limitation of their authority and, secondly, with a company of enlisted men with the egos and temperaments of professional performers. Lieutenant Koenig had no problem. Marc had that bad moment with Bob on the Atlantic crossing but, luckily, Koenig was able to set him straight. Captain Bentley should never have been assigned to anything but a straightforward infantry outfit where his authority was unlimited. It wasn't easy to deal with the conglomerate called *TITA:* wealthy sophisticates, raunchy-humored vaudeville types, ex-burlesque members, Catskill comedians, quite a few sensitive and intelligent middle class men, a few brash, rough types, several extremely literate writers and readers, upper crust and lower crust, blacks and whites, Catholics, Jews, Protestants, and independent believers—and among all these categories, heterosexuals and homosexuals, some who were blatant about their sexual orientation and others who were conventionally closeted, or at least silent. Bentley didn't try to get to know the company. Mr. B. told him his job was to get from the Army authorities what we needed. He occupied himself with that. Unfortunately, his rank wasn't high enough to impress the outside Army world. Berlin had to step in now and then.

☆ ☆ ☆ ☆ ☆ ☆ ☆ ☆ ☆ ☆ ☆

Our train pulled into St. Enoch's Station, Glasgow, at 4:40 p.m. Sunday, and busses took us to the US Army Hotspur transit camp.

My excitement to be in Scotland, having a good deal of Scottish blood, was soon flattened when we were led by a very cheerful Scottish sergeant into a huge gymnasium filled with double bunks, except for one corner which was occupied by a towering mountain of straw.

Next to the straw stack we discovered blankets and mattress covers.

The Sergeant said, "All right, lads, name's MacDougal. You can choose any of the bunks that take your fancy if there's no one ahead of you. There's fifty of 'em as already filled. Just take two blankets and a mattress cover and you can set about stuffin' all the straw you like into the cover. You'll get a call to supper soon, so you best get at it." He had such a lovely accent we were all delighted to hear him talk, although it was hard not to laugh at what he had to say. With his speech over, MacDougal left us before anyone could express their gratitude.

The transit camp's attempt to borrow some grandeur from Shakespeare's *Henry V* by reference to Hotspur did little to impress us. We decided we had no choice but to create our mattresses by busying ourselves with stuffing, until we found the air filled not only with wisecracks but straw dust.

Danny Longo made us an offer. "Anybody want your cover stuffed by an expert Hotspur five bucks!" Abner Silverstein looked at the hay in terror. "I get terrible rashes from dead grass!"

"This stuff isn't grass, honey," said Barclift. "I'll give you some real grass if you're worried about sleeping."

Julie Oshins spread his arms wide and cried out to us all, "Think of the goats going hungry just for us!"

Big Hank Henry growled his opinion.

"The goats already ate this stuff. It's second time around."

We were interrupted by a summons to the mess hall.

When we arrived, Marc Daniels announced that we were to remain in the mess hall until Mr. B. arrived. The food was better than the sleeping arrangements. I was scraping up the last of the lamb stew with a crust of bread when Mr. B. came in, followed by Marc, Johnny, Captain

Bentley and an officer with the golden leaves of a major on his shoulders. We started automatically to stand but Mr. B. stopped us with a gesture and everyone settled back in their seats.

"Don't get up. I've been asked by the Major not to disturb your meal. He knows you've had a tough twenty-four hours." Mr. B. looked at a piece of paper in his hand and then went on. "This is Major

Clifton G. Holmgren. He didn't tell me what the G stands for. I'll let him tell you."

Major Holmgren was tall, over six feet—or would be if he didn't stoop slightly, as if apologizing for his stature. His manner was almost deferential. He greeted Mr. B.'s introduction with a sheepish grin.

"I don't generally tell anyone about the G, Mr. Berlin. I've been kidded about it since the fourth grade. Maybe when we get to know each other better I'll tell you. I don't want to interrupt your meal, but I figured you might see me hanging around and wonder what I was doing here. I'll be real quick so you can finish your dinner."

"I'm from Minnesota. I'm not a theater man; I'm in newspapers. But I'm very pleased to be with you guys and I'll try to get into the swing of things as soon as I can. We'll all spend more time talking when we get settled here in Scotland. More than likely, most of you have never been here before. I've been in the Special Services Division in the European Theater for over a year, so I know my way around a little. They've given me a title for this assignment: Project Commanding Officer. I'm not sure yet what it entails. You've already got your Commanding Officer, Captain Donald Bentley." He acknowledged Bentley with a smile. "Don will take care of that part of it. But I may be able to facilitate things while you're moving around the British Isles. So get back to that food and we'll get to know each other later on."

I felt we ought to respond to this amiable introduction. "First Sergeant Anderson. Welcome aboard, sir!"

"Thank you, Sergeant. So you're the top kick?" He was squinting at the stripes on my arms.

"Yes, sir."

"I hope you and Captain Bentley will let me know if there's anything I can do for you."

"Actually, I'd like to invite you and Captain Bentley to visit our quarters here this evening, sir. They're rather unusual."

"Problem, Sergeant?"

"I don't want to influence your opinion, sir."

"We'll be there," he said, exchanging glances with Bentley.

There were some smiles and chuckles from the guys when I sat down. They appeared to be delighted to have visitors in the hay room.

Johnny Koenig was the first one on the scene. He took one look and reacted with his characteristic reserve, "Oh, kiddies, isn't this peachy! I can't wait to see you all snuggled down in your nests." A moment later Ben Washer and the other officers appeared with Holmgren and Mr. B. in the lead.

"What is this?" asked Mr. B. in disbelief.

"It's what they call a transit facility, Mr. B.," I explained. "They're designed as an overnight provision for troops on the move."

Mr. B. turned to the Major. "But we're going to be here a week!"

"I'll have a talk with someone," the Major said to Mr. B. and then he turned to me. "We'll find something more appropriate first thing tomorrow morning, Sergeant."

☆ ☆ ☆ ☆ ☆ ☆ ☆ ☆ ☆ ☆

Next morning, once again we were rescued by the American Red Cross. After breakfast, we were bussed to a Red Cross building at Charing Cross and assigned rooms—but not until we had returned all the straw and folded our mattress covers. From then on we had nothing to complain about. We were two to a room. Carl and I were next door to Pete and Rosie. Delicious meals—the Army supplied the food, the Red Cross cooked it. What a luxury to have butter, sugar and genuine meat. They took such good care of us that the guys volunteered to give a special show for them in their own home. Jus Addiss wrote his father,

Never has an audience been so demonstrative.

The Lord Provost of the City of Glasgow gave Mr. B. and all of us a great treat: a hearty midday dinner at Castle Balloch on Loch

Lomond. He delivered a welcoming speech and described the castle as "The Gateway to the Highlands." By each place was a small volume of Robert Burns songs, a sprig of heather and a pack of cigarettes, all tied together with a Tartan ribbon. The place cards were inscribed,

> Welcome, compliments of the Lord Provost and City of
> Glasgow Central War Fund.

It seemed a flattering generosity for them to spend precious "war funds" on the show.

Mr. B. responded to our host's speech and volunteered that we had some Scots among us. He took me by surprise by saying, with a hand on my shoulder, "In fact, Mr. Welsh, I've got one right here. Our top kick, Sergeant Anderson."

"Well, indeed, if he's an Anderson, sure he's a Scot," said the provost. "Welcome, to you," he said, with a wave.

"Thank you, sir," I replied. "I'm sorry I'm not wearing my colors, but I don't think the Army would encourage it."

"I wouldn't want you to offend your Army," he said with a smile. "The more Yanks are with us, the sooner it'll be over."

☆ ☆ ☆ ☆ ☆ ☆ ☆ ☆ ☆ ☆ ☆

We opened at Glasgow's Empire Theater the following night and played two shows each night, at 6:00 and at 8:30. Between shows there was a mighty traffic jam in front of the theatre, getting the first audience out and the second one in. It was a tiring schedule for the boys but it turned out to be roughly the same schedule for the rest of the British Isles.

As soon as Mr. B. was settled in a hotel, he started doing hospital appearances, with Morty Kahn accompanying him if there was a piano. Otherwise, we sometimes added Eddie O'Connor with his guitar or accordion. Mr. B. was often joined by the juggler, the magician, or another of the singers, musicians or comedians. As the tour went on, wherever we went, it became more and more the practice to put together four or five entertainers in various combinations so that they could reach those who could not get to the theater shows. Jus and Hayden became expert in putting such units together and scheduling them where they were needed.

☆ ☆ ☆ ☆ ☆ ☆ ☆ ☆ ☆ ☆ ☆

Going from city to city, playing the show a week in each, two shows each day, with varying distances to travel, places to live, food to eat and theaters into which Pete had to adapt the show physically, our life followed a pattern. The audience responses varied the least. There were never any empty seats and the performances were received throughout with tremendous enthusiasm. Also unvarying were the important civil and military guests who came backstage on opening nights and lavished praise on the cast. What varied the most was the weather. We weren't surprised to have rain in Scotland and we expected it would change wherever we went.

Mail call of course was always a vital part of our lives, and we learned that there was no pattern to that. Some days there was no mail. Some days we would get several letters. Now and then, we got packages. They excited general curiosity. "Hey, Abner, whad'ya get?" Abner received a stream of gifts from his wife, including medicines for his allergies.

It seemed somewhat of a miracle to me that the Army Post Office system could keep track of all the Army outfits around the world. The APO numbers changed when we moved and we had to keep our correspondents aware of any changes. We'd had two so far: 4995 and then suddenly, as we left London, 887. Every letter we wrote was censored. Our officers were designated as censor one at a time. They passed the job around depending on who was available. I gradually overcame my sensitivity to having every letter I wrote to

Nancy read by someone. I tried to put myself in their position and consider what I would do: Would I read every word, hoping for something interesting—maybe even juicy? Or would I skim through looking for some reference as to where we were or what we saw around us that might be dangerous information to have discovered by the enemy? It did become possible to forget about it and trust that our officers were also gentlemen, as they were supposed to be from the oath they took when they were commissioned. Letters we received from home were not censored, of course. It was assumed that there was nothing in them that would be useful to our enemies.

One thing I discovered was that when letters from home reached each of us, they animated our behavior as though fresh blood were flowing through our veins. Nancy and I wrote almost daily but, of course, they didn't arrive at either end with the same regularity in which they were mailed.

Papa Berlin came into the theater as I was opening two of the tiny envelopes.

"I got one today, too," he said happily. "How's that boy?"

"Oh, he's fine! I don't have any pictures yet, but I'm expecting some soon."

"It must be tough not watching him grow."

"The letters help."

"I get letters from my daughters now and then, although their mother's a little more dependable."

"She must worry about you."

"She does." He looked up from his letter after a moment. "You know, these guys love you. I had dinner with Jus and Hayden last night and they told me they think you're great."

"I'm glad to hear that. The guys have problems they want to talk about sometimes. Some of them are older than I am but they come to me anyway."

"How's your Dad?"

"Fine. He has a new play opening out of town but he finds time for a letter to me now and then."

"Good! I'll call him when I go back."

I tried to avoid any alarm in my question. "When will that be?"

"I don't know. Nothing's decided. I'll let you guys know as soon as I do."

☆ ☆ ☆ ☆ ☆ ☆ ☆ ☆ ☆ ☆

Then back to England, to Manchester—smoky, dirty, manufacturing city, the Pittsburgh of England. But they had a reception. Every mayor had to give us a reception, of course. An official greeter announced each of us with a bang of his staff and a hearty voice heard by all. Joe Wojcikowski, charmed by the procedure and the Manchester accent, couldn't let the opportunity pass. He gave his rank and name as Private Polish Princess. The staff banged and Joe was announced faithfully in a rolling country English: "Private Polish Princess!" The words rang through the great hall, followed by a wide variety of reactions. Joe walked down the steps into the room smiling and waving to us all. A bit naughty, but even Major Holmgren could not suppress a smile.

☆ ☆ ☆ ☆ ☆ ☆ ☆ ☆ ☆ ☆

Manchester's Palace Theater was a reasonably easy setup. Once again, thank goodness for the Red Cross living quarters and meals. Constant rain or fog kept us indoors. Daylight was the same at all hours, morning, afternoon or twilight. There was one continuing difference from London: We had not heard an air raid siren since we left the Palladium Theater.

On Thursday, December 9, Carl and I celebrated my twenty-sixth birthday by moving into a big room in the Midland Hotel—high ceilings, handsome furniture. I then enjoyed an excellent dinner provided by Carl, Pete and Rosie.

No mail. I thought about Nancy and the Punk, knowing that she would be thinking of what day it was.

We had to push hard in the move from Manchester to Liverpool. A Monday opening was scheduled meaning the crew and I would be up all Sunday night. The Empire Theater had 2,400 seats; the biggest we had played. Even so, every ticket was sold.

We knew little of Liverpool from our docking there except the waterfront and the railroad station. On returning, we had a more thorough view of the tremendous, dispiriting damage the city had suffered. Not only was it a dirty city, there appeared to be more prostitutes than pubs, and every other building was a pub. In the heart of the city, a huge department store had been bombed away except for the ground floor and the basement, which turned out to be a happy discovery. I described it to Nancy in a letter:

> There are no windows, no doors, no superstructure. But in the basement there is an enormous cafeteria which is incredibly popular. It's so cold that all the patrons sit wrapped in scarves and coats when eating their fish and chips. The wind whistles through the cellar at all hours, but they have two orchestras which play alternately for dancing and entertainment. One is a swinging jive five which features Pistol Packin' Mama complete with vocal, and the other is a string quartet led by a distinguished old gentleman who is the dead image of David Warfield in "The Music Master." His ensemble was featuring "God Rest Ye, Merry Gentlemen" and "Good King Wenceslaus" in honor of the holiday season, and somehow the whole picture of the English cross-section of life sitting huddled over their tea, in the poor shell of a building, humming Christmas carols seemed so typical of this country under stress that I could understand that they would never be beaten.

We had fourteen shows in the week and every one of the 2,400 seats were sold for every show. Again we had traffic jams because the two evening shows were so close together, but it didn't seem to bother them. I would have expected impatience and frustration, but there was an atmosphere of gaiety that precluded anything but good nature.

☆ ☆ ☆ ☆ ☆ ☆ ☆ ☆ ☆ ☆ ☆

Once again, Pete Feller had a killer schedule making the move and being ready for a Monday opening. They started to strike the show the moment the curtain fell, finished loading the railroad cars at 2:45 a.m., boarded a 10 a.m. train, Sunday, unloaded at Birmingham at 3:45 p.m., worked all night and all day Monday, played two shows, and then went to bed. Somehow Pete met impossible schedules over and over again, and the production looked like Broadway every time.

Our Birmingham quarters were unique. Since all the students had been sent home for the Christmas holiday, we lived in the King Edward School in very comfortable dormitory rooms. We had three Army cooks assigned to us for the week. They prepared our excellent meals in the school kitchen, with meats that were not available except from the Army or Red Cross. We were served on white tablecloths, and had linen napkins and shining silverware—unbelievable for an enlisted men's mess! Some of our guys decorated the dormitory with holly, mistletoe and several small Christmas trees. It was difficult to complain about being away from home!

Jus, Hayden, Carl and I took a train early Tuesday morning to see Coventry. Jus wrote a letter to his father about the experience:

> We all remember the newspaper accounts and photographs in
> American papers at the time. But we could have no conception
> of the actual damage until we stood in the midst of it—to see
> the crumpled mass of wreckage which is all that remains of the
> once magnificent Coventry Cathedral. The sensation is of utter
> futility, looking upward toward the beautiful spire which still

stands defiantly, towering over the remains. Only the bare
superstructure and transept stand. There is no roof, no interior,
no altar. What a prodigious waste of heart and craftsmanship.
We stood staring, helpless, outraged. Seven incendiaries obliter-
ated nine centuries!

Before the Wednesday matinee in Birmingham, I made my customary visit to Mr. B. in his dressing room. He looked up when I came in
and handed me a letter, smiling broadly. The page of stationery bore
the imprint of the words,

> Her Royal Highness, Queen Mary.

"The Queen Mother," I said in awe.
"This was enclosed." He held up the musical score of "Alexander's
Ragtime Band." I looked at that and then read the letter.

> My dear Mr. Berlin: I am so delighted at the prospect of seeing
> your wonderful Army show when it plays at the Victoria
> Rooms in Bristol. We have purchased tickets for the Tuesday
> matinee. I have taken the liberty of enclosing a musical score
> which I have had for many years. I hoped you might be good
> enough to sign it for me.

I alerted Pete and made a suggestion. "Hadn't you better get down
there and find out what problems you're going to face with the Victoria
Rooms? Pete agreed, left word with his crew and caught a train to
Bristol. He returned the next morning and called me right away.
"Blubber, we have to have a meeting with Mr. B. right away." We
called Ben and the committee met with Mr. B. in his hotel room.
"Mr. Berlin, we have a problem," Pete said solemnly. Hearing his
tone, Mr. B. sat down and then spoke. "What do you mean?"
"The Victoria Rooms in Bristol is not a theater."

"What is it?"

"It's a big, beautiful room with a small platform at one end—not really a stage. There's no curtain, no spotlights. It's just a great big, beautiful—*room*."

Mr. B. said nothing for a moment, looking at Pete. Finally he looked up.

"Pete, we're scheduled to open Monday night. We've sold out every performance for the week—and the Queen Mother is coming to see the Tuesday matinee."

"I know," Pete said. "Alan told me about your letter. I just have one question."

"Yes?"

"Can I spend some money?"

"If I say spend anything you have to, can we open on time?"

"Yes, sir!" Pete said.

"Spend it!" said Mr. B.

Pete nodded and then began giving orders. "Marc—John—get to the city fathers and arrange to have extra electrical power wired into the building. Have the local amateur theater groups and schools lend us lighting equipment. Get me a charge account at a lumber store and a hardware store in Bristol. I'm going to get some paper and pencils and make a design and tomorrow morning I'm going to Bristol. Merry Christmas!"

Our final performances in Birmingham were on Friday, December 24th. We took down the show Friday night and shipped it to Bristol. There were no shows on Saturday, Christmas day. Most of the company spent the day at the Red Cross, totally surprised to be served a holiday dinner of turkey with all the fixings by Bristol community supporters of the show. Tables had been set up in the ballroom area and Joe Fretwell and other designer talents in the show had decorated the tables and the room in festive elegance.

While they were at that, Major Holmgren distributed European theater combat ribbons and Good Conduct ribbons to each of us with our turkey dinner. The ribbons were assigned to anyone who had served in London during these months. "I guess some day we can show these to our kids," Rosie said, and gave us one of his barking chuckles.

In the meantime, Pete and his crew built substitute scenery and curtain assembly that would fit into the Victoria Rooms. Pete and crew worked all day Sunday, Sunday night and all day Monday until Monday night, when we opened the curtain and Rosie struck up the overture. The opening performance that evening went off without any disasters. The bright lights, costumes, music and vigor of the cast were enough to generate enormous enthusiasm from our audience of only a thousand people.

After the show, Mr. B. found Pete backstage, and grabbed his hand. "Thank you, Peter, a thousand times! Unbelievable job." And then he leaned close to Pete's ear. "She's going to love it." Pete thought for a moment and then smiled when he realized he meant the Queen Mother. "Good!" He said. "I'll tell the boys. They'll get a kick out of that!"

Pete and his crew went to bed and weren't seen again until Tuesday afternoon, in time to open the curtain for a sold-out matinee and Queen Mary.

During the intermission, the Lord Mayor stood up in the third row and introduced the British naval officer next to him and acknowledged the presence of the Queen Mother.

"Your Majesty, Ladies and Gentlemen, may I present one of our great heroes, the First Lord of the Admiralty, A. V. Alexander, a hero to Great Britain and all her allies." The Admiral stood and acknowledged the tremendous applause and made a brief speech. We couldn't hear it, but he uttered a few words of encouragement that was met with more applause.

At the end of the show, Mr. B. was as nervous as the proverbial schoolboy. Queen Mary came to the stage entrance with her entourage, including two US Army generals and the Duke of Beaufort, a brigadier general in the British Army.

For the second time, I performed my duty to the royal family by asking the Queen Mother if she would care to visit backstage. She graciously accepted. Mr. B. introduced her to the cast. She thanked him for his autograph and commended the cast on their fine performance, ending with: "My, my, do you do this performance twice a day? You must be very tired." And then with a twinkle in her eyes, "Perhaps I'd better leave, so you can rest." The boys broke into applause as she departed with the Brigadier.

☆ ☆ ☆ ☆ ☆ ☆ ☆ ☆ ☆ ☆ ☆

The schools were closed for vacation. We enjoyed the comfort of the boy's school dorm in Birmingham and then Manor Hall, the girl's dorm in Bristol with very comfortable beds, gas heaters and rugs in every room and coffee percolators with hot breakfast coffee ready each morning. Leaving the theater, the uphill approach to Manor Hall would have made an ideal setting for a Hitchcock thriller: winding steeply upward on a street dotted with shops, until it reached the crest. Through a swirling mist you looked down a darkened valley at an ancient graveyard dotted with hoary tombstones. To enter the school, you swung open a squeaking iron gate, descended a long string of narrow steps and went under a ponderous overpass of dark masonry. All it lacked was a moat and drawbridge.

Friday was New Year's Eve. The Lord Mayor invited us to a breakfast of pancakes, sausages and coffee, followed by yet another reception. This did not quite satisfy my need to be an ocean away where I could hold Nancy's hand and sing "Auld Lang Syne." Pete and many of us were probably feeling the same.

Mr. B. supped with us in the mess hall after the second show. Johnny Koenig told Pete, Carl, Rosie, Mr. B. and me that he had made a friend of a Colonel Gunn, who had invited us to a New Year's Eve party at an inn outside of town. It was our best and only offer. We all accepted except for Pete who was reluctant. I said I wouldn't go without him so he finally came. Ben Washer and Marc were missing. They had gone ahead to Belfast, Northern Ireland, to check the theater and housing facilities.

Colonel Gunn said he would send a car for us. Mr. B. said he would meet us later. This is how I described it to my wife and son in a two-page V-Mail.

Dearest: The New Year's Eve was indescribable. I know I was fated to find little enjoyment in anything so far away from you both, but there were many factors that contributed to the horror of the evening in addition to being as lonesome as if I were the last vestige of the human race alone on earth. John, Carl, Pete and I rode out of town to an inn, very drab indeed, and walked into a room filled with regular Army colonels, each one accompanied by a sorry representative of the fair sex. John spotted our host's table and led us to Colonel Gunn. Gunn welcomed us cheerfully but he failed to offer us a drink or a morsel of food. We scrounged around and found some nibbles under the glares of the Eagle-bedecked gentlemen of West Point. We decided to get our own liquor, and Pete, clever fellow, volunteered. He sent the driver back with a bottle and a message. He was going to bed. We started nipping at the scotch and looking for a way to get home. When midnight came Carl said, very quietly, "To the wives and little ones, God Bless them" and with a clink of our two glasses we drank to you both—to Carl's daughter and to Lil's expectations. 1:00 a.m. came and Mr. B did not. We had done nothing but sit and wait for a car and think about what we should have liked to be doing. The colonels were trying to be gay but it was a disgusting picture of mixed desires and habits. They wanted to have fun with their girls but they remembered occasionally that they were married; they wanted to be children but they kept discovering they were middle-aged; they wanted to relax but they couldn't forget to become their rank. The result depended individually on the balance between character and emotions. We left finally, and no one said good-bye. I was rather hoping they'd say something. As it was, they would never know that any attempt at civility would have been ignored.

The year had started at the bottom. It had nowhere to go but up. We went back to our billets and sat about talking about the extraordinary behavior of the colonels, finished the bottle Pete had provided, felt better and went to bed at 3:00 a.m. To end on a positive note, I'm fine and I miss you both so very, very much on this New Year's morning. All my love, Husband and Pappy.

THE

PALLADIUM

★

"THIS
IS
THE
ARMY"

★

Programme **FREE**

Chapter 14

THE WAR
—*Dec 7, 1943: US 5th Army begins its big offensive northward toward Rome, Italy, on a broad front.*
—*Dec 20, 1943: 1,000 Allied aircraft drop 2,000 tons of bombs on Frankfurt, Mannheim and other industrial cities in Germany.*
—*Dec 27, 1943: Secret planning for landing on French coast is complete. Eisenhower to be Supreme Allied Commander.*

Once I finished writing my V-Mail to Nancy early on New Year's morning, I had no trouble deciding how to spend the rest of the day: start packing, do two shows, finish loading the show onto trucks, off to the station, load the railroad cars, go to bed at midnight. It was routine for us by now. However, our next stop was Bournemouth—a summer holiday city—a dramatic change after the manufacturing cities we had been in. Another letter to Nancy describes it best:

Darlings, Bournemouth on the sea—what a wonderful change. I can't think of anything but how much I want you here. Our Red Cross club is a hotel facing the ocean; the moon is silvering the water to the south, the stars are doing their utmost to outshine the moon, and the sky has a brilliant blue gown. The windows of the club look out through tall evergreens over a fairyland and a fairy sea. Walking in from the trucks tonight the moon silhouetted the slim trees high over our heads and all the stars that we've seen together standing on the lawn where you are. In a moment I will look down in your dear beloved eyes—so you see I'm dreaming, darling—this is a dream place and I want you both here with me.

The trip from Bristol took us through my imagining of English countryside—farmland and grazing land, all of it

clothed in green right up to the stonewalls that border the
fields. No space wasted and something growing everywhere,
and fields where Kett could run and play.

Carl, Pete and I are sharing a room here. I could have had the
only single in the house but I gave it to Rosie so that Pete
wouldn't have to live with him. He's getting too weird for Pete.
He's working hard on arrangements for a couple of songs he
wrote — the most abominable garble of words ever combined in
sentences. I told him gently, as long ago as last spring, that they
were gobbledygook, but there they are still. I fear he believes
them immortal.

Poor Rosie. Why did I pick on him for trying to keep his mind busy?
The show had become routine for him as it had for all of us. I was try-
ing to write stories, and bad poetry. Why should I complain about
Rosie?

None of us had imagined how different the southern coast would
be from the rain and chill just a few hours to the north. Our whole
week was actually warm and sunny. Our companions were the elderly
British enjoying a holiday, some couples, some singles, walking along
the ocean front, sunning themselves in beach chairs, dozing off with a
book in hand.

We had breakfast each morning with a view through white lace curtains of the sea. We discovered the routine was to purchase a jar of
marmalade, put your name on it and it would appear on the breakfast
table each morning. We got exercise exploring the neighborhood on
rented bicycles. Mr. B., whose B and B was just two doors away, joined
in some of our explorations.

One of the only reminders of war was the guns booming far off in
the Channel at almost any hour, day or night. The other was the number of wounded in the hospital wards where Mr. B. and some of our
boys entertained almost every day. Marc Daniels and Ben Washer
were still in Belfast. Mr. B. confirmed that we were booked there for

the next two weeks which was to be followed by a ten day furlough in London!

Pete and I had one hitch with our roommate, Carl. It involved over-active testosterone. The sunny weather drove him into the arms of the wives of absent British fighting men. On Thursday afternoon our keys to the room were of no avail, the door was double-locked. A broadly smiling Carl appeared at dinner time to explain that the battleship *Duke of York* had been at sea for months without leave for a young gun-ner whose bride was beside herself with loneliness.

"I'm having dinner with her. She wants to cook me something special."

"Did you say the *Duke of York?*" Pete asked.

"Right. She married the guy about six months ago and she hasn't seen him since," said Carl.

"Do you ever look at the news, you dumbkopf?" Pete asked.

"I've been pretty busy," Carl replied with a satiric grin. "What did I miss?"

Pete produced the daily paper, and summarized the front page as he handed it to Carl. "That ship, with that Navy gunner whose bride you've been screwing, just sank the last operational German battle-cruiser *Scharnhorst.*" He quoted:

> "This was a critical victory since it amounted to the end of the German High Seas Fleet!"

Pete gave Carl a grim smile. "Do you think those heroes aren't going to get a furlough tonight? And do you know the first thing that Navy gunner is thinking about!"

Carl grabbed the paper. "You're making this up!" He looked at the story. "I'll be a son of a gun!" He said.

Rosie couldn't stop laughing. "You poor bastard!"

Pete summed up the situation.

"Think of it this way, lover boy: the second thing the navy gunner's

got on his mind is that good dinner she was cooking for you, so you
did him a favor!"

"Thanks a lot," said Carl. He looked at the paper once more.
"Unbelievable!"

"Would you like to join us for dinner?" I said.

We saw a lot of Carl for the rest of the week.

☆ ☆ ☆ ☆ ☆ ☆ ☆ ☆ ☆ ☆

Bournemouth spoiled us. We went from the "semitropical" warmth
created by the Gulf Stream, to the frigid Arctic winds off the North
Sea. To reach Belfast, Ireland, we first had to travel seventeen hours by
train to Stranraer, Scotland. I wrote to my Scottish father to describe
the scene:

> We traveled all day and all night, five to a compartment, eating
> K-rations from our mess kits, freezing from the penetrating
> cold. The trip was followed by a fantastic night in a Nissen hut
> in a British transit camp in Stranraer.
>
> A Nissen hut has the general appearance of a blimp hangar.
> The unlined walls and ceiling are composed of corrugated tin,
> wrinkled like a washboard. Our particular hut was outstanding
> because of the many gaping openings, never planned by the
> architect. All night long, the wind whistled through those holes
> furiously. There was one small iron belly stove which threw a
> little heat up to four feet within its circumference. Our beds
> were wooden slabs, set about two feet over the cement floor.
> Of course, there were no mattresses, sheets or blankets. We
> could have used that hay!
>
> Everyone made an attempt to sleep, but no go. The sight of
> all the bodies laid out resembled a well-stocked morgue. All
> that was missing was the identification tags tied around the
> ankles. We wore everything we owned: shoes, socks, leggings,

full uniform, overcoat and hat, but to no avail. In an attempt to improve the fire we broke up bunks and shoved wood in the stove. The only added heat was from the exercise. The damp wood made more smoke than heat.

Everyone resorted to keeping their circulation going either by jumping up and down, flailing their arms, singing loudly, or huddling close together by the pitiful fire, the cold air penetrating to the marrow. I recalled Emily Dickinson's poem, "The Snake." Her last line, "Zero to the Bone." Of course she was describing fear, but it did as well for our condition.

We talked, laughed, argued, and agreed at least that it was an experience we would never forget. Outside, the moon shone bright and beautiful, making luminous the miles of marshy wasteland, leading down to the sea.

At last, the morning sun crept tentatively above the eastern mountains and we rushed to the mess hall to devour hot porridge, hot creamed chipped beef on toast and steaming hot tea. We would have eaten anything that would heat us up.

We were not in Belfast yet. The northern approach to the Irish Sea lay between us and our goal. That body of water had won the international seasick record over and over again. The Twyckenham Ferry was tossed high on the waves and dropped into the troughs, our stomachs following the same motion. The queasy among us clung desperately to the leeward rail, stomachs rejecting what had been so eagerly devoured. Some of the land lubbers mistakenly chose the windward side and then staggered across the deck wiping away puke thrown back by the nor'wester.

At one point a plane flew overhead toward Northern Ireland and Julie Oshins cried to the sky, "Ben Baby, Mr. B. — come and get me before I'm all gone!"

At last the ferry cut engines and drifted into the lee of the docks of Larne, Northern Ireland. I was about to set foot on ancestral soil. My mother, Margaret Haskett, was conceived somewhat further south on this island before my grandparents set sail for Canada in the 1880's.

☆ ☆ ☆ ☆ ☆ ☆ ☆ ☆ ☆ ☆ ☆

It was a short train ride from Larne to Belfast. Busses took us straight to the Grand Opera House where we were to perform. They must not have our billets quite ready. Surely the beds should have been made, the pillows puffed up invitingly and a good hot shower waiting. The chill was deep in our bones. We proceeded to get good and warm unloading the trucks, then the busses took us to a dank, dark, abandoned four story building with a grand old identification on the ancient brick walls, "McConnell's Brewery."

I had misread the delay. It wasn't true about the pillows. In the dim, cold, dreary twilight we could see that there were plenty of mattresses, a few beds and no pillows. The good news was that the hay had already been put in the mattresses.

How was it that our advance men always found these unusual places? They never thought of going straight to the Red Cross to begin with instead of having to move us there the next day. This time there could be an excuse. We were in Ireland, land of the blarney—and Marc and Ben fell for it. They might even have been fed a little Irish whiskey to wash down the blather. Major Holmgren, dear old Swampy, took one look at the room and went to find Mr. B., who in turn found Brigadier General LeRoy P. Collins, the CO of all American troops in Northern Ireland.

The General was embarrassed, "Mr. Berlin, there must be some mistake. I'll take care of it immediately."

Papa still had a way with generals.

There were no complaints about the food. We discovered that in Northern Ireland there was a plentiful supply of fresh eggs, fresh milk, real baked potatoes and all manner of delicious meats. We ate royally and slept in comfort in a Red Cross dormitory.

Northern Ireland appeared to be bursting with American soldiers and now we knew why: it was the food.

Mr. B. was called upon for a heavy schedule of appearances in the hospital wards, together with the usual comedy, juggling, magic and soloists—both singers and musicians from our outfit. Harry Rosoff didn't know any Irish songs, but he was always popular with spirited Hungarian rhapsodies on the violin.

In Belfast's Grand Opera House, the audiences roared and stamped and laughed. There was such a demand for more tickets that they extended our run for a third week.

Mr. B. addressed us that night after the show. He said nothing about our furloughs but he announced that we were going to play two performances at Her Majesty's Theater in London on Sunday, February 6, to an audience of service men and women, and no civilians.

Everyone was mystified. I decided to ask. "Just two performances?"

"That's right," said Papa and left us in the dark.

The trip back to London was a delightful change. The Irish Sea was as smooth as a millpond. We got on a sleeper and arrived in London without going near a Nissen hut.

Back in beautiful London! Mr. B. and Major Holmgren had made sure we started off with comfortable quarters. We were in four residential buildings, numbers 77, 82, 83 and 84 on Cadogan Place, S. W. We had a charming landlady, Mrs. Tillie Lenihan, who welcomed us warmly.

"If there's anything you want that you don't have, sing out. I'll sure take a stab at getting it for you."

The furlough was cut to a four-day pass for those who didn't have to hang the show. The rest of us got ready for the two Sunday performances. Jus and Hayden and other theater lovers rushed to see plays and musicals and to have a last visit with friends in London town. I had a drink with Burgess Meredith in a pub in Piccadilly. He was having a ball in London. It was not hard for a handsome, dashing American actor-lieutenant to find attractive, lonely wives and sweethearts whose husbands or lovers were in Africa or the China-Burma-Indian theater. It was a sore point between the U. S. and our British allies.

Our officer complement was changed again. Marc called us together on stage—those that were not on furlough—and announced that Captain Bentley, with great regret, was going back to an Infantry Regiment. Major Holmgren was now going to be the commanding officer, and he, Marc, would be his executive officer. This was met with general relief, although the boys were sensible enough not to overreact to their pleasure. Bentley was stiff and remote. Marc was too close to our ages and too anxious to be involved with us and the show. A comfortable, easygoing, jolly type CO like Holmgren suited us better.

On Sunday, February 6, as soon as the curtain went up with an all-service audience, we felt a special electricity in the air. The responses to humor were more boisterous and a little restrained to the emotional moments in songs. The applause was stronger than it had been with mixed audiences. But the mystery of why just two shows was not solved until Mr. B. came out on stage after the last curtain call and held his arms up. "Don't move, boys," he said looking very pleased. The mystery was over when everyone automatically snapped to attention as an officer entered briskly from stage left, and shook hands with Mr. B. at center stage. We were looking at General of the Armies Dwight D. Eisenhower.

"At ease, gentlemen," said the five-star general, turning to us with a smile.

It was an incredibly impressive experience for all of us. It's true that our meeting President Roosevelt was of the same order, but because we were in the war zone, the General's presence was stunning. He was not just a man from Abilene. He was the embodiment of our whole purpose—the purpose given to millions of men and women in uniform to save the world from savagery.

I deliberately avoid using the word "strode," which would have applied to many of the generals who visited us backstage. He felt no need to enlarge his presence. In those few steps, after putting us "at ease" he held his hand out to shake hands with Mr. B. We could hear him say "Thank you" and then he turned to us once more. He had seen the show as one of an audience of service men and women, as he requested. He spoke to us at length. No one could write it all down, but many of us tried to reconstruct it. I filled out my notes and saved them.

"Men, there is nothing I can say in praise of the performance you gave today which has not already been said many times. But I can make you realize the very important job you are accomplishing with This Is the Army.

"This war is a far-flung and far-reaching enterprise. It extends to all our people everywhere. You must never feel for an instant that because you are not manning a machine gun in the front lines, your work is unimportant or unessential, or that you are not in the midst of the war effort. Because it *just isn't true.*"

After those words there was a momentary pause — and I felt myself take in a breath. Indeed, many of us had felt just that on several occasions. It helped to have his reassurance.

"War is fought in many ways, by fighting at the front, by transportation, communication, supply lines and by maintaining the morale of the soldiers who must bear the brunt of it. It extends right back to the little town in America from which you came and affects the lives of those behind, who contribute in different but important ways.

"I was particularly pleased with the feeling of comradeship and partnership in the show — a sense that it is a joint venture with our British allies, the British who have proved themselves fine soldiers and superb allies. When you get to the African and Italian theaters of war you will be entertaining troops who have been through front line action. I assure you, from my own experience, *This Is the Army* will mean far more to them than any of you can imagine. So never feel that your contribution is not vitally important — so important, in fact, that I am going to recommend to General Marshall that you be sent around the world to perform this show for every American soldier and every one of our Allies, wherever they are.

"I leave you with my honest appraisal: you are great performers, great troopers, and—this is the highest compliment I can pay—*great soldiers.*"

A second's pause, and he was gone.

After all these years, when I ask members of *TITA* for impressive moments in the life of the show, they remember the directness and sincerity of General Eisenhower. In the aftermath of his words to us, the whole company was so lifted, they would have done *anything* they were asked, cheerfully. I went to Mr. B.'s dressing room and he looked up with a smile. "Well, we've been given quite an assignment!"

A grin took over my face. All I could think of was, "Yes, sir!"

The next day, we started to act out the future that Eisenhower had projected for us. His mention of Africa and Italy left little doubt about where we would begin. We took down the show and started getting ready to leave England. The company was gathered at the Red Cross building. Major Holmgren, now our new CO, announced that all furloughs had to be canceled so we could be ready to move out at a moment's notice. Pete would have to postpone doing any work on the scenery.

Mr. B. talked about his plans.

"Boys, I've got to say good-bye to you for a while. As you know from the General's speech, you've done a terrific job with the show. And you heard him tell you where we're going next. While you move everything down there by ship, I've got some jobs to clean up back home and then I'm going to rejoin you for the next opening. In the meantime, I have all your addresses and I'm going to get in touch with as many of your families as I can reach and let them know what General Eisenhower thinks of you—and of course, I'll let them know how handsome you all look."

He got his laugh and then he and Ben left for New York and Hollywood.

Papa had left us on our own. We weren't used to that and I think everyone felt a little worried. He'd been with us since we got to London. Now we weren't sure just when and where he would rejoin us. He looked good in his official correspondent's uniform. They were exactly like the uniforms of the commissioned officers except that they did not have the hardware that indicated rank. But in our lives, Mr. B. outranked them all!

☆ ☆ ☆ ☆ ☆ ☆ ☆ ☆ ☆ ☆ ☆

On February 18, twelve days after our performance for General Eisenhower, our train pulled into Liverpool, our third visit to that beleaguered city, and we boarded the S. S. *Ormonde*, an Orient Line ship. After he saw us aboard, Marc flew back to London. From there he was to fly to Africa and arrange for our arrival. He took with him all the letters we had written to mail them for us in London.

Before sailing, we had a boat drill and ship's officers gave everyone considerable lectures on safety measures of all kinds. Life jackets were to be worn or carried at all times. Everyone on board was instructed not to let anyone know our identity, duty or destination. From the orders that were posted, it was clear that our ship was carrying far more personnel than would fit into the lifeboats:

IN THE EVENT OF ORDERS TO ABANDON SHIP, WE WERE INSTRUCTED
TO CLIMB DOWN A ROPE LADDER AND SWIM TO THE NEAREST BOAT
OR RAFT.

Immediately after receiving this helpful instruction, at 5:30 p.m., February 18, we left Liverpool dock so other ships could use it and dropped anchor in the harbor opposite the pier for the night. There was no sign of our convoy as yet.

Our detachment was assigned to space in E deck, in what was formerly cargo space. We were to sleep in hammocks and store them each morning at 6:30 a.m., replacing them with folding tables for our meals. Major Holmgren and Lieutenant Koenig were assigned a cabin on B deck. At 7:15 p.m., we stored the tables and rehung the hammocks in time for lights out at ten o'clock. At 9:30 a.m., February 19, after that night at anchor, the PA instructed everyone to put on life jackets, cartridge belt with canteen filled with fresh water, and to take places at assigned table seats. Various emergency alarms were explained and demonstrated over the PA system. Boat drill announced for 1:45 p.m.; all manner of safety details were described and demonstrated.

After that meeting, when Rosie, Pete, Carl and I were standing at the rail watching the ships moving around us, the PA came on once more. "Attention—attention. An air raid on London during the night by an estimated one hundred or more Luftwaffe aircraft destroyed many buildings in central London with incendiary bombs."

"What the hell!" Rosie said. "We got out of there just in time." The voice continued. "For full details of the news, they are posted on C deck bulletin board.

"Let's go take a look," Pete said. We made our way down to C deck. A ship's officer was just pinning a sheet up on the board. When he had finished, Pete went close to the board and started to read to us:

"V-2 BOMBS DESTROY SEVERAL BUILDINGS. CADOGAN PLACE SUFFERS DIRECT HITS."

Pete stopped reading and exclaimed, "Son of a bitch!" We all got close and went on reading the details. Those house numbers—that's where we were! Out of the whole bloody city, they bombed the buildings we had been living in for seventeen days!

"What was her name? Pete said.

"Oh, my God!" Rosie said. "The landlady!"

"She took care of us night and day!" Pete said.

"Tillie Lenihan," Carl produced a piece of paper from his wallet.

"When we were leaving I promised her I was going to write her a letter."

"And we were bitching because they took away our furlough," Rosie said. We all stared at each other.

"She gave me a slug of Jameson's when I helped her carry a box of food one day," Pete said. "I was bellyaching because they made us leave town before I could get that stuff into the scene shop."

"That would have wiped out the show," I said. "We would all have been in bed."

The word spread through our outfit fast. I kept warning them not to give away our identity in talking about the V-2 damage, but it was hard to get it out of our minds. How long could our luck hold? We wondered if Axis Sally would talk about it—if she knew that we had been there. The shock of that bad news went through the whole outfit that morning, and I felt it would probably stick in our memory forever.

☆ ☆ ☆ ☆ ☆ ☆ ☆ ☆ ☆ ☆ ☆

While the boat drill was still going at 2:45 p.m., we pulled up anchor and sailed north along the shore. Lights out at 10:00 p.m., still heading north. At about 11:00 a.m. on Sunday, February 20, we dropped anchor in the Firth of Clyde, off of Glasgow. From the number of ships at anchor, it appeared that our convoy was forming. We continued to have boat drills.

We spent the next day, Monday, at anchor until 10:00 p.m., when we raised anchor and sailed south accompanied by other ships. It was February 21, 1944. For the next eight days we proceeded south along the coast in a large convoy, guarded once more by destroyers, carriers and at least two battleships. We were offered classes in French; a speech on journalism was given by our CO, Major Holmgren. We had to watch training films about behavior in strange lands. These were British. It was entertaining to hear the eloquence of British voices. Anyone who wanted to could take French lessons given by our French officers. Our black platoon leader, Sergeant Clyde Turner, sang at two religious services on Sunday morning. On the eighth day, February 28, we were issued an anti-mosquito cream.

The day before we were due in Algiers our cheerful Lieutenant John Koenig came bubbling up to us. "Kiddies," he said, "you've been challenged!"

The challenge turned out to be from the ship's champion tug-of-war team, the "King Kongs." We were limited to a team of nine men. I appointed Sergeant Leander Berg, known in Hollywood where he had appeared in several movies as Gene Nelson, as our team captain. Gene was a very strong and athletic dancer, very handsome and well liked. He chose the eight other men. Corporal Marion "Spoons" Brown, a specialty dancer and spoons player. (Spoons are played by holding two large dinner spoons, bowl to bowl and shaking them together in the manner of castanets.) Spoons, who was black, did this while dancing with great rhythmic agility considering he weighed about two hundred twenty-five pounds. Gene's next two choices were Geno Erbisti and Angelo Buono, the under-stander and middleman, respectively, of the Allon Trio, an acrobatic tumbler team. They were extremely powerful men. Angelo weighed one hundred seventy-five. Next he chose Robert Jackson and George Johnston, two large black dancers; Eddie O'Connor and Ralph Kessler, two hefty musicians; and Richard Reeves, a big basso profundo. All of them exercised regularly. I would guess the team weight was about 1,800 pounds.

Although I'm not aware that we did anything as a group to provoke such competitiveness, it was hard for a one hundred sixty-five interracial show folks to be seen as "regular guys." Perhaps we were perceived as a self-assured bunch of Yanks who needed a little taking-down.

A space was cleared on the afterdeck. The rest of our whole company came to watch and cheer. The Kongs were a rugged group. We discovered later that there were farmers and steel workers among them. Their captain, with a heavy Cornish accent said that it was customary to make it "the best two out of three rounds." Gene said that was agreeable. The Kongs and the *TITA*'s picked up the rope. A white line on the deck was about six feet from each team. One of the ship's officers dropped a white handkerchief to start the tugging. Everyone shouted encouragement to their favorites. The Kongs tried a surge of brute force to finish us off. The *TITA*'s seemed not to feel it. They quivered a little but then Captain Gene said, "Pull!" and the Kongs came sliding across the white line until the referee said, "Stop!"

"The 'Titans' scored the first point," the officer announced, having added an "n" to our name. The Kongs' captain pulled his men together for a quick, mumbled instruction. Gene just nodded to our boys. The teams lined up again. The Kongs now had their jaws set, looking a bit grim. The *TITA*'s were calm, trying not to look smug. After all, we had been lectured by Major Holmgren to be friendly to our Allies. The handkerchief fluttered down. The Kongs threw themselves immediately into an enormous tug with a great roaring cry, having decided to take us by surprise. Again there was a quiver, then nothing. Then Gene said, "Go!" and the Kongs came flying over the line tumbling into a heap.

That, we thought, was that. All the guys shook hands with the Kongs and complimented them on good sportsmanship and so forth. There was a moment of milling about and then the ship's officer said to Gene, "Would you be ready for another challenge or do you need a rest?" Gene looked at the guys. They all shrugged and said, "No, we're fine."

"The champion team of the ship, the unbeaten Ship's Officers Dozen, would like to have a match."

Gene looked at his boys again. "Okay?" he asked.

Geno said, "We're just warmin' up, Sarge!"

It took a few minutes for them to get the other team together. Some of them had some smudges from working in the engine room. They were a solid, heavier bunch—the term "Officer" being used loosely.

The handkerchief fluttered down. For a few moments there was a little movement one way and then the other, and then Gene said, "Go!" again and the Dozen began to slide a little, and then faster. You could see Geno throw himself backward; the Dozen were grunting and groaning and sliding across the line and it was over.

"You win!" said the Ship's Officers leader. "We've never lost before."

"Isn't it two out of three?" Gene asked.

"Not necessary," said the Dozen's captain. "We default."

After all hands were shaken, the *TITA*'s were offered anything they wanted from the bar. By the time supper was called, a good deal had been consumed and Mr. B. would have been proud of the graciousness of his team toward the losers—and also, perhaps, of their ability to hold their liquor.

The next day the convoy passed through the Straits of Gibraltar without incident.

"That's two convoys without a ship being hit," said Rosie to Carl, Pete and me as we looked south at the rows and rows of gleaming white buildings that were the city of Algiers.

Chapter 15

THE WAR

—*Feb 15, 1944: Monastery at the summit of Monte Cassino bombed. Germans occupy it immediately afterward.*

—*Feb 16, 1944: Germans fail to drive Allied forces from Anzio beach-head.*

—*Feb 18, 1944: At Monte Cassino, strong German defense and strategic position stop all attempts to take the monastery hill.*

—*Mar 6, 1944: US 8th Army Air Force bombers make first large-scale daylight raids on Berlin.*

All the way into the harbor of Algiers, it was like a dream or a childhood storybook: successive tiers of white houses and buildings towering over each other.

The convoy gradually worked its way into harbor. By two o'clock we were boarding trucks and winding through the city. After weeks in the British Isles, the shock of a totally different culture—Muslim women swathed in white robes, veiled, faces covered, their eyes peering; the men dressed in djellaba and fezz (the long robe and red cap). There were swarms of children, beggars—considerable filth and noise. Mixed among native clothing were the uniforms of France, Britain, America—every Allied country. Above, a brilliant blue sky and below, dirt, turmoil and clamor in the ancient city.

We piled into trucks and drove out of the city for a mile or so through open desert and entered a huge tent city, through an archway—two metal towers with a horizontal structure which displayed the words "Maison Blanche." It was the beginning of March, nearing the end of the rainy season. The tents stood in drying mud, connected by rough board sidewalks with street signs at the intersections.

The trucks stopped on 6th Street between Avenues E and F. This was home for the duration of our stay. Following instructions from our officers who had been briefed, we assigned eight men to a tent, four metal double bunks in each tent. Pete took possession of the first tent for us, at the corner of 6th and E. We made up our bunks with our shelter-halves, a straw mattress and two blankets for each bunk. We were warned that it was cold at night in this desert world and we might find it comfortable to keep on all our wool clothing. The warning was well advised. Rosie discovered that the legs of our metal bunks stood in cans. "What the hell is this?" he asked, sticking his finger into a can. Pete grabbed his hand and sniffed.

"That's kerosene, you jerk. It's to keep the ants from crawling into bed with you. It's not for putting out your cigarettes."

Carl was smiling at the luxury of a half-burned candle standing on the table in the center of the tent. "This is what we get to read by."

Camp Maison Blanche may have been named by the Algerian French, but when we got there it was another British transit camp and, like the Nissen huts in Stranraer, Scotland, it was simple, bare, utilitarian. We set up our own strict Army routine for reveille, guard duty, meals and had formations to announce the day's activities, one of which was watching more training films — the routine method of informing troops about unfamiliar environments. A lot of writers, actors, directors and cameramen spent the war producing those films — some in Hollywood, some in Astoria, Long Island.

In many respects, we had a good deal. The cooking, KP duty and fatigue details in the camp were done by a squad of very cheerful, friendly Italian prisoners of war who were assigned exclusively to *TITA*. They were absolutely delighted to be out of the war and well cared for.

The morning after our arrival, Major Holmgren announced that because the Allies had advanced more rapidly than expected we would not be playing shows in Africa and would sail to Naples as soon as a ship was available. In the meantime, we were on our own. A truck schedule was posted so that we could get into town and out again without hiking. Most of the detachment stayed in camp the first night for the five o'clock dinner.

The next night there were many who decided to climb in a truck and start exploring Algiers. We asked our truck driver, an affable Welshman, if he knew where we could get a drink. I never knew what he said but his smile and demeanor were encouraging. He dropped us in front of a lively and very popular establishment called *Le Cochon Aveugler*. Sergeant Jus Addiss assured us it meant The Blind Pig, immediately appealing to all. The huge room was fully occupied by sailors and soldiers with a wide variety of uniforms, a few civilians, older men, and here and there, young and not so young women, whose occupation seemed to be to entertain the soldiers and sailors.

We worked our way to the bar and Rosie got the attention of a bartender who asked for our order in French. Rosie looked up at the rows of bottles and said "brandy," and then Pete said "cognac," which brought an immediate response from our host, who said "*eau de vie*," which even I understood. I was reasonably sure that it covered a whole range of low quality alcoholic liquids.

Our bartender filled glasses for all of us with a brownish liquid, said *eau de vie*, took our money, and the evening continued that way for some time. We started chatting with several Brits.

"You can't go wrong with *eau de vie*, mate. Nothin' can live in it to do you harm except maybe the alcy." This wise advice from a hardy Devonshire sergeant.

We got directions to a restaurant from our Devonshire pal and after paying up, set out to find food. We ran into Jus, Hayden, Joe Bush and Art Gilmore, who had left the bar earlier in pursuit of food. They were just leaving something called, the *Place Delicat*, or something of the sort. We knew them to be knowledgeable in judging *haute cuisine*.

"We were told," said Jus, "that it was the best in town."

"God help the town!" said Hayden. "Jus's French is fabulous so he ordered for us. The main course consisted of—and I'm not kidding—

one lone pathetic sparrow for each of us. I lifted my fork and knife but I couldn't bring myself to attack the poor thing."

"I've decided," Joe Bush said, "to stick to our Italian prisoner chef at camp and save Algiers for the drinks."

We followed Joe's suggestion and ate in camp. We made a couple more trips into our favorite bar for *eau de vie* while we were in Algiers and actually found a couple of wines that were pretty good.

After visiting the Casbah with Charles Boyer on the silver screen, we decided we must see it ourselves. The bartender gave us directions and we found our way to the romantic district. The sidewalks were crowded, the streets narrow and winding, most of the natives were busy trying to get some money out of the soldiers, especially the Yanks—prostitutes waiting in every doorway, grotesque caricatures of women, branded on the forehead, slash scars on the cheeks, pockmarked faces. We found our way back to our favorite bar and sat at a table next to some elegantly robed Algerians. Some of our boys were at the table next to ours, including Bob Summerlin, a young dancer who was shy, very handsome, slim, rather delicate, feminine features—and homosexual. There was a good deal of chatter back and forth between tables. Rosie was admiring the handsome and ornate cape which one of the Arabs wore over his shoulders. He appeared to be the high ranking member of the Arab group. His English was quite good and he and Rosie talked about the show—the music, the dancing.

"What does that young man do?" the chief wanted to know.

"That's one of our dancers," said Rosie, his eyes going back to the cape.

"Ah! A dancer," said the chief. It was clear to Rosie that the chief couldn't take his eyes off Bob Summerlin.

"Where could I get a cape like yours?" Rosie asked. "It's beautiful."

"It was made for me," said the chief.

"Could I buy it from you?" Rosie asked.

"Oh!" The chief was somewhat taken aback. But then his eyes

fell once more on the beautiful young man. He leaned over close to Rosie. "What would I have to do to acquire the dancer?" the chief asked more quietly.

Rosie looked at the man for a moment, then at Summerlin, and then turned to the chief.

"It's a deal!" said Rosie, putting out his hand. The chief looked at the young man once more, shook Rosie's hand and then took off the cape and handed it to Rosie.

"Bob," Rosie called. Summerlin looked up at Rosie's beckoning finger. He came around to Rosie who whispered in his ear, "The Chief there wants to talk to you about dancing, Bob."

"Oh, sure," Bob said obediently. He went over and sat down next to the Chief who had cleared a seat for him with a gesture to his friends.

We finished our round, and Bob and the chief were deep in conversation. Rosie said to us that he thought it was time we got back to camp.

Once we were outside there were no trucks waiting. Rosie started moving quickly. Pete complained, "What's your hurry? Let's wait for a truck."

"Can't wait! Just keep moving. I'll tell you in a minute." Rosie hustled us down the block and around the corner. Then, walking fast with us in pursuit, he told us the deal he had made for the cape.

"You crazy bastard!" said Pete. "When he finds out Summerlin's not for sale, he's gonna kill you!"

Rosie glanced over his shoulder and then started jogging along the dark road to camp. We had kept this up for several minutes, fearing for our lives, when we heard running feet behind us. We sped up and for the first time, felt really scared. Suddenly a figure went flying past us, his face chalky white in the dim light. It was Summerlin. We tried to keep up with him but he had terror on his side. When we got to camp, we raced down to 6th Street and Summerlin disappeared into his tent. I followed him in and he turned, looking at me, panting, trying to catch his breath.

"Bob, are you okay?"

"Yeah, I'm fine! But I had to get away from that crazy son of a bitch of an Arab!"

"What happened, Bob? How'd you get away?"

"He was gonna take me home with him. I said I had to pee. I went into the men's room and climbed out the window!"

I went to our tent. Pete and Carl were holding Rosie down. Pete was giving it to him.

"I want to hear you say it! I'll never drink that crap again! Promise! I will never in my life touch eau de vie! Say it!"

Our crazy buddy was laughing so hard he couldn't stop but he kept nodding his head in the affirmative, gasping for air. Carl wanted to tie his wrists to the bunk but we couldn't find any rope so we hid the cape under the tent floor and went to bed.

We told Rosie he was not to leave camp until we left for Italy. He didn't argue. I think by morning, he decided we were right. He'd seen the last of Algiers.

☆ ☆ ☆ ☆ ☆ ☆ ☆ ☆ ☆ ☆ ☆

The V-Mail from home came in every couple of days and we wrote a lot home. There was a steady supply of Hollywood films shown in the camp each evening. Hollywood sent all its best films out to all the services around the globe. We saw *Miracle of Morgan's Creek*, *Holy Matrimony* and several other feature films. The titles of the training films we saw probably won't stir many memories, titles like *Why We Fight*, *The Battle of Russia*, *Malaria*—this last reminding you to take your Atabrine pill every day—and Sucker Bait to warn servicemen against buying junk from fast talkers or chancing a venereal disease with the camp followers.

Jus and Hayden didn't try any more restaurants. However, Jus was a big opera fan and when he saw a poster for *Carmen*, insisted that we should see it. It was a wonderful experience in the midst of chaos and poverty to see and hear an extremely spirited and tasteful production, with some good voices and a quite good orchestra. Jus wrote his father about it:

> There is a red plush opera house which seats 1,100. It's a jewel box with an ample stage and extraordinary facilities backstage.
>
> We arrived early and drank at the bar a la Metropolitan, except that this bar is six feet long and presided over by a Frenchwoman, full of joie de vivre. The curtain went up on a setting far more effective than the Met ever had! Carmen was the toughest gypsy ever to enact the role. But with drive, fire and great energy. But Micaela was the treat of the evening— really thrilling in her third act aria. She had perfect control, beautiful clarity and simplicity. But also, alas, a mustache. I shall never see *Carmen* again without thinking of the Algiers Opera House—a vivid and extraordinary experience.

On Friday, March 11, after eleven days in Algiers, we were put on alert and Saturday morning we loaded our show and ourselves onto a British attack transport, the S.S. *Winchester Castle*, a high speed troop carrier bound for Naples.

The passengers on the ship were much needed either for replacement of overworked fighting troops or medical support groups—doctors, nurses, aides. Except for *TITA*. We were flattered to be included in such precious cargo. With our orders emanating from General Eisenhower's headquarters, we must have been regarded as emergency morale support.

The Germans were anxious to interrupt the flow of ships into the Naples Harbor to supply the Italian front. The attack transports, like ours, were designed to move faster than the submarines. We boarded at 10:00 a.m. on March 11, and as dinner approached, were told we wouldn't sail until morning. The committee got hold of the major and arranged some after dinner music for the evening. Rosie introduced a string quartet in the officer's lounge and a jazz band in the mess. They were both anxious to have a chance to play without the other. They each did a two hour concert, acknowledged the applause and the thanks, and put their instruments away for the night.

At 7:30 the next morning, the *Winchester Castle* slipped out of port and started north. We've all heard that "the way to a man's heart is through his stomach" and that "an army marches on its stomach." I decided after our breakfast that the ship's British cook must have taken these age-old observations seriously. The main course every morning of that voyage was one of my father's favorite breakfasts—smoked kippered herring. I decided my father and my British companions were right.

After breakfast, my pals and I were at the rail and Rosie observed that we seemed to be going due north instead of toward Naples, which lay east of us. "Don't these guys know where we're going?"

A ship's officer was going by and heard Rosie questioning our route. The officer laughed and came over to us. He recognized Rosie from last night's performance. "You'd better stick to music, Sergeant. The Captain likes to avoid the subs. We'll get to Naples eventually. It's more prudent to obscure our intentions."

Rosie covered his face with both hands before replying. "Wow! Don't tell him I said that! He runs a great ship!"

"I happen to know he liked your music last night," he said. "Incidentally, Sergeant Conductor, your life jacket is coming untied." He smiled at Rosie and headed for the bridge.

"Ouch," Rosie said, retying his jacket. As could be expected, we had had a boat drill as soon as we were under way and were told to wear life jackets at all times.

The committee arranged a variety of activities for Monday afternoon and evening. After lunch, orchestra members and several of our singers entertained on each deck and some of the dancers and comedians joined them. At three o'clock, Rosie and his dance band played continuously for three hours on E deck square and as many as three hundred were on the dance floor all the time. British women—Army nurses and Auxiliary Territorial Service girls—danced with the troops. The rest of our guys kept the comedy, song and dance going everywhere else. After dinner, the British troop commander made a speech and introduced our show, which consisted of many elements of our full show. It was received with great enthusiasm by an audience of over four hundred troops.

Tuesday, March 14, preparations for arrival in Naples were made by all on board. We entered Naples Harbor after just three days at sea. It was jammed with ships. The captain edged in, and found that our best choice was to tie up alongside another ship. There was no food waiting for us in Naples so they served another meal and at 5:00 p.m. they gave us some K-rations. All the ship's passengers, including *TITA* Detachment, disembarked except for Marc, Pete and Jus, the stage crew and a squad of able guys to help load the show into trucks.

The rest of our detachment marched a couple of blocks to Garibaldi Railroad Station. Even having seen the devastation of Liverpool, what we saw of Naples as we left the ship and marched to the station was heartbreaking. There was nothing to be seen of dwellings near the harbor. The workmen were dressed in the remnants of clothing. Urchins rushed up to us with their hands out, offering to shine our shoes with a brush and a dirty rag, or offering us their sister in exchange for a cigarette.

We climbed into box cars, forty men to a car, and in a few minutes were in a suburb called Bagnoli, where we were to sleep.

Our first night reminded me of an ancient song, "I Dreamt I Slept in Marble Halls," which is exactly what we did with the help of our blanket rolls. We bedded down on the third floor of a building which Mussolini had built for the recuperation of his soldiers when they were discharged from hospital care. Herbie Shifrin got out his violin and played it for us while we were spreading our bedding. The air was filled with irony, sarcasm and considerable laughter. It wasn't bad, because it wasn't cold in southern Italy. We were under orders to blow out our candles at ten o'clock. Shortly after the room went dark, the German fighter-bombers put on a show as the air-raid sirens wailed. We were told to descend to the shelter under the building. Joe Fretwell was so moved by the spectacular view we had of the tracer light of strafing, and the antiaircraft fire, that he had to be persuaded three times to give up the spectacle and seek safety. Bob Sidney prevailed with, "Miss Fretwell, you will get your ass down to the shelter this instant and that's an order!"

"Yes, mother," Fretwell replied and followed us down.

Ominously, the sounds of bombing were heaviest in the direction of the harbor where Pete and all our guys were unloading the show. Obviously, Naples Harbor was a primary target, with all the supply ships coming in day and night.

Half an hour later we returned to our marble beds and because there was nothing we could do about our guys, we got some sleep. When Pete and the whole unloading gang rejoined us the next morning, it was a huge relief. Pete's usual bombast was missing when he told Carl, Rosie and me about their night. "Every crazy Kraut pilot was after a medal for blowing us out of the water. Just after we made it to the shelter, they sank the ship next to us. Axis Sally just barely missed, but she sure was there last night."

Mr. B.'s show was still being watched over by a special angel. At least a dozen Junkers or Heinkels had attacked the harbor at 2100 hours, the thirty-second such attack in the past two weeks—and not one of our guys was injured. Out of the three ships that were sunk, only one was a close call for our men.

The next day, Wednesday, March 15, it was clear that orders from Washington had ordered us to Italy to give shows, but preparations for where we would live and where the shows would be presented had not been determined. They found cots for us to sleep on instead of the marble floor, and they decided that the production could be stored in the basement of the Royal Palace. Marc used his limited clout to get trucks and Pete and his gang were able to move the entire show production, in the crates, to the basement of the palace. They set up a temporary guard roster for the show production until someone in Naples headquarters could decide what to do with us.

On Thursday morning, March 16, Major Holmgren was able to get the Peninsular Base Services (PBS), to which we were attached for administrative purposes, to assign MP's for that duty. That night, the USO was supposed to give a show in the post theater, but they were delayed and a thousand soldiers were sitting in their seats waiting for the curtain to go up. So Jus, Hayden and I rounded up the guys. Rosie got enough musicians to make a tolerable noise and we all hurried down from our third floor encampment to see what we could do.

Rosie started things off with some band music. Bob Sidney rounded up some dancers and we started feeding guys out onto the stage to do their thing. Our audience was cheering us on and laughing at the adlib material from Dick Bernie, Julie Oshins and Hank Henry.

The USO gang turned up an hour and a half later and, between us, we made a clever segue from our show into theirs. When the entertainment ended, we all got a huge hand. We said good night and went back to our marble floor.

☆ ☆ ☆ ☆ ☆ ☆ ☆ ☆ ☆ ☆ ☆

PBS supplied us with rations, administration and supply, under the command of a major general. Our direct contact was the Special Services officer under the general, Colonel Maurice J. Meyer. It was his job to decide where we could live and put on the show. Colonel Meyer decided on the world famous San Carlo Opera House. We would have to wait, therefore, until the opera season ended with performances of *La Forza del Destino*, *La Bohème*, and *Madame Butterfly*. We would not be able to bring our production to the opera house until March 31. In the meantime, we would be able to rehearse our show during the day, leaving the opera company time to set up for the evening.

For our living quarters, the Colonel decided we would share the Royal Palace of Naples with units of French and Polish troops. The palace had been bombed and strafed many times, partly because there were antiaircraft gun emplacements in the palace courtyards and troops living there, but also because it stood so close to the ships unloading in the harbor, it often became the victim of inaccuracy. Using the third floor for our living quarters was only possible if Pete Feller was able to construct various facilities to create our bathing, our eating and our sleeping necessities. Master Sergeant Peter Feller once again said, "I can do it!"

"Pete, you schmuck, you open your big mouth and make promises like that. How the hell are you going to do it?"

Pete looked at Rosie for a second, and then with his usual grace, said, "You just go on waving your stick at the orchestra and let me figure that out."

It was a challenge. While there were many rooms on the third and top floor, we were largely in the open air. The bombs had left debris, holes, open spaces and large areas of open terrace. There were no doors, no window glass, no running water or electricity. Mostly there was space. Peter and his crew constructed wash-stands, kitchen counters and did myriad repairs.

They managed enough roofing to shelter a cooking area. We ate under the sky. When it rained we would have to retreat with our mess gear to the sleeping areas.

In three days, we were living in a palace although little about it was palatial except its size. Once again we had marble floors, but happily we were sleeping on Army issue canvas cots that had been given to us in Bagnoli. Marc and I assigned rooms mostly by platoon and squad. Our lighting was from kerosene lanterns; our running water from the five-gallon jerry-cans we hauled up the stairs. I set up a company roster for that vital job and found lighter jobs for Abner Silverstein.

We had incredible views in every direction—of the sea, the city of

Naples, the sky, and to the east, the plains of Campania from which rose the famous volcanic peak, Mount Vesuvius.

In addition to hauling water, another problem about being on the third floor was the dash down three flights of stairs to get to the air-raid shelter under the palace basement. Peninsular Command insisted that everyone in the palace must use the shelter since the hospitals were already overloaded. The French troops on the second floor and the Poles on the ground floor beat us to the only seats more comfortable than stone. When there was a raid, the antiaircraft gun emplacements next to the palace let go their thunderous blasts, attempting to drive off the German bombers. Our third floor perch was not a sensible place to remain during a raid: when they missed the ships or the gun emplacements, they might easily blow away our open air accommodations.

We soon got used to the sound of the air-raid sirens. We hated to roll out of bed, slip into shoes and dash for the shelters, so we learned to pause long enough to determine if it was one of the occasional false alarms. We had one very reliable clue—Private Herbert Fluker, a young, black dancer who was fleet of foot and seemed to have an instinct for the real thing. Fluker slept in the room next to ours which included Hayden, Jus, Pete, Carl, Rosie and me. Hayden was next to the door with a view of the passageway. When there was a raid, first there was the sound of the sirens, then there was indecision, then there was the voice of Hayden, trained to throw his speech clearly to the back of any theater: "There goes Fluker!" And everyone followed.

Much of the interior of the Palazzo Real had been designed by Giovanni Bernini. Although there was little to make the palace habitable, we discovered that there was a great deal to effect enormous grandeur: countless marble statues, paintings, tapestries and silk-lined walls. What ceilings remained were covered with beautiful paintings and miraculously, a great deal of a glorious chapel remained. We found many treasures that were worth the search. There was nothing to carry away. That had been done long since!

As we settled in, we learned that Mr. B. would not return to us until March 28th. Clearly we had to begin rehearsals before that. After his arrival we would have only seven days before the opening on April 3. Holmgren, quite properly, left it to the committee to organize the show activities.

By Wednesday, March 22, we felt settled in enough to start rehearsals. The opera house was available to us until late afternoon when they had to get ready for the evening opera. We started at nine in the morning. Bob Sidney and Milt Rosenstock had the major responsibilities: Bob directing or supervising all the big numbers and dances; Rosie working with the orchestra, rehearsing the chorus numbers and soloists. I rehearsed the second act sketch and Jus, Hayden and Joe Bush coordinated the scheduling and made sure all the specialty numbers went through their routines and lines.

Pete, meanwhile, made small repairs and was ready early to load in the production. We would have to wait until Friday, March 31, for the operas to end their season.

Although we were officially attached to the Peninsular Command, we had not expected to be involved with them. We were taken by surprise when Holmgren announced that Colonel Meyer would be conducting a full General Inspection the next day, Saturday, March 25 at 11:00 a.m. Since we usually started rehearsals at 9:00, this was going to wreck our schedule. Mr. B. would not have let this happen. I spoke to Holmgren in private.

"Major, could you explain to the Colonel that it would be better for our rehearsal schedule if we could have the inspection either early in the morning or at the end of the day?"

The Major thought for a moment. He looked as if he was standing in the middle of a busy road and had to decide which way to run. "He seemed pretty definite about the time he wanted to do it. Since we're new here, I thought we ought to go along with his request."

"With respect, sir, this would not happen if Mr. Berlin were here. Perhaps if the Colonel had known our schedule—"

He was shaking his head. He knew I was right but he wasn't going to tell the Colonel what to do. "Well, when Berlin gets here, I guess we'll do it his way. But for now, I think we'd better keep the Colonel happy." I pointed out that by then we would be near the end of our rehearsal time. Obviously, our dear Swampy turned to jelly when he was out-ranked, a weakness we have experienced with far off Dixie.

The Colonel arrived promptly at 11:00 with his driver, a sharp look-ing corporal. I recognized the type: his pants a little too well creased, a hard look in the eyes. I would guess he had kissed ass to get to be the Colonel's driver and he was bucking for sergeant.

"Stand by, Larry," Meyer said to the driver. "Be ready to leave as soon as we finish."

"Yes, suh!" Larry replied in an accent I recognized as North Carolina. The inspection team consisted of Colonel Meyer, Major Holmgren, Lieutenant Daniels and First Sergeant Anderson.

"Lead the way, Sergeant," Meyer said. I glanced at Holmgren and he nodded to me. The Colonel checked every cot, and all clothing and equipment in every room. I was glad to see the guys had put on a real show. They could smell their audience and they knew he was GI (Government Issue) to the core. When we finished up back at the orderly room, the Colonel said, "Good work, Sergeant. Considering the conditions, your men are first rate."

"Thank you, sir," I said temporarily relieved. This guy had the poten-tial of being a real pain in the ass.

Corporal Larry was waiting for us at the orderly room. He was talk-ing to Bachner. He took pains to be sure we all heard him. "Looks like you've got a bunch of fruits in this outfit, Corporal."

I was pleased to hear Bachner's reply. "I wouldn't let them hear you say that, kiddo," said Bachner.

Sergeant Artie Steiner happened to walk in the door right behind me and heard the whole exchange. Artie was a very muscular, hand-some, smiling guy, a favorite of everyone in the show. And he'd earned his sergeant stripes in an infantry outfit. In show business, he was an acrobatic dancer—strong, fast, good natured. His nose gave evidence of boxing experience. "There something you don't like about our out-fit, young fella?" said Artie, smiling.

"Uh, no, Sergeant," the driver said. The driver's uniform looked as though he had some nice Italian woman ironing his stuff every day. And he probably slapped her around if she complained about what he paid her. I could smell a homophobe and a bully, all rolled into one.

Artie turned to me. "Sarge, what time do we start rehearsals this afternoon?"

"Two o'clock, Artie. We'll only have two hours left before we have to get out of the opera house."

"That's all you gotta do—rehearse?" says the driver.

"You've got a tough job? You drive the Colonel around in a car, right, buddy boy? You want to know who sent us down here to do our job, little fella?" said Artie.

"The USO," said the driver, with a slightly twisted smile.

"General Dwight Eisenhower, buddy boy. Is that good enough for you?" The driver didn't say anything. "Just watch your manners around here, buddy boy," Artie said.

Colonel Meyer came to the orderly room door.

"Atten-*tion!*" I said sharply. Everyone came to attention. There was an atmosphere produced not only by the driver but by the Colonel that warned me about the Peninsular Base makeup.

"At ease," the Colonel said. "Thank you, Sergeant."

"Sir," I said, all business. I wasn't going to relax around this guy. No familiarity! He and the driver left.

☆ ☆ ☆ ☆ ☆ ☆ ☆ ☆ ☆ ☆ ☆

When we sat down for dinner, Bob came over to our table with his tray. "Can you imagine what Mr. B. would have done if he'd been here?"

"It would never have happened," I said. "I asked Holmgren if we couldn't schedule the inspection at the beginning or the end of the day. He was afraid to offend Meyer."

Pete said, "If he had a little guts, Meyer might give him some respect. He treats him like he wasn't there."

"He's not!" Carl said. "All that Swampy can think about is getting back to the *Minneapolis Daily Bugle*."

☆ ☆ ☆ ☆ ☆ ☆ ☆ ☆ ☆ ☆ ☆

Bob had told everyone we would start rehearsals the next morning at 9:00., as usual. Rosie and I finished breakfast and started for the opera house. Bob Sidney was ahead of us. When we checked the bulletin board where all scheduling was posted, Bob and I were both aware of an unfamiliar notice. Bob reached it first.

"What is this: Rehearsal of the Navy Number, signed Lieutenant Marc Daniels? Our executive officer is playing producer!" Bob pulled the notice off the corkboard and went straight for the orderly room. I thought I'd better go with him. Arnold Bachner was working on the morning report at his desk. The officers' doors were closed. Bob opened Marc's door and charged in. I stayed close to him. Marc was sitting at his desk. Bob tossed the notice down on the desk.

"What's this supposed to mean: Rehearsal of the Navy number?" Bob asked.

"It means just what it says: I scheduled a rehearsal of the Navy Number — and you shouldn't take it down."

"Since when do you start scheduling rehearsals?"

"There are changes in the Navy number and we should be rehearsing them," Marc said, picking up the notice and holding it out to Bob. "Just put this back where you found it."

"For your information," Bob said, ignoring the notice, "I know all about the changes. Have you talked to Mr. Berlin about this?"

"Of course not. He's on the way here and I'm meeting him at the airport on Tuesday. But we should rehearse the Navy number — before he gets here. Just put it back."

"I want a committee meeting, Lieutenant. We all agreed that the offi-cers have nothing to do with running the show. You know nothing about the Navy number. You have no business scheduling anything."

"I called a rehearsal of the Navy number, Sergeant, and I want it done. That's an order."

"Marc," I said, hoping to save the situation, "I think Mr. Berlin—"

Bob cut me off. "Go to the Officers' Club and have a good time, Lieutenant! But don't butt in on the show."

Marc stood up with the paper in his hand. "You aren't listening. I'm ordering this rehearsal. That's what I want."

"Lieutenant Daniels, you're forgetting our agreement. This is none of your business!"

"For the last time: I want the Navy Number in rehearsal, today!"

"And I said you're not getting it!"

Bob started out of the room. Marc's face was going red. "Sergeant Sidney, I told you—I'm not asking you, I'm telling you: This is an order!"

Bob stopped and turned. "And I say, kiss my ass!" And turned again to go.

"Come back here, Sergeant! You are not going anywhere!" Bob turned at the door. Marc pulled himself up and crossed his arms. "You are confined to your quarters!"

Bob gave him a derisive laugh, "Well, aren't we grand! My quarters! Is that what you call them!"

"You are sequestered! Right now! You are to go to your quarters and remain there until further orders." He turned to me. He was in a fury. "Sergeant Anderson, you will see that he obeys my order!"

I looked at him and then at Bob, who was standing with his hands on hips, looking confused.

I said, "Yes, sir," and started toward Bob.

"You're making a big mistake, Lieutenant," Bob said, smirking.

"Let's go," I said to Bob and when I was close enough for him to see, I gave him a wink. He followed me out and back to our sleeping quarters. When we were in Bob's room, I closed the door, he turned around and held his palms up helplessly.

"What does he expect to do now?" Bob said. "Berlin will kill him when he finds out about this."

"Jesus, Bob! I don't know. But I wish we could have handled it some other way. I mean we should have insisted on a committee meeting."

"I suggested that and he ignored me. Why should we have to *handle* it? He's way out of line. Berlin will be furious."

"I know he's completely out of line, but Berlin's not here! And Marc's nose is out of joint! He's likely to do anything."

"When does Berlin get here?" Bob asked.

"Tuesday afternoon. The day after tomorrow. A lot can happen."

"This is ridiculous. We have to rehearse."

"Bob, forget rehearsals! He's so goddamned mad, he's just as likely to call for a court martial!"

"Court martial?"

"I'm not kidding! He's put you under arrest! This is serious! Who knows! You'd better stay here so he doesn't try to get Military Police or some damn thing."

Bob looked at me, "What shall I do?"

"Just stay here. I'll go and see what's going on. Don't move — please!"

I went back to the orderly room. Marc saw me and came out of his office.

"Is he in his room?"

"Yes, sir" I said. I wasn't taking any chances. "Do you want me to have someone stay with him?"

"Assign a guard roster, four on and four off, so there's someone with him at all times. I'm going to get Eddie Barclift to take over rehearsals. Arnold, go get Barclift."

Bachner went after Barclift. I assigned Eddie O'Connor, one of the tug-of-war team, to stay with Bob for four hours. "I'll have someone spell you at three o'clock, Eddie."

"What am I supposed to do?"

"You're supposed to make sure he stays in his quarters. He can go to the john, he can go to meals. That's it."

"What the hell did he do?"

"I'll tell you later. He disobeyed an order."

"Oh, for Christ's sake! Big fuckin' deal!"

"It could be," I said.

"No shit?"

"Don't tell anybody about it. I don't want to start a panic. Get him anything he wants—except out!"

"Right."

When I got back to the orderly room, Bachner was at his desk. "Did you get hold of Barclift?"

"Sure."

"Where's Marc now?" He gestured toward Swampy's door. "I got Barclift and he told Marc he didn't know anything about the changes in the Navy number. He said Bob and Berlin discussed it in England and they decided they should do it before the opening here."

Holmgren opened his door. "Alan, would you come in here?"

I went in. Marc was sitting. Swampy was looking sad. "We've got a problem here, Sergeant."

He never called me Sergeant. This was serious.

"Sergeant, Sidney seems to have been insubordinate. That could be a court martial offense."

"I know, sir. I hope we can find a way to avoid that. If Mr. Berlin were here, I'm sure he would want us to find a way around a court martial, sir."

"It's out of his hands," said Swampy. "Berlin's a civilian. This is an official Army matter."

"Is there any chance we could keep it unofficial until Mr. Berlin arrives?"

"I'd like to do that. It's up to Marc. Sidney disobeyed Marc's direct order, and he used abusive language."

"We have to go ahead with rehearsals, Alan," Marc said. "If Sidney refuses to obey my order to rehearse the Navy number. I want him punished."

"Marc," I said, taking a chance I could reach him on a personal basis, "if we had put this matter with the committee, we could solve it in a minute."

"I want Bob to obey my order—and I *want* his apology."

"I think I can get him to apologize. If I can, would that do it?"

"Not unless he obeys my order."

"But Marc, you know Bob and Mr. Berlin discussed the Navy number, and Berlin's the only one who can solve that. I would think this calls for a committee meeting."

"The committee has nothing to do with what Bob has done!"

"This is a serious matter, Alan," said Swampy. "If this is a war zone, and a noncom refuses to obey an order—that's punishable by death. That's in every soldier's manual."

I must have been staring at him in shock, in total disbelief. His expression changed from a kind of matter-of-fact acceptance to concern.

"We're not talking about anything like that, of course." The Major finally realized how his statement sounded in the context of Sidney's crime.

Marc said, "Of course not. But I do want him punished."

Holmgren opened his office door, "Corporal, would you see if you can get Colonel Meyer on the phone?"

He came back and sat down, leaving the door open.

"Sir, wouldn't it be better to keep this thing within the company for now? If we could just take care of it ourselves for a day or a day and a half? That's all it would be."

Arnold came to the door, "He's on the line, sir." Arnold closed the door. The Major turned away from me and picked up the phone.

"Major—" He wouldn't look at me. I turned to Marc. Marc wouldn't meet my eyes. I shook my head at him. "Don't do this," I said quietly. Marc looked at me and then stood up and looked out the window toward the east. I could see he was shaking a little. From anger or fear?

"Colonel, I'm sorry to bother you but we have a problem. . . . No, no one's sick. We had a little insubordination problem. . . . Yeah, one of our noncoms refused an order. . . . A written report? Yeah, we can do that. . . . Yes, sir. I'll take care of it right away." He listened for a moment. "Of course, it might not have to go that far right away, sir. The Sergeant might apologize if he knew how serious—" A pause again. "Oh. Yes, sir. Of course, I'll take your advice on that. I'll send you the report, sir. Thank you."

He hung up. He looked like a guy who had just pulled the plug out of a dam and couldn't get it back in. "Jesus. He wants you to write out your complaint and get it over to him pronto," he said to Marc. "He wants all the facts—the full story."

"Okay," said Marc. "I can do that." Marc left to go to his office and start writing it all out. "I guess that's it, Alan. The Colonel was pretty upset. I guess he feels anything that happens with the show could reflect on him."

"Jesus," I said. "Berlin's going to be furious."

"You think so?" Swampy looked even more worried.

"Sir,"—I held his look for a long moment—"this is going to affect our relationship with General Dwight Eisenhower, sir—" Swampy stared at me, frozen—"and also General George C. Marshall, the Chief of Staff."

"I know who General Marshall is, Sergeant."

"Yes, sir. I thought you did, sir." I saluted him and held it for his reply.

"Jeez, Alan—I'm sorry about all this."

I was so goddamned mad I wasn't going to let him feel better by trying to apologize to me. "Yes, sir," I said, holding my salute. He finally had to acknowledge it. When he did, I did a neat one-eighty, opened the door and then turned back to him.

"Sir, I wonder if Colonel Meyer is aware of the five-star generals who will be concerned about any repercussions on the Irving Berlin show."

I left him alone to think that one over.

Chapter 16

THE WAR

—*Mar 15, 1944: In Italy, huge bombardment of Cassino and immediate ground attack. Progress hampered by vigorous defense and mountains of rubble produced by bombs.*

—*Mar 17, 1944: German paratroops defending Monte Cassino with great resolve. Slight Allied gains.*

—*Mar 22, 1944: New Zealand Corps makes final assault to no avail. Makes partial withdrawal.*

I picked another guy to spell Eddie O'Connor in keeping Bob confined to his quarters—Dick Reeves, a hefty baritone, also about two hundred pounds, mostly muscle. Not that they really needed muscle. Bob wasn't going anywhere. He was allowed to get in the chow line for all meals. Where the hell could he go anyway? Besides, they both admired Bob a hell of a lot more than they did Lieutenant Daniels.

Monday seemed to drag on forever. Jus and I rehearsed all the specialty numbers and I got Eddie Barclift to rehearse the Stage Door Canteen dancers. Rosie rehearsed the soloists and the orchestra. The Navy number, needless to say, would wait for Mr. B.

I kept wondering what the Major had said in his memo to the Colonel and whether the phone would ring and blow up the show at any minute.

On the way to lunch, I went to Bob's room. He was lying on his cot.

"Sergeant," he asked wryly, "am I allowed to have visitors? And by the way, you can tell the lieutenant that our library doesn't have one book I want to read." Marc was very proud of having set up a library for the company. Norman Stuart and Bill Roerick were the librarians, both well-read.

"I'll see what I can do," I said. "We had James Joyce last time I looked. You've got time to finish *Ulysses*."

"You'd better be wrong. I never could read the damn book!"

"I suggest you do a little praying. Something like, 'I hope to God the phone don't ring.' Or maybe, 'I sure hope Mr. B. ain't late.' "

"The Lieutenant better pray that he's not in the infantry when Mr. Berlin gets through with him."

"I'm hungry. Can I take you to lunch? I know a nice place looking out to sea."

We got our mess gear and stood on the chow line. I looked around to be sure there was no one listening and then continued to lecture Bob. "I'll tell you one thing: This is a lesson to be learned. When Mr. B. isn't with us, we have to play the Army game. There's always some jealous hard-ass who wants to play GI." This time it was one of ours. It could be worse. Marc let it get out of his hands, the jerk. And Swampy was afraid to tell Marc to cool it. Never—never depend on the power of Mr. B. unless he's here to exert it. We can't do anything without bars on our shoulders, and Mr. B. doesn't want us to have bars. So, be prepared to eat shit once in a while when Mr. B. isn't with us. You've got no choice."

I knew I was asking a lot. Bob tended to explode, ignoring the consequences. It went against his grain to "play soldier" when you had to. I explained my own technique. "As a first sergeant, officers expect me to work with them. But they also expect me to realize that they are in charge. In other words, I can argue but I can't say 'no.' *And neither can you!*" He looked at me with a smirk. But he didn't say no. Maybe he would try.

We finished lunch and we still hadn't heard anything from Meyer, thank God. Maybe Mr. B. would get here before he takes any action.

Bob went back to his sumptuous quarters. I went to rehearsal. Judging from his staff, Meyer is straight out of the rule book. He may be a tough case but Mr. B. will stop him cold. He won't want to cross him. I can't have started any action yet. It was a complicated procedure and you had to "go through channels." Meyer would have a hard time scheduling a court martial. With Berlin involved, he might think he'd better talk to his superior. What's his name? General Wilson?

We were in the middle of rehearsing "Daddy's Furlough," the second act sketch, when Larry Weeks came running down the aisle yelling incoherently. Larry was a juggler, so you would imagine he was deft—good with his hands. But somehow he wasn't good at juggling words.

"It's—the mountain—the whole mountain's blowing up!"

"What?—Larry! Calm down. What's happening?"

"It's the volcano! Come on," he said. "I'm not kidding!"

As we ran out of the opera house, the townspeople were running down to the harbor so they could see the mountain. We knew an even better view. We ran into the palace and up to our third floor balcony where we had the best view of an exploding volcano of anyone in the world. It was an absolutely phenomenal sight.

Mount Vesuvius rose steeply from the flat plain barely ten miles away. As we watched, a fresh explosion of fiery red flame and lava shot upwards out of the crater. Red-hot rivers of lava and ash roared down the Western slope toward the Bay of Naples. The peak was only a little over 4,000 feet high but it rose straight up from the surrounding low hills. The stupendous, scene was like a theatrical extravaganza being produced on a gigantic stage, just for us.

"Wowie! It's Pompeii all over again!" Rosie shouted.

"Not yet," said Bill Roerick, our resident history expert. Just three days ago, Bill had taken a busload of *TITA*'s on a tour of Pompeii. "Pompeii exploded last in 79 AD and buried three cities. It hasn't done that since—at least not this big."

"Just enjoy it," Pete said to Rosie. "You'll be able to tell your kids, 'I saw a volcano erupt!' And you'll probably never see one again!"

"What happens to the people living in the valley?"

"It depends on how long it goes on!" Bill said.

"How long ago was the last one?" Rosie asked.

"Nineteen-hundred, I think," said Bill.

We forgot about Meyer and court martials and rehearsing. We were mesmerized by having first row balcony seats for what was bound to be an incredible geological-historical event! They'd be hearing about it everywhere — even on South Mountain Road. I could tell my son I was there — almost!

I stood there thinking how ironic it was to have these two events overlapping each other: fascinating history and a potential tragic mess. General Marshall — General Eisenhower — all the letters and speeches of praise — that could all blow up, too. Shame. Insubordination. Direct defiance of an order in wartime. You know what you can do with your Good Conduct ribbons, you fruits! How would they act with us — the little snot-nosed guys who were jealous of us?

We'd be dumped in no time. Berlin wouldn't be able to deal with the finger-pointing.

Why didn't we have a CO with some balls? Why was Marc such a jealous bastard he had to stick his nose in everything? "Swampy Homegrown" and his precious *Minnesota Daily Bugle!* Scared of his own shadow! Scared of Marc Daniels! Our nice, talented artist, Johnny Koenig? He wouldn't have a chance with the stuffy administrative gang — the Army bureaucrats.

John was a great guy. We knew it. Our guys loved him. He joked and laughed with the guys and did more for morale than Marc or the Major ever could. He was also very resourceful and a damned good designer. He had done a great job on the show. He and Pete could work very efficiently together when there were emergencies — problems that arose just before curtain time or in the middle of the show that had to be solved quickly. But the last thing John could do was to try to explain to Colonel Meyer that the problem between Marc and Bob was something that should be solved as a show problem, not an Army one.

Tuesday dawned without any word from the Peninsular Base Services. Vesuvius had quieted down; it wasn't going to be another Pompeii. But there had been many killed and great damage. We heard

US Army troops were helping people to escape the area. But the spectacular show was over. An incredible memory.

Once again, Rosie went through the solos with the singers and I did a run through of the sketch.

We were standing in line for lunch when I suddenly heard some excited voices—something going on—from the direction of the stairs to the lower floors. Was it Meyer with the Military Police? Then Marc appeared and right behind him Ben Washer and finally, Mr. B. wearing his correspondent's regulation uniform, looking very handsome. He pulled off his Army cap and walked up to Rosie, Pete, Carl and me in line.

"All you guys do is eat!" he said with a big smile. If Marc was with him, why was he smiling?

"Where's Bob," said Mr. B.

I looked at Marc. "Didn't you tell him?" Marc was silent.

"Tell me what?"

"Mr. Berlin, uh, let's all go into the office for a minute," I said and led them to the orderly room. Ben and Mr. B. followed me in, Marc was behind us. The Major was in his office with the door closed.

"Is something wrong?" said Mr. B. "Is Bob sick?"

"No. Bob is okay. He's perfectly healthy." I decided since Marc hadn't tried to plunge in, I would.

"Marc and Bob had a quarrel and Marc arrested Bob. Bob has to stay in his room." "Arrested him! What?!" He looked at Marc. "We've got a show to put on!" He turned back to me.

I almost laughed—I did smile—it was so characteristic of Mr. B.

"It's more complicated than that, sir," Marc said. "We've been rehearsing without Bob." "How can you rehearse without Bob?" He said.

"We started rehearsals with Bob," I said.

He looked at me. Marc still didn't have the guts to tell the story so I plunged again.

"We started rehearsing—everyone. Bob was working hard. On Sunday, Marc put a rehearsal call up on the board for the Navy number."

Berlin turned around and looked at Marc. "How could you do that? There are changes in the Navy number Bob that I have to work on."

"I thought we should get going on it, sir. The days were going by—"

"Well, you should keep your nose out of the show. You should let the committee make the decisions. We agreed on that—you agreed on that. You can't rehearse Navy without me. Bob knew that and if you didn't you should have gone to the committee."

Marc threw up his hands. I explained again.

"Bob told Marc he couldn't rehearse the number until you got here."

"Of course not!" said Mr. B. and walked around the room in a fury.

I went on. "So Bob asked for a committee meeting and Marc refused and ordered Bob to rehearse the number." Mr. B. turned to Marc again. "So you broke the rules and ignored the committee and you're holding up the whole show."

"Well, Mr. Berlin, there are certain Army rules which must be obeyed. When I give a soldier an order and he refuses to obey and says "kiss my ass," that's abusive language. I had to put him under arrest."

"If Bob said that, it was because he was upset because you were interfering with the show. 'Kiss my ass' is far too nice a phrase to use for your behavior. So if that's the problem, then that's the end of it and we will get on with rehearsals tomorrow morning."

Mr. B. started to leave. I spoke up quickly. "Mr. Berlin, Marc made an official complaint to Major Holmgren."

Mr. B. stopped and turned to Marc. "What complaint?"

"Mr. Berlin, I think you'd better talk to Major Holmgren. The matter is in his hands now."

I thought I'd better give him the whole story. "Mr. B., I have to tell you this so we can move quickly. We may not have much time. Major Holmgren called the commander of Base Services Command, Colonel Meyer."

Berlin looked at Marc. "Young man, you're going to be punished if you hold up our rehearsals. Why the hell did you involve Holmgren?"

Marc looked at him blankly but said nothing.

He didn't speak so I goosed him. "Marc?"

Marc finally spoke. "I guess you don't understand this, Mr. Berlin, but an officer can't allow an enlisted man to talk to him the way Sergeant Sidney spoke to me. I was listening to him quietly enough. I was doing everything I could not to provoke a confrontation. But he wouldn't let me. He had to be insubordinate and then he had to be abusive. He knew perfectly well what he was doing. There was no excuse for the belligerence and the insult."

"There was no excuse for you to suddenly interfere with committee rules. When you did that, you made it impossible for Bob to function according to my orders. How did Holmgren get involved?"

"I reported the whole confrontation to Major Holmgren and I demanded he take action."

"And he told the Colonel?"

"Yes, sir," said Marc, "that was his decision." Holmgren's door opened and he stood in the doorway. He was smiling.

"Welcome back, Mr. Berlin." He put his hand out. Mr. B. ignored it. Swampy started turning to jelly.

"I couldn't help hearing some of this, Mr. Berlin. I'm afraid we've got a problem here, sir." The smile had turned upside down and looked more like tragedy.

"It sounds to me as though you fellows have forgotten who's in charge of the show when I'm not here. You should have let the committee make the decisions," Mr. B. said to the major.

"The Sergeant got out of hand, sir," the Major replied, in full grimace. "It's a bad situation — matter of insubordination and improper language to an officer."

"And what are you contemplating, Major?" Ben asked.

"Well, it's not just up to me. This is a matter for Peninsular Base Services. We're just attached here."

"You mean you've got the headquarters here involved?" Berlin asked.

"Couldn't be helped, Mr. Berlin. Serious charges here, uh, have to be dealt with."

"Do you want to sabotage the whole show, Major?"

"No, no, sir. Nothing like that."

"What do you expect local authority to do about it, Major?"

"Well, uh, I guess we'll have to leave that up to them."

"What?!" Mr. B. exploded.

"You're not talking about court martial?" Ben asked with alarm.

"Court martial!" Mr. B. repeated with horror.

"The Lieutenant insists that he have some punishment for his behavior," Holmgren said.

"You insist?" Mr. B. leapt up and shouted at Marc. "Who the hell do you think you are!"

"We'd better get on the phone," Ben said to Mr. B. quietly. "Let's talk to Colonel Meyer before he does anything." Ben was looking at me. "Can you get the Colonel for Mr. B.?" I picked up the phone and dialed PBS.

"Colonel Meyer please, for Mr. Irving Berlin."

"I don't think I'd jump the gun on this thing, Mr. Berlin." The Major was in pain.

Berlin glanced at him. "You've already done that!" He turned away, waiting for the Colonel's voice.

"Colonel Meyer?... Irving Berlin. I just returned and I find some complaint has been made against my director for the show. . . . Well, if you want to talk about it, let's move. We don't have time to waste. . . . Ten minutes? All right." He hung up the phone and said to Holmgren, "Call me when he gets here. And Marc, you stay right here. I want you both here when I talk to this guy. You, too, Bob. Where's my office, Alan?"

"I know," Ben said and led Mr. B. to his office which was right next door.

"You fellows had better stay right here," Swampy said. Marc, Bob and I had not moved. "I wouldn't miss it for the world, sir," Bob said quietly.

"It seems to me this whole matter could have been avoided, Sergeant."

"I couldn't agree more, sir," Bob said.

A few minutes went by and Colonel Meyer was announced by Corporal Emil Skarda. Mr. B. and Ben heard the activity and came in on their heels and I introduced everyone. "Close the door, Alan."

"Is there anyone who is in a position to outline the sequence of events?" Colonel Meyer asked. Ben spoke up. "I think First Sergeant Anderson is in the best position. He was present at all events."

"Including the events about which Lieutenant Daniels is charging Sergeant Sidney?" the colonel asked. "Yes, sir," Ben replied.

"Very well, let's start with that," the Colonel said.

I went through all the events, including our conversations that discussed the fact that the committee would have been in a position to solve any differences. The Colonel then asked Marc to state in detail the words of insubordination to follow Marc's orders and the language which Marc regarded as improper. When Marc had completed his statement, the Colonel stood up.

"I've heard enough. This is a very clear case of refusal to obey orders and improper language from an enlisted man to an officer. Major Holmgren, I can trust you to keep Sergeant Sidney on base until action is taken. I don't think imprisonment is necessary. I will proceed with suitable action. Thank you for clarifying everything by getting everyone together, Mr. Berlin.

"Just a minute, Colonel," Mr. B. said. "This won't do. Lieutenant Daniels had no right to be giving orders having to do with the show. He was entirely out of order—or whatever you want to call it. I think Bob should apologize to Marc if he didn't like the language he used and we ought to get on with rehearsals."

"In all due respect, Mr. Berlin, you are a civilian and highly as I may regard you for your professional importance, in your correspondent's uniform you have no authority to speak in this matter. To be blunt: don't butt in."

"What?! Did you say butt in? Who the hell do you think you are?"

"I won't even dignify your remarks by responding to them, Mr. Berlin. Just don't butt in! Good-bye. Major Holmgren, you will hear from me through regular channels. Follow my orders.

"Yes, sir," said the Major, without much spirit. Colonel Meyer left the building.

Ben and Mr. B. started for the door. Ben gave Bob and me a signal to follow them. I closed the door on the Major and the Lieutenant. Mr. B., Ben, Bob and I were in Mr. B's office. Ben was trying to reach Washington. Forget Base Services Command—talk to the Boss!

"They're ringing." Ben handed the phone to Mr. B., who took it and waited.

Ben said, "Couldn't you stop this?"

"I tried, Ben, I tried. Marc just totally lost control of his judgment. And Bob did nothing to help. I pleaded with both of them. And when Marc realized what he'd done, it was too late."

Ben just shook his head. "Awful!"

"I tried to calm them down, all of them, even Holmgren. Marc secretly thinks he could run everything better. Bob gets bitchy when he's in an argument. Holmgren is afraid he's going to look soft in front of Marc."

"Colonel McCarthy, please. Oh, hello, Frank. It's Irving Berlin. I'm calling from Naples." There was a pause. "Not so good." We listened while Mr. B. told him the story.

"Frank, can you have someone stop this thing? Here, I'll let Alan tell you." He handed me the phone. "He wants to know who received the story from Holmgren."

"Hello, Colonel. Fine, sir, thank you. Our CO, Major Holmgren, called the Special Services officer, Colonel Maurice Meyer in Peninsular Base Services, sir. We're attached to them for administrative purposes. We haven't heard anything yet, but it appears he was going to try to convene a court martial. Yes, sir."

I held the phone out to Mr. B. and mouthed the name General Marshall.

Mr. B. took the phone. "Hello, General. . . . Thank you, sir. It's going wonderfully. Frank is taking care of us beautifully. Thank you. I'm most grateful." He hung up. "Alan, would you ask those guys to come in here?"

Marc and Holmgren came in. "I'm going to tell you both. First of all, Bob will apologize to you, Marc. Secondly, we just talked to General Marshall. There will be no action beyond the apology. And from now on it must be clear that any decisions that relate to the show will be acted upon by majority vote of the committee unless I am with you, in which case I will make all decisions having to do with the show. The immediate plans are as follows: I want to start rehearsing with the show tomorrow morning at ten o'clock. Bob is in charge. I want Bob to direct. I'll make sure he doesn't run away. We'll take care of the problem of the apology when it does not interfere with rehearsal scheduling. It will be taken care of within the next few days. Colonel Meyer will receive orders from General Marshall's office in regard to any matters in regard to the show. I don't want to interrupt the show and neither does General Marshall. Now, if that's all clear, Alan will put up a notice about the rehearsal and I'm going to talk to Bob about the show and then I'd like to meet with the whole company." Mr. B. rose and started out of the office.

"Before we leave it there, sir, I'm not going to let Bob off without a proper apology."

Mr. B. froze. And then he spoke each word loud and separate. "I TOLD YOU, WE WILL TAKE CARE OF THAT LATER! RIGHT NOW WE'RE GOING TO WORK ON THE SHOW! PERIOD!" Mr. B. drank a glass of water, pulled himself together, literally. "Let's take a walk around the place, say hello to the guys and then I'll talk to them all at dinner. Alan, take us around."

I led Mr. B. and Ben Holmgren and Marc followed. The guys were smiling and relaxed now that the boss was with us. Mr. B. was smiling, too, pleased at the warmth he heard and saw in their voices and faces. "I'm going to have dinner with you as soon as the banquet is ready!" We ended up at Bob's space and he joined us for the walk to dinner.

☆ ☆ ☆ ☆ ☆ ☆ ☆ ☆ ☆ ☆ ☆

Mr. B. kept his fork in his hand after cleaning his plate. I could never understand how he stayed so slim when he loved to eat so much. Except that he never stopped doing something; he was always in motion. He stood up and rapped his plate with the fork. We had no glasses to rap. Everyone drank out of mess gear cups.

"You remember I told you I was going to try to get hold of your families. And I did. I have to tell you, though, two of you gave me the phone number for the same girl." Everybody roared. "Wait! That's not all. When I called her number, some guy answered the phone!" Another laugh, then he continued, "I said I was sending greetings from two guys who were overseas, serving their country, and I gave him both names. 'Gee,' the guy said, 'she told me they were both killed in action.' 'No,' I said, 'They're okay, but *you'd* better keep your eyes open!' The truth is, the phone calls I made for you guys were some of the best experiences I had while I was away. I have a few messages for some of you. I'll get to you with those."

"Mr. B.," Rosie called out.

"Quiet, everyone. Yes, Rosie?"

"I'm glad you're back!"

Everyone started to applaud. Mr. B. looked happy, considering the day he'd had.

☆ ☆ ☆ ☆ ☆ ☆ ☆ ☆ ☆ ☆ ☆

We went through most of the show on Wednesday, including Mr. B.'s number. The sound was great in the opera house. Rosie felt like a king, whipping the orchestra with his stick, as Pete called it. I couldn't remember a better rehearsal.

After dinner, Mr. B. met in the Orderly Room with the whole committee except for Marc. "I talked to Frank McCarthy just a few minutes ago. He talked to Major General Wilson, who's the boss of the Base Services Command. They agreed to drop the court martial charges provided Bob agreed to apologize to Marc for his language. So, Ben and I will get together with the two of them in the morning. I'll let you know as soon as that's done. Let's all get a good sleep and keep going."

Ben gave the committee a report the next morning, without the two combatants. "Honestly, sometimes I could wring Bob's neck. Mr. B. got them together this morning and you can just imagine what Bob did. He pulls his shoulders back and stands like a puppet and says, 'Lieutenant, your Highness, I apologize.' Marc doesn't even look at him and he says, 'Mr. Berlin, I want a formal apology in front of the whole company.' Mr. B. is really furious at both of them. So he said, 'All right, Marc, write it out for him, just what you want to hear and he'll do it!' and he gave Bob a good hard look."

☆ ☆ ☆ ☆ ☆ ☆ ☆ ☆ ☆ ☆ ☆

On Thursday, after lunch, we had the usual 1:15 p.m. formation. Mr. B. spoke again, this time telling the guys that when he visited General Marshall in Washington and Lieutenant General Jacob Devers in Algiers, they had both commended the detachment very highly for their service.

Bob then stood up, and said good and loud, "May I have your attention!" Everyone was quiet. Bob started to read and he played it straight, with no kidding around: "I have been ordered to make the following statement and I have also been told to request that Lieutenant Marc Daniels rise so it is clear that the statement is directed to him." Marc stood.

Bob pulled himself up as though his mother had said, "Bobbie, stand up good and tall." And then, as though he was being sworn in as the President of the United States, he said "I, Master Sergeant Robert Sidney, do hereby admit to having refused to obey a direct order given me by Lieutenant Marc Daniels, not once but repeatedly, and in so doing did use foul and improper language in connection with such refusal, and that I do, therefore, now, in all *solemnity* make a full and unqualified apology to *Lieutenant—Marc—Daniels!*" The emphases and pauses were Bob's.

Marc turned to Berlin and burst out angrily, "I refuse to accept this! This is not an apology! He doesn't mean a word of it!"

"Oh, but I *do!*" Bob says, terribly hurt. Mr. B. rose and there was complete silence until he said, firmly, "Marc, you have had your apology. You wrote it and he read every word of it and that's the end of it!"

Marc stared at him for a moment and then left the area. Mr. B. broke the silence.

"Boys, the show looks good and once the opera gives us the stage and Pete can hang the scenery and the lights, we're going to have a great opening. Have a good rehearsal this afternoon. I'm going to take a nap. Thanks for the lunch. I've never eaten in a palace before." He left us with a grin.

☆ ☆ ☆ ☆ ☆ ☆ ☆ ☆ ☆ ☆ ☆

Friday was devoted to the revisions in the Navy number, adding the semaphore routine. Bob staged the handling of the semaphores, which spelled out, "This Is the Navy!" and the number that started all the trouble between Marc and Bob was ready.

Friday night the opera company gave its final performance of *Madame Butterfly* and Pete and his crew spent the night loading in and setting up. Starting at noon on Saturday, we did our first rehearsal in the full set. Sunday, we did a complete technical run-through. There was an air raid alert at 8:15 Sunday evening in the beginning of "Daddy's Coming Home On a Furlough." His three cute kids were in the middle of their song, dancing in a circle: two darling hairy-legged, five foot ten "girls" and their older brother in his sailor suit.

> KIDS (singing)
> After Daddy's through with his furlough
> He must sail away 'cross the foam;
> He'll be glad to face a bomb
> When he takes a look at Mom—
> There'll be hell when Daddy comes home.

At that moment, the sirens began to wail and the antiaircraft guns sent up a few bursts. Then it was quiet so we finished the rehearsal.

☆ ☆ ☆ ☆ ☆ ☆ ☆ ☆ ☆ ☆

Mr. B. took great pains to eliminate any resentment that might have arisen toward him in the detachment and in the Base Services Command for having gone over everyone's head to squash the court martial. Before rehearsal Sunday morning, he invited Marc Daniels and Ben Washer to a friendly breakfast of home-cooked bacon and eggs. He then invited Colonel Meyer to have dinner with him at his hotel before the dress rehearsal. On the other hand, he didn't bother to appease Swampy. He was sore as hell at the Major for taking the problem outside the company.

☆ ☆ ☆ ☆ ☆ ☆ ☆ ☆ ☆ ☆

Monday, we put up a big sign outside the theater that read:

> All Allied forces, free tickets, reserve now, 9:00 a.m. to
> 9:00 p.m.

There was a party atmosphere in all the faces — service men and women were lined up all day, patiently, getting reservations for the show. There were 1,800 seats to fill for each of the two daily performances. A few seats were reserved for special guests: generals, admirals, heads of state. The long lines around the opera house kept being refilled right up to 9:00 p.m. every day.

Playing almost exclusively to audiences of service men and women, their responses were tremendous: the laughs wilder, a little closer to raucous, the emotions deeper, vigorous applause, whistling, stamping, robust laughter.

On opening day, Colonel Meyer, our court martial-happy friend, and the generals in command of Naples and the southern Italian region came backstage to praise the company. The homophobia or macho attitudes we had sensed from some individuals did not appear.

The fear that Mr. B. might be too late to save the show from a catastrophe was almost forgotten. The result was a dramatic reminder of the potency of his protection and the delicate balance of authority in the outfit when he was away.

☆ ☆ ☆ ☆ ☆ ☆ ☆ ☆ ☆ ☆ ☆

Mr. B. was tireless. In addition to the two shows every evening, he went from hospital to hospital almost every day, talking to the wounded soldiers and singing them songs they requested. If there was a piano anywhere nearby, he'd take Morty Kahn to accompany him. If there was a recreation hall or a library — any kind of space — Larry Weeks would juggle; John "Prince" Mendes would do magic; Jimmy Burrell or Stu Churchill, superb tenors, would sing; and Hank Henry's, Julie Oshins' or Dick Bernie's jokes produced smiles and laughter that would evaporate some of the loneliness and depression.

At the time the Allies had taken Naples, we had still been at Camp Upton, rehearsing the overseas version of the show. Now the troops had started the long battle toward Rome, against a determined

German defense. Mussolini had long since been taken captive by one of his generals, then kidnapped by Hitler and spirited out of the country. Italy had declared war on Germany the day we arrived in Camp Shanks.

General Mark Clark's Fifth Army and the British Eighth Army, based just north of Naples, had been the largest forces battling toward Rome, although the burden had been heavy also on smaller, but vigorous, units from New Zealand, Canada, India and Poland. They had all been in combat in Italy for many months. The Fifth Army's most recent battle had been the largely successful beachhead landing at Anzio. Success notwithstanding, the casualties were heavy. Now the challenge was to overcome the increased resistance as they moved inland. The Allied troops were exhausted and frustrated by the slow progress.

What the allies still faced was the most difficult of all: the dislodging of the Germans from their hold on Monte Cassino, a mountain fortress which lay in the way of any attempt to recapture Rome. Ironically, the German's position had been improved by attempts to bomb them. The bombing had only succeeded in providing fresh barricades of rubble in the destruction of the monastery buildings and the surrounding rocky cliffs. The attempts to break through the horrendous advantage the Germans held stretched the long, exhausting weeks into months. Clark pushed them hard but there was only so much they could do. Casualties were high and the morale seeped away.

When Eisenhower copied Special Services of all European commands, Lieutenant Colonel Raymond Novotny, the Special Services officer for the Fifth Army, learned that *This Is the Army* was being sent to Africa and Italy, specifically for morale purposes of all Allied combat troops. Novotny drove down to Naples for our opening performance and after making a short congratulatory speech to the cast, told Mr. B. what he was going to report back to his boss. "We must find a place to perform Irving Berlin's show, *This Is the Army*, close enough to the front so all those guys will have a chance to get off their bellies and climb into trucks and, truckload by truckload, sit down in front of that orchestra, those singers and dancers and comedians and those great songs, and just let go like I did! I can't think of one other damned medicine that would do them as much good!" Mr. B. relayed this message to the committee. We knew that when we had finished our two weeks in Naples, we would be going somewhere near the front.

☆☆☆☆☆☆☆☆☆☆☆

We had two kinds of audience during our stay in Naples. One, the combat troops who were temporarily away from the front on rest leave, or recuperating after hospitalization, and also the nurses and doctors who were running the hospitals. They were all a great audience, giving us a sense of what it would be like when we were up even closer to the front lines. The second kind of audience was the support services, the "behind the lines" forces — headquarters, administrative, supply — those doing the very necessary jobs of supplying the fighting men. The majority of them were great. They knew what their job was and they respected the ones who were up front. It was to their headquarters, Base Services, that we were attached for our supplies and administrative purposes. I made many trips there with Carl, our supply sergeant, to sign forms and make official requests. They were a somewhat different audience.

As an example of the difference, there was, for instance, Supply Master Sergeant Clayton Embrey in Naples. Clayton's accent reminded me of Beaufort, South Carolina, where Nancy's mother and stepfather had been for just a year and that I'd visited once. Clayton had the rather soft, slow speech of the region — its gentle, rolling style.

"Mornin', Sergeant. Y'all had your grits today?"

"I wish you could get us some, Clayton. Be a good change from the oatmeal you send out of supply."

"How'd it go down with those dancer fellas? They'd pro'bly want somethin' a little more delicate?"

"You got a problem with dancers, Clayton?"

"Hell, no, Sarge! It's a damn good show. I got no kicks. Not like some of the guys'll just get all wound up when they see queers in an outfit."

"Well, I know a lot of queers, as you call 'em, that I'd rather be around than some creeps I've met."

"Don't get me wrong, Sarge. I say live and let live."

"That's a good philosophy. Maybe you oughta preach it to your outfit."

I started to leave him and turned back. "I don't suppose you know how many homosexuals there are in your outfit?"

"Not a damn one! What the hell you talkin' about!"

"Maybe I should use your word—queer. None?"

"Hell, no! Not in my outfit!"

"All your closet doors are tight closed?"

"Ain't anybody in any closets!"

"How do you know, Sergeant? Do you listen to the bedsprings at night? Excuse me, you wouldn't do that. You just said live and let live."

"For damn sure, we got no officers like your Lieutenant Swish. I can't say his name. Something like 'Ko-nig.' "

"You're referring to Lieutenant John Koenig—that's how you pronounce it. He's a damned good officer and a damned good designer."

"All I know is Colonel Meyer calls him and that Warrant Officer that tags around with him—"

"Warrant Officer Ben Washer?"

"That's it. The two of 'em, Meyer calls 'em Swish and Swash." He laughed contentedly at his boss's cleverness.

"But not to their faces, I dare say."

He just kept chuckling. I smiled at my curtain line and left him. I had known it was pointless to discuss the subject with a bigot and I kicked myself for trying. As I drove back to the palace in our jeep, I made a vow to keep a level head with bigots. Arguing was useless. Let the show shut them up. Nobody thought about Swish and Swash when the curtain was up.

Within a few days of Novotny's message to General Clark, the Colonel found what he was looking for—a tiny opera house just a short drive from the front line troops. Pete, John and Marc drove up there to check it out.

"Anderson, wait'll you see the place. It will only seat a little over a thousand guys, but it's a beauty, like a miniature of the San Carlo. Of course, I don't know how the hell we'll get the show in there, but we can figure it out."

"Is it near Monte Cassino?"

"About twenty-five miles. It's a little town called Santa Maria. The plan is they're gonna have trucks going back and forth twice a day from the front, bringing those guys down to the shows and then right back to where they're dug in."

What we learned was that Santa Maria would put us within a short drive from over 100,000 combat troops. There were no transit camps in the region. We would put up our own tent city in Santa Maria's little Garibaldi Park, set up a kitchen and washing facilities and call upon Peter Feller once again. He would have to not only squeeze our production into a tiny theater but, as before, construct washing, cooking and eating facilities at the tent area.

☆ ☆ ☆ ☆ ☆ ☆ ☆ ☆ ☆ ☆ ☆

Our two weeks in Naples in the magnificent San Carlo allowed us to play two shows a day, except on Sunday, for a total of 40,000 troops. The first show was at 2:30. That left the morning for Mr. B. and various members of the cast to work with him, doing intimate shows in hospital wards. The detachment rose in the morning, watched the sun rise behind Mount Vesuvius, washed at our outdoor Feller washstands and ate breakfast on Feller tables with the sunlight slanting across the palace's open terraces. Mail from home was still distributed by our trusty Alan Lowell, mail clerk by day, basso-profundo under the spotlight. Everyone checked to see what Arnold Bachner had posted on the bulletin board for the day's duty roster before the hospital show units got together with instruments and props. Mr. B. arrived and off they went in squad cars and jeeps.

Work parties were trucked to Santa Maria each day to prepare the camp and the opera house. Pete and his crew got damned little sleep.

Late at night, his most creative time, Irving Berlin sat at the Buick's keyboard in his palace office high over the Bay of Naples, writing a new song for General Mark Clark's Fifth Army.

R. TEATRO S. CARLO

NAPOLI

THE UNITED STATES ARMY

presents

Irving Berlin's

All-Soldier Musical Show

" THIS IS THE ARMY "

Music and Lyrics by **IRVING BERLIN**

" This Is The Army „ is presented overseas under
the supervision of the Special Service Division of
the United States Army.

MAURICE J. MEYER
Colonel, J.A.G.D.
Special Service Officer
Peninsular Base Section

Chapter 17

THE WAR

—*Apr 5, 1944: US bombers fly from Foggia in southern Italy to attack the Rumanian oilfields.*

—*Apr 14, 1944: In Burma the Allied offensive proves a morale boosting victory despite heavy casualties.*

—*Apr 18, 1944: Over 2,000 Allied bombers fly missions over Germany, dropping more than 4,000 tons of bombs, the largest quantity dropped in one day since war began.*

Now that we were leaving Naples, Colonel Meyer suffered some remarkable change of attitude. From his first contacts with us, before Mr. B. rejoined us and before we had given any performances, when in his book we appeared to be a weird bunch of misfits to the time we left for Santa Maria, the show had such an impact that it inspired him to write a letter to Mr. B. on our very last day. It read in part:

> From everywhere and everyone, privates to generals, have come the voluntary testimonials to the sheer greatness of "This Is the Army." The technical and professional perfection of the show has taken them closer to their homes than anything that has happened to them since they have been away.

It closed by saying to Mr. B.,

> As to your personal contribution, enough cannot be said.

And yet he went on to try to say it. It may have been a record in the eating of crow.

☆ ☆ ☆ ☆ ☆ ☆ ☆ ☆ ☆ ☆ ☆

At the close of the Saturday night performance, Pete had to strike the whole show before 8 a.m. the next morning, so the opera company could resume their cycle with a matinee performance of *La Bohème*.

On Sunday morning we sent the first platoon off to Santa Maria to pitch our tents, dig garbage and latrine pits and install the kitchen tables and washing facilities that Pete had built for use in the palace. Pete and Johnny had figured out just what little scenery would fit in the theater and the second platoon spent the day trucking in the usable scenery. The excess production, which we might make use of after Santa Maria, was put in storage in the Bagnoli Fair Grounds outside of Naples where we had spent two nights before moving into the palace.

On Monday at 5:30 a.m., the second platoon did a final cleaning of the palace area and went in convoy with all remaining equipment to Santa Maria. By Monday afternoon, there remained only the challenging job of installing the show in the extremely limited space.

Mr. B. and Major Holmgren were taken on a tour of our living area in Garibaldi Park and then, before returning to Naples for the night, Mr. B. and Ben Washer visited the rooms the Army had secured for him with a family in town.

Tuesday the Fifth Army issued us our own motor pool. It consisted of two trucks, two jeeps, one weapons carrier and one command car. I assigned our very smooth, handsome, staff sergeant, tap dancer Maurice Kelly, to run the motor pool. We gave tests and issued driving permits to several of the boys and all of the committee.

For the past forty-eight hours the detachment had done a lot of manual labor, no entertaining and very little sleeping; the sentries reported no disturbing incidents but an unusual volume of snores Tuesday night. There was no mention of the level of body odor but immediately following Wednesday breakfast the schedule read:

8:30 A.M., FIRST TRANSPORT LEAVES FOR SHOWER BATHS AT FIFTH
ARMY REST CAMP IN ROYAL PALACE, CASERTA. SHUTTLE SERVICE
CONTINUES UNTIL ALL REQUESTS FOR SHOWERS ARE SATISFIED.

At 2 p.m., Wednesday, the completely washed company began the
first and only rehearsal in the Santa Maria Opera House.
We had to provide our own electric power with two antiaircraft
searchlight generators, borrowed from the Signal Corps. Johnny
Cooper and I had to simplify the lighting plot because of somewhat
reduced amperage and a limited number of light units. The rehearsal
was a bit rough because a great many space adjustments had to be
made, especially by the dancers and the acrobats.

It was our first opportunity to hear Mr. B.'s new song dedicated to
the Fifth Army. The boss was greatly cheered by the ovation we gave
him.

An hour before curtain time we had the whole company on stage so
that Ben Washer could give us some last minute information.
"Fellows," he said, "you should know this about your audience today.
Colonel Novotny has been hoping to make the show available to the
Fifth Army combat troops and he's got it all organized. Trucks are
going to be bringing the guys right from the front on Monte Cassino to
each show. We have no idea how they'll respond, so don't be surprised
at the reactions. Just don't let it throw you. Give 'em the best you've
got and we'll see what happens."

It was half an hour before curtain. Bob was still working with some
of the dancers on some space problems. Johnny Cooper was running
some new cables to left stage. Jus was helping me focus some side
spots. He stopped moving suddenly. "I wonder if we're going to have
to start late. I don't hear much noise with those guys coming in."

"As soon as we finish these lights, I'll take a look out front. I'll let you
know."

I went through the stage door into the auditorium and started up
the side aisle toward the lobby. I was surprised to find that the house

seemed nearly full. Usually so many men entering a theater would be pretty noisy—full of wisecracks and joking. I couldn't see their faces very well. But they were quiet, subdued.

As I approached the lobby, the light was brighter and I could see their expressions for the first time. It was startling: men straight from the front wearing combat boots and helmets, faces drained of expression, eyes unfocused. Men who a few hours ago had been dug into the hills facing Monte Cassino. The only sounds were low murmurs, boots clumping, the occasional squeak of the old wooden floor, seats thumping down as the men sat, olive drab against the damask and velvet of the small, elegant auditorium—our audience, here to see the show. Once seated they just waited, staring.

What would they do? Yell? Throw stuff? Riot? Sit in silence?

Johnny Koenig was across the lobby in a corner, watching, too. He gestured to me, echoing my helplessness, as if to say, "What the hell would they want with singing and dancing?" I turned and hurried backstage. Might as well get going, quick.

When I got there, Jus was looking at me, waiting for orders.

"Let's go!" I said.

He looked a little surprised. I realized why. There was none of the usual chatter coming through the curtain. He shrugged, said, "Okay!" and hurried across to his side of the proscenium. I took a deep breath, signaled Cooper to dim the house to half and bring the lights up on the curtain. At the same time, I signaled Rosie to start the overture.

Thank God for the orchestra! They played like angels. Johnny Mince's sweet hot clarinet, Nate Gottschalk's vivid and flowing violin, Judy Burke's drums, the heartbeat of the whole band. The opera house was filled with the glorious, synchronous beat of harmony and melody that lifted me onto another plane every time I heard it. I looked through my peep hole at the auditorium and a sea of pale faces. Were they hearing what I heard?

The music rose to full volume and the overture came to a crashing

Mr. B. serving soup to comedian Hank Henry.

The Committee in session. *Clockwise:* Mr. B. standing, WO Ben Washer, Lt. Marc Daniels, M/Sgt. Robert Sidney, M/Sgt. Milton Rosenstock, First Sgt. Alan Anderson, Tech. Sgt. Carl Fisher. (Missing, Lt. John Koenig.)

First Sgt. Alan Anderson to comedian Hank Henry: "The boss would like you to stick to the script, Hank."

M/Sgt. Robert Sidney, our choreographer, chatting with glorious Egyptian belly dancer Carioca between shows. We were in Cairo playing to an audience of King Farouk and our allies.

After Egypt we played in a very different world — Persia, traveling between camps by truck, winding and roasting through the desert world, and then through the barren mountains in the north.

Shows in the Pacific Islands were in huge amphitheaters that provided movies for anywhere from 5,000 to 10,000 service men and women.

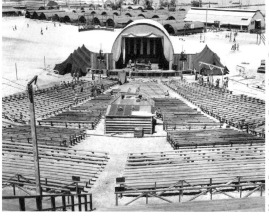

We went ashore to the islands by climbing down rope nets and into LCM's. We had our own ship for several months, S.S. *El Libertador*.

Me and my pals at sea posing for a picture for Zinn. *Back row, left to right:* Conductor Rosenstock and Stage Manager Anderson. *Sitting, left to right:* Technician Pete and Business Manager Carl.

"Swampy," the friendly name everyone used for our CO when he wasn't present.

Warning sign posted on a tree next to where we were performing in Saipan.

Little school girls singing with our chorus and Mr. B., "Heaven Watch the Philippines," the song he wrote for and presented to the Philippine nation.

In New Guinea, we gave an outdoor show. The native dancers then entertained us.

Ladies singing "Ladies of the Chorus" in the Jungle Bowl theatre in New Guinea.

Mr. B. singing "Oh! How I Hate to Get Up in the Morning" with chorus behind him, in Santa Maria, Italy.

On board the *Haleakala* when the war is over. The meals are banquet-style.

end. There was a moment—maybe half a moment—of silence. Void. Where were they?

And then it started like a wave. First applause, then whistling, stamping, yelling. It felt almost like hysteria. Just keep going! I dimmed the house to black and Rosie gave the downbeat into the opening number. I dropped my hand and as the curtain opened the stamping and yelling was miraculously snuffed out. The faces were staring but focused now. One thousand men were listening, watching, hungry. We had them!

Jus waved from the other wing, a grin all the way across his face. I waved and grinned back to stop the tears.

As each number came and went, the whole house was alive. The laughter was all belly. They yelled and cheered and then, for a ballad, grew still, rapt, silent, as though they were letting love and homesickness engulf them in the darkness. And then strong, grateful applause—the emotions up and down, the laughter open and happy. And then deep in act two, when the curtain opened and the spotlight found the small, forlorn figure of Irving Berlin sitting center stage on an Army cot, wearing a 1917 uniform, singing in his tiny, quavering voice, "Oh! How I Hate to Get Up in the Morning," they opened up to him like a visit from home.

This was an evening Mr. B. had never expected but unconsciously *always* hoped for. He had come a long journey from being a five-year-old on Ellis Island. Fifty years later, caring deeply for America and the winning of the war, he must have felt closer to helping at that moment than he ever dreamt could happen. When he finished ". . . And then I'll get that other pup, the one that wakes the bugler up, and spend the rest of my life in bed." They cheered and cheered until he quieted them again, walking right down to the edge of the stage.

It was time for his new song.

Al Gorta's spotlight was bright on the small figure. Rosie, watching Mr. B. carefully, saw him take one last step and gave the downbeat for the first quiet notes and Mr. B. sang: "I met her in America about a month ago;"—the audience absolutely silent—"She asked me if I'd give her love to a certain GI Joe. She said, 'When he returns, I'll be his bride.' I asked her where he was, and she replied,"—a beat of silence in the music and then Mr. B. started up the ladder, firmly but quietly—"'Not the First, not the Second, not the Third,'"—louder and louder—"'Not the Fourth, but THE FIFTH ARMY'S WHERE MY HEART IS.'" The faces were all ready to cheer! They had no idea what was coming next: "'He's somewhere on a beachhead, which must be lots of fun.'"—Mr. B. romanticized that one so they burst out with a laugh, a sudden recognition that he was playing with them—"'I can see him in a bathing suit basking in the sun.'" Another laugh. "'From a cute signorina he's been learning to talk like a real native of Rome; she's a very tasty dish, but my baby no capish till the Fifth Army comes home.'" And then they cheer! And off he goes into the chorus, inviting them to join in with a gesture of his hands—"'Not the First'"—now they're all singing with him—"'not the Second, not the Third'"—louder and louder—"'Not the Fourth, but THE FIFTH ARMY'S WHERE MY HEART IS!'" Big, big finish and great howls of laughter and applause, whistles and stomps!

And then on to the rest of the show and the closing chorus. At the final curtain, there was pandemonium again. And now it all felt good. They stamped, yelled and applauded through a whole string of curtain calls and Mr. B. had taken about six solo bows, until they finally came down to talking, smiling, slaps on the back. I kept the house lights full up.

I slipped out into the auditorium by the side door and worked my way to the lobby again.

Johnny was there in the same corner. The men were surging through the lobby and out to the waiting trucks. They pounded each other on the back or yelled a joke. Their movements were loose, relaxed. Their faces were alive, open, the eyes bright and focused. I looked across the lobby at Johnny. He waved, his face scrunched, trying not to blubber.

The guys were clambering back into the trucks, the truck engines roaring as they went off, still filling the area with emotion, wisecracks, laughter.

I went backstage and found Mr. B. in his dressing room. Bob was with him.

"She wasn't there tonight, Mr. B.," I said.

"Who?"

"Axis Sally," I said. "She can't match it. Nothing could match what you've brought to those guys."

It was hard for him to speak. He smiled at me in his mirror as he wiped at the makeup and his eyes.

"Wasn't it beautiful?" Bob said. "Alan, did you ever see anything so beautiful?"

"Never."

"I guess it was worth the trip," said Mr. B.

"It's going to be a tough month," I said. "But you can be so proud of this show."

And then Bob said quietly, "I hope they can keep some of it inside them – when they have to jump out of the trucks with their rifles."

☆ ☆ ☆ ☆ ☆ ☆ ☆ ☆ ☆ ☆ ☆

When we arrived at the theater for the evening performance, we were faced with an enormous six-layer cake, crowned with the Fifth Army insignia, inscribed tier by tier with:

The Fifth Army Welcomes This Is the Army

It was worthy of statistics: weighing about seventy-five pounds, close to a yard wide, a yard high and over two feet deep. Considering its size, we discovered later that it was remarkably tasty.

After the performance — and this one took us through the same emotional sleigh ride — Major General Gruenther, Clark's Chief of

Staff of the Fifth Army, explained the absence of his boss. He was occupied with matters of war. Gruenther also said simply that it was the first show he had ever seen which he wanted to see twice, proving himself more original than most of his brethren, whose compliments were too often fulsome and repetitious.

The second performance was as difficult to get over as the first, but we toughened gradually as the days went by. And then it got really heartbreaking when we began to have trucks arriving from the many hospital units; as the days passed, they came on crutches, in wheel chairs, in their pajamas. They were in seats right down front of course.

We watched the routine each day for each show. Their emotional response continued. In their perspective, they came to us right from the rim of hell and were plunged into the revelry of a big Broadway revue, the orchestra, dancers, comedians, variety acts, singers, huge chorus and then the extraordinary little guy with his very special songs, every soldier's complaint: "Oh! How I Hate to Get Up in the Morning," and the surprise involvement he gave them with their own song, "The Fifth Army's Where My Heart Is."

Lieutenant General Mark Clark, their commanding general, was finally able to see the show. He came to the twenty-second performance for his guys and expressed his gratitude warmly. To paraphrase him: "You know we don't get many laughs here—I've heard nothing but praise—You have done wonders for their morale—The casualties have been many. They have been fighting a well-seasoned and determined enemy and the going has been rough. We're going to hit them soon and we're going to hit them hard, and when the time comes our morale is going to be higher and our chins a little more confident because of the lift you have given us with this show. By the time you get through here, you will have entertained 100,000 men of the Fifth Army. When you get back, you will know that you have done more than your bit. Thanks a million. Good-bye."

His speech almost made me shiver. I tried to hear his words from the point of view of the guys who were climbing out of the trucks and walking into the opera house. I talked about it to a private who had come backstage after the show a couple of days later. He had been at Anzio, was wounded and was on leave, recuperating. He was using a cane and he limped a bit. Ray Simpson from Newark, New Jersey.

"It's a great show, Sergeant. I wanted to come back stage because I've been to some shows in New York. I was reminded of that. Were you in the theater?"

"Yeah. I was doing the same thing, stage managing. All these guys were in entertainment of one kind or another."

We talked about our lives and I had him join us for our Red Cross meal between shows. He'd been at Dix after I had left there. We talked about his being drafted, how he'd ended up in the infantry and the Fifth Army. He dropped by a few days later.

"I brought you a souvenir." He had it in a paper bag. It was a combat knife — leather handle, two-sided blade, heavy steel in a leather scabbard meant to be worn on a combat belt. "I'm not going to need it. They're sending me home. My knee is no good."

I slipped the knife out of the scabbard and checked the edge with a thumbnail. It was sharp — very sharp.

"Thank you, Ray." I looked at him. "I hope I don't have to use it."

"It's been used," he said.

"Jesus!" I couldn't help saying. I decided not to ask him just how, because I doubted that he wanted to talk about it. "I guess you won't mind going home. Will they discharge you?"

"I don't think so. I'll be in some kind of desk job they think. But in case I don't see you again, I wanted to wish you luck — all of you. You're doing a great thing."

"What do you think of your boss?" I asked.

"Clark?" I nodded.

"Some of the guys call him 'The Butcher.' They think he sacrifices a lot of lives for ground."

"Do you think it's true?"

"I don't know." Ray said. "I wouldn't want to have his job."

I told him about the speech he had made to us and his statement about "hitting them hard soon."

Ray stared at the ground. "I've got a lot of friends up there." He shook his head a little and then looked up and waved his cane. "I suppose I'm lucky."

When he was leaving I thanked him again for the knife. We shook hands.

"Maybe you can take it camping with your son some day."

"Yeah." I never took it camping, but I still have it.

✩ ✩ ✩ ✩ ✩ ✩ ✩ ✩ ✩ ✩ ✩

Mr. B. could not contain his usual impulse to write songs. He would play and sing his new songs for Rosie or Bob or whoever was within earshot. The officers he met discovered this and were flattered by having the great composer try out a song on them. They invited Mr. B. to social occasions regularly, and they learned to include Ben. They plied Mr. B. with scotch or his favorite — gin martinis.

The Army officers couldn't get enough of Mr. B and when they realized that he got enormous satisfaction out of being able to give any comfort he could to the hospital cases which were everywhere about us, they kept him on a busy schedule, from one hospital to another, where he could talk to the soldiers or sing them a song. In Santa Maria, when Ben was driving him to the 56th Station Hospital to entertain the patients, he had the idea of a song about the most famous Army transportation of World War II — the jeep that he was riding in.

The wounded kept arriving from the north by ambulance: He was busy almost every day traveling to hospitals, some of them within a few miles of the front. Ben Washer's Italian diary records many details of those visits because he was invariably with Mr. B. wherever he went.

☆ ☆ ☆ ☆ ☆ ☆ ☆ ☆ ☆ ☆ ☆

I was with Mr. B. and Ben on May 12, the morning after "the push" as they called it. We visited one of the field hospitals. Mr. B. described it as "the morning after the night before." There was still the sound of artillery in the north. The beds were filled. When the battle for control of Monte Cassino was at its height, there were so many wounded there were not beds to put them in nor enough nurses and doctors to keep up.

Many of the wounded were sitting on benches—if they were able to sit. Those who could not were lying down; some on cots, some on the ground. The boys who could walk to a bench were called "leg cases" because they were marginally ambulatory. Most had bleeding hands, heads or legs. With the help of a medic, they would draw water from a jerrycan and try to wash the blood off. Some who were not in much pain would joke or smile and feel lucky because they were away from enemy fire.

There were two German prisoners among the wounded. They sat on a bench in their heavy gray uniforms with knapsacks at their side. The older one held his drooping head with a scarred hand. One of the sergeants guarding the pair asked about the scar, it was so apparent, and was told the soldier got it in Russia. The German prisoners kept peering about furtively at their captors as the Sergeant questioned them about where they had been and what outfit they had been with. The younger man was smiling and trying to be cooperative. He volunteered information in broken but passable English. The Sergeant continued to question the older man in German. He continued to be silent and sullen.

Nurses were tending men in pain: one gently bathing the face of a man who had just come out of surgery, was strapped to his bed and was whimpering quietly. The stump of his leg stuck out of the blanket, bandaged and bloody. The long, narrow tent held cot after cot, side by side, all filled.

The doctor who was accompanying us, a major, said, "It would be good if those at home could see what these doctors and nurses are able to do. This crew set up the hospital in two and a half hours. They're some of the best doctors in America."

The doctor led us out to a hillside across the road, where a mass of men who were able to move around were gathered to hear Mr. B. They had placed a piano and a microphone on a small platform. Mr. B. sat at the keyboard playing and singing while the planes flew overhead and the cannons boomed in the distance.

☆ ☆ ☆ ☆ ☆ ☆ ☆ ☆ ☆ ☆ ☆

Ten days later, on Monday morning, May 22, about 10:30, our sound man, Corporal John Tolbutt, crawled under the stage in the opera house to check his wiring and found a suspicious-looking box with wire coming out of one side. He reported this to one of the MP's on duty who relayed the information to Marc Daniels with the suggestion that we delay the matinee until we could have the bomb squad check it out. At 1:15 p.m., with the audience for the matinee gathering and no bomb squad in evidence, we decided we'd better give a show outdoors in Garibaldi Park, with costumes and no scenery. We used the top platform of the Garibaldi monument for a modest stage area. The chorus of singers sat on the steps in front of the statue. I helped Rosie set up the orchestra next to the monument. Dances were eliminated. We found enough folding chairs for the hospital cases in the audience. The rest of the guys had to sit on the grass. Mr. B had to sit on a little camp stool for the beginning of his number. The applause was as wild as ever through the whole performance.

☆ ☆ ☆ ☆ ☆ ☆ ☆ ☆ ☆ ☆ ☆

During the show, Marc and the MP's got tired of waiting for the bomb squad. They got Johnny Cooper to shine some big lights under the stage. Marc crawled in while the MP's watched. Two minutes later Marc crawled out dragging a portable phonograph behind him and the scare was over.

I was standing watching the show when one of the MP's said there was a captain looking for me. He pointed to a very tall figure with two other men at the edge of the park. I told Jus I'd be back and I walked up behind the three officers who were busy watching the show and said, "Excuse me, sir. Was somebody looking for me?" The tall officer turned around and I was looking at six foot two Bill Agar, who Nancy and I had last seen in the fall of 1941 with his lovely bride, Nan. I grabbed his hand and we grinned at each other, saying things like, "I'll be damned! I don't believe it."

That night, I wrote Nancy about Bill's visit:

> May 22—Darling: Extraordinary news! Bill Agar is here—
> arrived at camp about 3 o'clock with two other officers—a
> couple of friends. Bill looks wonderful. But after the joy of see-
> ing him, I had to hide a chill which ran down my spine, seeing
> him here, wearing a captain's uniform and the insignia of
> Armored Infantry. I don't like the idea of his coming here. His
> job isn't like mine, but like me, he has a wife and child—Nan
> and Raymond.

When we met them that summer before we were at war, in Fort Dix, they couldn't make up their minds about whether to get married. After a few weeks of seeing us together and a little persuasion, they decided to do it. Nan's father was a judge so they got married in her home in Princeton, New Jersey, and I was the best man.

Two and a half years later, William Scott Agar was standing in front of me in Santa Maria, Italy. And just two weeks ago, Nancy had written me that Nan had invited her to visit her on Cape Cod so the kids could be together.

"What are you doing here?" I asked, standing back to get a good look at him. "Two bars—a captain!"

"And you're a bloody topkick! And back in show business! That's how I found you! I've been hearing about this show from all over the map."

"Have you got time to hang around and see it? We'll do a real show tonight."

"Sure! I'm just waiting for orders."

"Let's go somewhere where we can talk."

"Good," Bill said.

"There's a little joint in town where we can have a drink."

We ordered a couple of beers and did some more catching up. "Rush got into the 82nd Airborne—just what he wanted—and they're coming here."

We talked until dinner time about how lucky we were and exchanged baby pictures and wife pictures. We walked back and joined Pete, Carl and Rosie for one of our good Red Cross dinners. Bill and his friends saw the show and came backstage afterward. Bill was very excited when I introduced him to Mr. B. Mr. B looked at him with surprise.

"Agar," said Mr. B. "I just met Herbert Agar in London in November." He looked at Bill questioningly.

"My father," Bill said simply.

"Someone told me he's a famous writer. We talked about the war and he seemed to know everything."

"Yes, he does. I only see him a couple of times a year when he's in New York. He remarried when I was fifteen. His wife is British. He spends most of his time in London. During the war he's been with the Office of War Information there."

When we left Mr. B. he told me he wanted to get together with Bill and me again. I got a Jeep out of the pool and drove Bill and his two friends home, and then Bill and I got to talking again. I described what happened then in my letter to Nancy.

We'd had a bit to drink and Bill felt pretty sentimental because of our meeting and began to tell me, in words that hurt him to say, that in case he shouldn't get home to Nan, I must tell her what I had seen of him — and you and I should try to help her and Raymond, their son. There was nothing I could say except that I was sure there would never be any reason why I would have to deliver any message — that he would be able to do it himself. Oh, Darl, I'm so worried! Bill's outfit will be going straight for Cassino. It all reminds me of your last letter telling me that my handsome cousin Keith was shot down over the Adriatic. Bill said to be sure to send his love to you.

Bill turned up for the show the next night and we talked again. When he came to the Thursday matinee, Mr. B. invited Bill and me to have a cocktail at his apartment. Mr. B. again brought up his father and mother — and then began questioning Bill about what he was doing. It dawned on me that he wanted to find out if Bill would like to be with the show. I knew that Mr. B. was sore as hell at Marc ever since the fight with Bob. Marc continued to assume authority in show decisions when he wasn't asked and didn't belong. He found Swampy was spineless just when Berlin needed his support for something. Bill was bright and personable and would certainly not want to interfere in show decisions.

Bill didn't respond to Mr. B's fishing expedition. When we were walking back to the tent area I decided to get his reaction.

"I think he wants you to join us, Bill. He wants to get rid of a couple of other guys." Bill was silent for some time.

"I don't think I could leave the guys I've been training. It's hard to explain. There's a lot that I've been prepared for in this assignment."

I didn't dare push him too hard. I knew what he was feeling: the same thing that made me go to our friend, Colonel Victor Rapport, in London and ask to be assigned to the D-Day landings in France. Eisenhower had stopped that idea. When Vic made a request for me

to be made a lieutenant on his staff he was told that our detachment
was frozen. No transfers. But I wanted to give it one more shot.

"I understand that, Bill. But you're a married man—and I think
Berlin really wants you."

He smiled at me. "I'll think about it, but there's a lot involved."

There was nothing more I could say to Bill. He would do it if he felt
he could—or should. I left it there, wondering if I should, thinking of
Nan, thinking of what Nancy would say.

Bill spent the whole next day with me, saw both shows, and we
talked between shows and again in the evening. I wrote Nancy after
he left.

> He finds a great deal of pleasure in hanging around the show
> and in our talking endlessly about our precious wives and chil-
> dren who have so much in common—and about how we gave
> them a sendoff after the wedding, having those martinis in their
> room at the New Weston. It relaxes him a great deal just to be
> here and talk. He's a fine person and I feel terrible remorse
> about the ultimate necessity for him to go to the front. I wish
> he had stayed with us. But he wouldn't do it. And I'm sure that
> Mr. B. wanted Marc out and Bill in. I sit here feeling it's so
> important that he get home to Nan. I think what it would be
> for us if I were in his position. Darling, do write Nan right away
> and go up to see her. Bill gave me a letter of hers to read. It was
> long and quite beautiful. It had so many things in it that yours
> have had, darling. There were innumerable things that we have
> experienced also. I didn't give him any of yours to read. I don't
> think I could let anyone in on our feelings to that extent, but
> I'm sure he did it because of the strain he is going through and
> because he feels that you and I are a big part of their marriage.

I didn't see Bill again after that night. He didn't come the next
day. The shows were canceled without warning. No trucks came

from the front. The show had played its last performance in Santa
Maria, and when we left for our next stop, there was no way to contact
him.

We knew something big had happened but no one knew what it
was. We found out later. It was the final grueling strike against the
Germans on Monte Cassino, the drive through from Anzio and the
real goal—the march into Rome.

In the meantime, we had gone back to Bagnoli, in the suburbs of
Naples. It was where all the wounded and the recovering soldiers
were being sent. We were playing in a big theater that was part of a
luxurious retreat Mussolini had built for the Italian Army to enjoy
after the victories that never happened. The park, the theater, all the
playgrounds and the Olympic swimming pool were used first by the
Germans and then the Allies for the recuperation of hospitalized
wounded. We spent two weeks, day and night, doing shows in the theater and in the wards and wherever our troops could be reached with
music, song, and every manner of entertainment we could provide.
Mr. B. was exhausted by the hours he spent entertaining in the wards
coupled with the shows in the theater.

✫ ✫ ✫ ✫ ✫ ✫ ✫ ✫ ✫ ✫ ✫

Letter from Nancy written on July 1:

> Nan Agar called me last night and wants us to come up
> Tuesday, July 4th for a week. . . . She hasn't heard from Bill since
> June 2. Let us know any news at once.

Now that we were in Bagnoli I had lost all contact with the guys that
might have heard from Bill. Then on July 3, I had a cable from Nancy:

> NAN CALLED. BILL KILLED ON JUNE 5TH. WE'RE TAKING TRAIN TO
> CAPE TOMORROW. LOVE, NANCY AND KETT.

When I told Mr. B. and my friends, it was as if we had all lost one of our own family. That beautiful man, gone.

☆ ☆ ☆ ☆ ☆ ☆ ☆ ☆ ☆ ☆ ☆

I didn't learn the whole story until it unwound gradually in Nancy's letters.

> Bill never reached the front. He was leading part of an armored convoy and was hit by artillery fire as he stood with other officers at an intersection, discussing the progress of the move. No one else was hit. Later she admitted: I got hysterical with my poor father. I was shrieking at him in tears, 'how can they do this! How can a man like that just be killed!' Poor Dad, he was trying to calm me down and I was blaming him for the whole war.

I kept looking at all the wounded men who were coming into the hospitals and then I thought of all those who never made it that far, like Bill.

My poor, damned, beautiful friend, robbed of any chance to strike a single blow. His life ended in bitter, profound waste.

Chapter 18

THE WAR
—May 18, 1944: *After months of failures, Allied forces walk into the remains of the abbey on Monte Cassino.*
—May 25, 1944: *US Forces break out of Anzio beachhead and drive east.*
—June 2, 1944, *The German withdrawal in Italy speeds the Allied advance.*
—June 4, 1944: *First Allied units enter Rome and the invasion convoys sail from southern England for the French coast.*

Once the push to Rome had begun, we woke each morning to new rumors about our own plans, most of which were denied before they could be confirmed.

We had left Santa Maria, the park and the little opera house — suddenly silent without the cries and laughter of our audiences and the grinding of their trucks. Cutting through the sounds of normalcy and peace — church bells, children's laughter, the squeak of the playground swings — was the roar of planes streaking northward and the booming of artillery far off.

The move to Bagnoli Medical Center had seemed anticlimactic. We put up a tent city once again and settled in. Pete hung the show in a characterless auditorium, Mussolini-modern, and on Friday, June 2, we started doing two shows a day, seven days a week. Our audiences were almost entirely recovering patients, many in their hospital bathrobes accompanied by nurses. And every day we sent small groups out to entertain the bedridden in the wards. An MP was assigned to drive Mr. B., Ben and pianist Morty Kahn from hospital to hospital. It was hard work and emotionally exhausting for Mr. B.

On Monday, June 5, I went into his dressing room during the intermission, his face a little more creased, tired. He was putting some pancake over the shadow of beard.

"You okay, boss?" I asked.

"I'm fine," he said with a smile. "How's your family?"

"Nancy just turned twenty-four," I said.

"I'll call her and say happy birthday when I get back."

"You're going back?"

He nodded with resignation, looking in the mirror. "I've got some work to do on a picture. And I also have a serious business problem in my office."

"I hope you can get some rest. You're on a hell of a schedule."

Ben came in, with a grin, excited, talking before he could catch his breath. "I just heard on the radio that we've taken Rome!"

The news traveled around the backstage. Before the overture, Mr. B. went out and announced the news to the audience and a great roar went up. The show was especially animated.

The next day, Mr. B. addressed the detachment at noon.

"I've got some news about our schedule for you, boys. The war news is heating up. We took Rome yesterday after a long siege. Today is the big one: D-Day and over 100,000 Allied troops have landed in France. Maybe this is the beginning of the end! As for us, we're still scheduled to play for the Air Force on the west coast in Foggia, Bari and Lecce through most of July." Then he read us some letters of high praise for what the show had accomplished in Italy: letters from the General in command of European Special Services, plus somewhat more impressive ones from Generals Eisenhower and Marshall.

"I can't give you any definite plans," he said, "but it's likely that the show will go from here to Cairo, India, Australia, New Zealand, New Guinea and Hawaii, possibly finishing with shows in the United States. That would take about nine months." Then he dropped the bomb. "I'm going to have to leave you about July first, following Foggia, but I'm hoping I'll be able to rejoin you somewhere." There was an unhappy moan and a mumbling "Oh, no!" before he went on. "I know you guys will continue to keep up the professional standard of the show." He finished by saying that he fully intended to write to as many of the families as he possibly could. Conscious of the enormous dismay, he attempted a slightly more hopeful note. "Look, fellas, I really think I'll be able to get back somewhere. I just don't think I should promise. You're doing a great job and I'm going to trust you to continue that."

Pete, Rosie, Carl and I got together after the meeting and I asked Bob to join us. I snagged a few bottles of beer from our mess sergeant. The discussion began with Mr. B's departure.

"We've had it!" Rosie said. "There's no way this show will make it with him gone."

"Rosie," I said, trying to calm him, "it's going to depend on us, guy. It'll work just fine if we believe in it." And then to pump up his ego, "But it can't last ten minutes without you!"

"Oh, yeah?"

"Yeah!" Pete said, gentle as always. "Just keep waving your stick at those guys and we'll kill 'em! And don't worry about the old man. He'll be back. He loves this goddamn show and he won't want to leave us alone with it!"

"I hope you're right," Rosie said.

"I'm always right, you Russke! Just keep playing!"

"Pete's absolutely right, Rosie. Mr. B. loves the show and he loves you."

"Besides," Carl said, "you're in the Army and you've got no choice, unless you'd rather be up front with those poor bastards who are slugging it out day after day praying for it to end."

"Well, I'll tell you one thing," said Bob. "If the committee doesn't keep Lieutenant Daniels under control when Mr. B. leaves, we'll never make it!"

"Bob, if we're diplomatic, Marc will go along with us," I said, with all the conviction I could muster. "And if he starts breaking the committee rules, you keep your trap shut and we'll get Swampy to set him straight. Besides, Berlin hasn't left yet. Let's see what happens. The fact is," and I panned around their faces, "we'd better take a very positive attitude. If Mr. B. thinks we can't do without him for a couple of months, he might give up."

"You know what?" Pete said, "We'd better start cheering up the whole damned outfit right now before they wonder what we're doing!"

We all looked at Rosie.

"I love you guys," he said.

☆ ☆ ☆ ☆ ☆ ☆ ☆ ☆ ☆ ☆ ☆

We all went to work on the rest of the men with: "Berlin will never leave the show for long. He's jealous of us for every minute he has to be away." The whole company responded. We began to believe it ourselves.

The opening in Foggia was scheduled for June 22. That gave us another week of performances in Bagnoli. And since we had Sunday off, some of the guys got passes for the weekend. Trucks were scheduled to take groups on various trips on Sunday. Few of us knew that Sunday morning what was unfolding in Mr. B.'s life. Ben Washer's diary tells the story:

> Sun, June 11 — Major John Morgan of General Wilson's staff, Special Services Command, calls on B. at 9:30 a.m., waking him, to inquire his reaction canceling remainder of Bagnoli and opening in Rome. B goes with Morgan to see General Wilson. Wilson not there. B. goes to camp to see committee to ask how soon Rome opening could be done. Decide possible to do on Wed. B. goes back to lunch at Parco (his hotel), finds Wilson has been there. B. finds Novotny at Parco after lunch. Morgan arrives to take B. to Wilson. B. has session with Wilson, all arranged. B. plays Wilson his new infantry song, which he promises to introduce in Rome. B. calls news to Novotny and Washer at Parco, then calls committee and tells them. B. to camp to arrange for move. Rehearses the infantry song with Rosie, Morty Kahn and Bob Sidney. B. announces change of

plans to which men are in camp. Most of men on pass. Move planned for Monday morning. B will fly to Rome in a.m. Washer and Fisher leave in Jeep at midnight drive to Rome to prepare for arrival of detachment. This was the day B. had planned to spend quietly motoring to Sorrento!

Back in camp, the committee informed Major Holmgren of plans. Pete and crew, with extra volunteers, takes the show down and all equipment is packed for morning departure. Reveille was at 6:00 a.m., Monday. We ate, loaded trucks and moved out at 11:30 with the entire production and detachment, except for Jus and Hayden who had not yet returned from Santa Maria!

☆ ☆ ☆ ☆ ☆ ☆ ☆ ☆ ☆ ☆ ☆

Eight p.m. the same day—Rome! We reached the Royal Opera House and set up a guard roster for the loaded trucks for the night. The detachment was billeted in the Fifth Army Rest Camp, a former Fascist Youth Center.

We were up at 6:00 a.m., the whole outfit full of excitement, and held a formation at 7:30 at the opera house, where we were informed that the opening would be on Thursday at 7:30 p.m., just two days away. We were then assigned to other billets: an unfinished luxury hotel, El Mediterraneo. It was just a concrete building with nothing finished but walls without doors. The walls had the odor of still drying concrete. There was no water or electricity.

We hooked up one of our antiaircraft electric generators we'd been pulling with a truck since Santa Maria and hauled water to our hotel site in five hundred-gallon trailer-tanks. It took some time to devise workable cooking and washing facilities. Pete Feller to the rescue!

Pete faced yet another challenge. He had a huge, magnificent opera house with more room than he needed for the whole show. We had only a day and a half before dress rehearsal to make sure everything was working. The opera house was under the command of Il Commandatori, the Italian title of the theater manager. He was a stern, fascist gent, loyal to Mussolini, used to classical opera, to whom a Broadway variety show was totally alien. For instance, he was appalled when I told him, with the aid of some of our Italian speaking members, that there were some comedy scenes which required a sudden, total blackout to support the "laugh" at the end of the scene. Blackouts were, I realized, unknown in the Commandatori's world of grand opera. He must have seen me as the embodiment of the crass American, an abomination to the pure Italian Fascisti, trained by Il Duce.

☆ ☆ ☆ ☆ ☆ ☆ ☆ ☆ ☆ ☆ ☆

Everyone worked feverishly to get ready. The magnificent Rome Opera House had 3,000 seats, the largest auditorium to which we had played indoors. As usual, Allied troops in uniform and in hospital robes filled every seat. We saw little of the Commandatori, who must have found it unbearable to see the blackouts and hear the lusty laughter, especially for the enormously successful WAC sketch. Mr. B's rendition of his new song, "No Wings on a Foxhole," that he dedicated to the infantry, drew strong and appreciative applause when he introduced it on opening night. Once again, we were a great hit.

Lieutenant Generals Devers and Eaker, serving directly under Eisenhower as heads of the ground and air forces respectively, addressed the cast in highly complimentary terms after the opening. Mr. B. sent the original score of "Foxhole" to General Marshall, who responded with a letter of thanks and a handwritten postscript:

> Please give my thanks and congratulations to the troop. GCM
> (George C. Marshall)

During the day, we started rehearsing a song and dance number to replace "Kick in the Pants," which had always had a cool reception. The replacement, "A Soldier's Dream," was actually a new staging of a number we had used in the last performances in the United States. We planned to have it ready for the opening in Foggia. It began with a song sung by Stuart Churchill. The dream was of Betty Grable, Hedy Lamarr and Carmen Miranda, three popular pinup stars found in many a soldier's treasured belongings. The three glamour goddesses were danced by Private First Class Charlie Tate and Privates Alfred Danieli and Charles "Bubbles" Dickson. These three guys did manage to be damned cute when shaved judiciously, made up, costumed by Johnny Koenig and choreographed by Bob Sidney.

As we began our second week, Mr. B. announced that our last Wednesday night performance would be reserved for an audience of Italian civilians. This had been arranged through our Allied Military Government Commissioner, Colonel Charles Poletti, with the cooperation of Prince Doria of Italy. All the proceeds would be turned over to an Italian charity fund.

When the Commandatori learned of the civilian audience, he gave a musical score of the fascist anthem to Rosie, intended for the overture. During our rehearsals Rosie had made contact with some Italian musicians and he asked them where he could get something more appropriate. They supplied him with the anthem of the Italian Republic, which had been used before Mussolini came into power. Rosie asked Mr. B. to listen to a run through of the music. Mr. B. listened, said, "Great," and went off to his dressing room. The Commandatori accosted Rosie as he finished the rehearsal and loosed a torrent of Italian. Rosie didn't understand much but he reported what he thought was the gist of it. "The fascist bastard blasted the shit out of me for five minutes straight." Frank D'Elia, a bass-baritone of Italian parentage, happened to be within earshot and corroborated Rosie's impression of what was said. "He don't like, you, Sarge," said Frank. "He says you'll start a riot if you play that depraved old crap." Rosie turned to Sergeant Willard Jones, who was in charge of his music library.

"Billy, lock that stuff up so that son of a bitch can't burn it! And give the fascist crap to the old fart and tell him where to put it."

Willard, who was about five foot six, begged off. "Hey, boss, he's just as likely to have somebody break my fingers and I won't be able to play the horn." Rosie turned to guitarist Eddie O'Connor, one of the tug-o-war team, shoving the pile of music scores in his hands. "Eddie, you do it."

"My Italian is lousy, Sarge." Danny Longo heard the by-play. "Hey, Goombah," said Danny, "you need a translator?"

"Yeah!" said Eddie eagerly. "Come with me, Paisan."

The two men went on their mission.

☆ ☆ ☆ ☆ ☆ ☆ ☆ ☆ ☆ ☆ ☆

Before the performance I ventured out front to see how the house was filling up with the citizens of Rome. They were an animated and talkative audience. I couldn't understand a word, but it was apparent from their expressions that their expectations were great. We had printed a special program in both English and Italian which included a thorough description of the show. We charged them fifteen lire, which was forgivable since it was a benefit performance.

They were wildly enthusiastic when they heard their anthem and they loved the opening music and song. But when the comedians came on, it became apparent they understood absolutely no English. Every joke was met with utter silence. It didn't matter. They applauded and cheered wildly after every scene. When it came time for Mr. B.'s appearance in act two, Frank D'Elia introduced Mr. B. in Italian. There was great applause. Mr. B. did his performance of "Oh! How I Hate to Get Up in the Morning" and again their applause was tremendous. Mr. B. had an inspiration. He grabbed Frank D'Elia, told him the idea and Frank relayed these words in Italian: "Mr. Berlin will sing, without orchestra, an Italian folk song he learned when he was a little boy, 'Oi Marie.'" He sang the first chorus and then when he talked the audience into singing the second chorus with him, it brought the house down. They yelled and applauded on and on and wouldn't stop until he sang it again. When we'd done the closing number and the curtain calls, nothing would stop the applause until I brought the house lights up on the closed curtain and the orchestra started packing their instruments.

The next day's matinee was for an all-British soldier audience and that evening we gave our final performance in Rome. At the end of the show, the curtain remained up. General Clark, commander of the Fifth Army was expected to attend but because of activity at the front, his Chief of Staff took his place. The Chief of Staff, Colonel Saltzman, then announced that he would like to make a formal presentation from the Fifth Army to *This Is the Army*. Mr. Berlin's reply took me completely by surprise.

Mr. B. said, "I would like First Sergeant Alan Anderson to accept this award on behalf of the whole company." I was standing, as usual, in the wings, but Mr. B. turned and looked at me and I thought I'd better get moving. So I walked out on to center stage to the Colonel and saluted. The Colonel returned my salute and then smiled and read the words on the plaque:

Presented by
Army Commander
(Fifth Army Insignia here)
for excellence in
Discipline
Performance
Merit
(clasp suspended by chain links)
This Is the Army
April–June 1944

Then the Colonel pinned the plaque on me and put out his hand. As we shook hands he said, "With this plaque and clasp goes the best wishes of the Fifth Army wherever it is and wherever it goes." The audience applauded and my guys applauded and I realized I'd better say something. So I said, according to our Company Clerk Davey Supple's notes, "Thank you, Colonel Saltzman, on behalf of Mr. Berlin and the entire detachment. We are all very grateful for this honor." And I then had the presence of mind to salute, which the Colonel returned and then, thank God, Jus Addiss had the presence of mind to lower the curtain.

☆ ☆ ☆ ☆ ☆ ☆ ☆ ☆ ☆ ☆ ☆

That ended our time in the command area of General Mark Clark, a major figure in the land war against Adolf Hitler. Our next move was to the southeast coast of Italy, to the area of the Fifteenth US Air Force command under Major General Twining. The Air Corps had been disappointed when we suddenly changed our schedule and went first to Rome, but they were so pleased we were coming that they offered to fly the whole company from Rome to Foggia. We accepted the invitation, although some of the men had to go by road to accompany the truck convoy carrying the show and all the equipment for the detachment. I volunteered to join Pete with the convoy. We finished loading the trucks at 1:30 a.m. Friday, departed immediately and drove for twenty-two hours and thirty minutes, chugging into the courtyard of the Albergo Cicolella at midnight. We had dealt with rough roads, detours, breakdowns and blown tires. At Saturday morning breakfast, Rosie and Carl, well-fed and rested, regaled us with the details of their 10:30 a.m. departure: smooth seventy-five minute flight in the Army transport planes and excellent air force dinner.

Foggia and Bari were disappointing after Rome. Dusty, hot as blazes, they had been the center of Italy's Air Force and the Germans did their best to devastate them both. Unfortunately, we were required to increase the damage in our effort to dislodge them.

Our opening performance in Foggia marked the second anniversary of the opening of *This Is the Army*. However, the difference in the response to the show—leaving the infantry companies and being with the Air Force was startling—I thought of the guys we had met and talked to who had been in the Anzio landing—or lying in trenches below Monte Cassino when Rome was still so far away. If a battle ended and you were wet and muddy and cold, the best of it was, at least you were alive. The infantry seldom had the chance to feel the exhilaration of an Air Force crew that has just come back from a successful mission—where there happened to be no casualties—to good food, a warm bed and no one shooting at you.

Their demeanor was utterly different. They were not stunned by the sudden freedom of feeling safe, blinded by bright theater lights that might give away their position, vulnerable, emotionally wiped out by anything in the show that touched them sentimentally as were the infantry troops.

In Foggia and Bari, they walked into the theater chatting, laughing and sat down relaxed, comfortable, confident, ready to enjoy a show. The result was they were open and spontaneous from the first notes of the orchestra. In a way, I felt sad thinking of the comparative lives of Bill Mauldin's *Willie and Joe* that Bill knew so well and brought alive for us in his cartoons of the fighting men in the trenches of the Italian campaigns. We had seen a lot of those guys before we got close to the Air Force and we understood why Bill's characterizations went so straight to the heart of the infantryman, who were lucky enough to be where they could read *Stars and Stripes*, the Army newspaper that ran Bill's cartoons.

We couldn't, of course, help enjoying the chow, the living quarters and the audiences in Foggia and Bari. This, in spite of the theater in Foggia, which was barely adequate for Pete to give them a show. It was one of those theaters that was built with movies in mind, not big stage musicals. Cooper and I lit the show fully, although by now it was all white light. By the second week in Santa Maria we had used the last of the color gelatins that are standard in the lighting of a Broadway show.

The takedown, load out and eighty mile trip to Bari took a day; then three more days to set up again.

In the thirty performances we gave—seventeen in Foggia with 1,800 seats, thirteen in Bari with 2,600 seats, we played to 64,400 Air Force personnel or guests.. They were extremely responsive audiences and took special pains to show us how welcome we were by feeding us extremely well, enjoying the show a lot and taking us up on special flights. I discovered that the view of the world from a bombardier's seat is a rare experience. You can see everything up, down and side-ways! Jus was impressed enough with the flying to write about it to his father:

> One of the highlights of our time with the Air Force occurred during the few minutes we stood waiting on the field in Rome. Seven Flying Fortresses came over in formation, streaking across the sky, peeled off one at a time, and landed, almost at our feet—a beautiful sight. And then we boarded our Air Transports and took off and within minutes flew into Foggia in formation, landed and stepped down on the ground feeling like guests of honor. We discovered that's the way the Air Corps does things.

As we finished our performances in Foggia and Bari, it seemed a good moment to assess the condition of our show equipment.

As to costumes, Tony Paglia and his assistant had kept everything in remarkably good shape. Makeup: there was still enough for Bert Whitley to portion it out for the "Ladies of the Chorus." Musical instruments: Rosie's musicians had to keep mailing orders into New York for strings for the string section and reeds for the woodwinds. Cooper and I discovered that we could replace a burnt out 500-Watt bulb in our spotlights with a 750-Watt movie projection bulb sent for the movie projectors that were everywhere the Armed Forces showed Hollywood movies. Our crew members would write home for special things they needed and get someone to supply them. Al Gorta had to get someone to send him carbon rods for his follow-spots. Somehow the crew managed to keep it looking enough like a Broadway production to amaze all the professionals we ran into overseas.

☆ ☆ ☆ ☆ ☆ ☆ ☆ ☆ ☆ ☆ ☆

The day that Mr. B. had warned us about was getting closer. When we finished in Bari, he was going home "for a while." We had played the show several times without him and it had gone well. We'd had to do it once in England when he had been unable to return from a hospital show because of weather, so we knew that the show was complete even without Mr. B. The audience didn't know what they were missing.

The performance wasn't the only problem with having him absent. The more critical one was that all show decisions must be made by the committee. Our officers had to know that and truly accept that. Even more delicate a problem—the outside Army structure must not know that. They had to deal with our officers, not knowing that they were not in charge of the show.

"Alan, have you got a minute?" Mr. B. said to me after we had opened in Bari. "Yes, sir," I responded as usual, but with some instinctive foreboding. We went into his dressing room. "Could you get me an up-to-date list of the boys addresses and phone numbers before we close here? I want to be able to get in touch with as many families as I can."

"We've been working at it, Mr. B. Dave and Arnold will probably have one ready tomorrow. The Air Force has been doing some mimeographing for us."

"Be sure to give me your Dad's, too. I want to call him. And, of course, I'm going to talk to your son and his mother."

Mr. B. talked to Bob and several of the guys. He kept hopping around to one after another, assuring, complimenting, being cheerful.

I felt his concern about leaving the show in spite of his pretense. He didn't want another Naples. All of a sudden, it was Sunday night and the Red Cross was giving us all a good-bye party with ice cream, cookies and coffee, and Mr. B. was making a farewell speech.

On Wednesday, July 26, Warrant Officer Ben Washer and Technical Sergeant Carl Fisher flew to Cairo, Egypt, as advance cadre for our next assignment. Irving Berlin climbed into a US Air Corps fighter plane and began the first leg of his journey to New York City.

This Is the Army Detachment packed up, getting ready to board the US Liberty ship *James J. Hill* in the morning, bound for Cairo.

☆ ☆ ☆ ☆ ☆ ☆ ☆ ☆ ☆ ☆ ☆

As we boarded the ship in Bari, I looked east across the Adriatic towards the shores of Yugoslavia and Albania. Beyond them lay Bulgaria and Rumania and so many of the targets of our bombers that took off from Bari and Foggia. Nancy had written me in March, when we had just arrived in Algiers:

> Darling, your cousin Keith was shot down when he was on a
> bombing mission in Rumania. He had flown over the Adriatic
> from Foggia, Italy, and his whole crew was lost.

Keith was my age and my favorite cousin. Aunt Lela always told me that he wanted to be like me. I never knew what that meant, but I liked to hear it because he was a handsome guy whom everyone liked. When he walked into a room, all the girls would go crazy. Nancy's letter went on to read:

> Poor Aunt Lela and Uncle Dan. Two sons gone.

Keith's older brother, Lee, had died in a flight training accident just month's before Keith's death.

Chapter 19

THE WAR

—July 21, 1944: In the Pacific, US forces land on Guam, the largest of the Mariana Islands.

—July 23, 1944: In Italy, the Americans have reached the outskirts of Pisa, Italy.

—July 27, 1944: In France, US forces continue to advance, taking Marigny, Saint-Gilles, Lessay and Periers.

—July 28, 1944: The long battle on Biak, off New Guinea, is finally won.

—July 31, 1944: Soviet forces move ever closer to Warsaw.

One of the most productive things Carl, or more properly, Technical Sergeant Carl Fisher, Supply Clerk of *This Is the Army* Detachment, nephew of George Abbott, experienced general manager of Broadway shows, did was to "write off" a piece of Army equipment formerly in the possession of a Fifth Army Motor Pool in Bagnoli, Italy, now in our possession. Because of its condition our supply clerk judged it to be of no further use, and said clerk sent a memo through channels to that effect. Making such judgments is the valid responsibility of supply clerks. Said item was therefore removed from the Fifth Army list and then listed by Carl as Item Number 62 on the equipment list of our detachment. We watched breathlessly as Item 62, an Army jeep, swung high out over the harbor, held by one of the loading cranes of S.S. *James J. Hill*, bound for Egypt.

"Take good care of her, guys," Carl had said, as Marc, Pete and I stood on the dock watching our vehicle do a graceful swoop and then disappear almost silently into the forward hold. Carl had handed the inventory papers to Marc, which would authorize us to repossess everything on the list when we reached Alexandria. Carl and Ben left us for Bari Airport, where they hopped a plane to Cairo as our advance party.

☆ ☆ ☆ ☆ ☆ ☆ ☆ ☆ ☆ ☆ ☆

We were the only troops on board the Liberty ship so we didn't have a lot of entertaining to do. The ship's complement were the ship's officers, crew, galley crew—very important to us three times a day—a squad of Navy gunners to man the gun turrets—of enormous potential value—and TITA. On the sixth day out, partly just to keep ourselves in shape, we gave an impromptu show on the afterdeck for about an hour and a half. It was heavily attended.

There were a lot of daily chores I had to assign: KP, including potato peeling and baking; hatch opening in the morning, closing at night; and there were regular lifeboat drills.

The *James J. Hill* was one of thousands of Liberty ships specially and hastily built during World War II to move supplies from the US to our armed forces and allies all around the globe. The Hill's cargo was bound for Egypt and neighboring areas. Our quarters were comfortable—double bunks in several cabins and one large room also equipped with double bunks for moving troops. We were eating merchant marine chow, which is about as good as you can get unless you're in the US.

Marc was in his element, putting up schedules and lecturing us on the emergencies for which we must be prepared: fire drill, boat drill, air attack, submarine attack, and lastly, abandon ship. We were assigned by platoon to lifeboat stations, instructed in how to throw rafts overboard and in the use of nets thrown over each side when abandoning ship.

Our Port of Call was Alexandria, Egypt, but after one night out of Bari we anchored off Augusta, Sicily, waiting to join a convoy. Twice during the remaining voyage our convoy was put on alert and we were ordered to remain below. In each case, "suspicious" aircraft approached us; both times, they were friendly planes. In our passage from the realm of Axis Sally towards that of Tokyo Rose, our ship's guns were fired only for practice.

One of our best hoofers, Sergeant Artie Steiner, conducted calisthenics each morning. The rest of the time we devoted to reading or lying in the sun, which was in those days filtered through a more protective ozone layer than we enjoy today.

We were plunging off into parts of the world we had never seen before, while our leader—boss, surrogate Papa—Mr. B. was flying back home to the familiar ground of Bing Crosby, Fred Astaire, and to his wife and three daughters, much to their relief. When we asked him if he wanted someone to sing his songs while he was away he said emphatically, "No!" His songs were not to be heard unless he was in the show. This was reassuring since it suggested that he intended to rejoin us. Warrant Officer Ben Washer traveled with us this time to help with the advance arrangements. He was valuable as an active member of the committee and his close association with Mr. B. added strength to the committee's power in the boss's absence.

It was a seven day voyage to the busy harbor of Alexandria, Egypt. We dropped anchor at 4 p.m. and had to transfer all our belongings and the whole production onto an LCT (Landing Craft Tanks), a bigger barge than the LCM (Landing Craft Medium) we had used previously. Then we were visited by three patrol boats carrying representatives of British, American and Egyptian port authorities. An hour later, after they had all checked us out, Ben and Carl came aboard with our mail and assured us it wouldn't be long now. Half an hour later, we all boarded another LCT and headed for the dock through the busy harbor traffic. By 6:15 p.m. we stepped ashore in Egypt into a bustle of activity. We piled onto US Army trucks and by midnight were in the Russell B. Huckstep casual transit camp in Cairo. They gave us some food in the casual mess that was better than the name suggests. Casual was the word the Army chose meaning "temporary." Bumming around the globe by ourselves, having to attach ourselves to more permanent units, relegated us to temporary, casual, food and lodging. Johnny informed us that orders from Washington were as follows: 1. The barracks of Camp Huckstep would be our lodging in Egypt; 2. We would

have a six day furlough before we set up the show in the Cairo Opera
House; 3. We could spend the furlough either on a trip to Palestine
and Tel Aviv or somewhere of our own choice within easy reach of
Cairo.

My usual pals and I — except for Pete — decided on Palestine and Tel
Aviv, so after a night at Huckstep about thirty of us, including Johnny
Koenig, trucked to a tiny airport just outside of town in the early
morning. There was a two-engine plane, a DC-3, with US stars on the
wing sitting silent outside the only hangar. A couple of Army Air
Force pilots strolled up, scratching and yawning.

"You guys from the show?"

"That's right," said Johnny.

"Okay. Climb aboard."

We all piled in carrying our overnight gear. There was something so
casual about the crew's behavior that it made me almost wonder if
they were real pilots who knew what they were doing. However, once
they got the engines running and not sputtering, I stopped worrying.
Ten minutes later we were on the runway, going full tilt for takeoff.
The casual look disappeared.

☆ ☆ ☆ ☆ ☆ ☆ ☆ ☆ ☆ ☆ ☆

Carl, Rosie and I found a nice hotel room on the beach in Tel Aviv. The
first thing we chose was a plunge in the surf and a brief walk around
the city before settling into a restaurant and a good dinner. The next
day we spent touring Jerusalem. These are bits from a long letter to
Nancy:

> The city was about 1,200 years old. I was startled to find several
> Jews wailing on the Wailing Wall. Little, narrow streets, packed
> with buildings — vendors and hawkers on each side of the ten
> foot street so there is barely room to walk. No room for carts.
> Every four feet there is a new odor or aroma — take your pick:

cheese, fish, fruit, bake shop, shoe leather, and a hundred others. Crowded but clean, as are the people. I felt I was in a movie. The whole of Old Jerusalem is visible beyond this great wall, which runs entirely around the city. By contrast, Tel Aviv is entirely modern, about twenty-five years old. The city itself was very plain with hastily erected buildings, a sort of Coney Island or perhaps Atlantic City. Outside the city of Jerusalem are the collective farms. And they must farm collectively; the earth is so hard to cultivate that a man would be helpless by himself.

We saw most of the historical places of the Old and New Testament. It meant riding and looking for eleven hours straight. After the Wailing Wall, we visited the thirteen stations of Christ, the lovely little town of Bethlehem, the Church of the Nativity, and finally, the Mount of Olives and the Garden of Gethsemane, where The Church of All Nations now stands, with twelve domes, each dedicated to a different nation. Even though many are left out, it is a church of rare beauty which continues to receive donations from all over the world.

Each night we knocked back several glasses of Tom Collins in the hotel bar and then had a fine dinner. We flew in to Alexandria, stayed with the Red Cross, found the most beautiful beach in the world, more swimming, went to the horse races and ate well. Back to Cairo by truck to ride on camels and see the Sphinx and the pyramids. Walking toward the Great Pyramid, thinking it quite close, we kept going closer and closer, and then realized it was still half a mile away, it was so huge! Finally we stood beside it, looking up and up, overwhelmed by its incredible mass.

Then our furlough was over and we were back in Cairo with Pete, setting up the show in the Cairo Opera House.

Cairo is a real city. Like New York, it has everything, but it is unique because it is at a crossroads for the world that draws on a wider assortment of races, nationalities and languages than any other single city. It was also hot as hell in August! Like all desert heat, it drops quickly after sundown.

The opening night performance was only for civilians, including King Farouk and his party. All proceeds went to charity—half of it to the Red Crescent, which was their name for the Red Cross. I had to hold the curtain for twenty-five minutes, until 9:10 p.m., for the arrival of King Farouk and his party. Evidently English was understood well enough to allow the civilian audience to enjoy the show, judging by the laughter, the applause and the quiet during the romantic or sentimental moments of the show. The next twenty-six performances were for American and Allied troops, two shows per night, and the one thousand seats were filled for every performance. There were as many British troops as American in the audiences. King George V, King of Greece, attended a week after the opening and came backstage to congratulate the cast.

He surprised us by saying, "I saw the show in New York and thought it was wonderful. I notice you have some new scenes and I enjoyed it even more!"

The company morale soared when the boys realized that they could be a hit even without Mr. B. The generals—and kings—still came backstage to congratulate us. But Mr. B. sent us a congratulatory telegram which was read to us by Ben Washer. The boss hadn't forgotten us.

✰ ✰ ✰ ✰ ✰ ✰ ✰ ✰ ✰ ✰ ✰

The next stop on our tour would be Iran, which was an unknown entity. Therefore, while the rest of us carried on a very standard production in the Cairo Opera House, Ben, Johnny, Pete and Bob flew to Iran to figure out how we would play in a very primitive situation. They all returned in five days except for Johnny, who stayed to draw diagrams and take measurements. Once again, we couldn't have done it without Pete's ingenuity. We gathered the company for a meeting and Bob

Sidney described the plan to us with a flourish.

"It's simple," said Bob. "Simple but marvelous! You see, each one of these camps where the troops live has a movie projector and an out-door amphitheater. Before we get to each stop, the Army guys build a platform for the show where the screen is usually hanging. Pete builds a proscenium arch—just enough to hang our gorgeous yellow show curtain. We put up pipes with guy wires to hold the lights on each side of the stage and pipes on each side of the audience for front lights. Al Gorta uses the movie projection platform way out front for his follow spot. The orchestra sits in front of the platform. The audience sits on chairs or benches, or whatever they use when they watch movies. We wait until it's dark and cool. And we play outdoors once a night to at least a couple of thousand men. Lieutenant Koenig stayed behind to make working drawings for each stop; they'll be ready for us when we arrive. We can pull into a camp during the day and start playing the show that night." Bob folded his arms and lifted his head proudly. "How about that?" he finished, with a flourish characteristic of our staging director.

He got a big hand for his presentation.

"Question," I said. "Coop hangs the lights when we get to each camp?" I asked.

"Right," said Bob.

"It's daylight outdoors, right?" Bob looks around for help. He sees Pete.

"Pete, take over, will you? We've got a troublemaker."

"No, no!" I said. "Just want to be clear. Johnny Cooper and I focus the lights in broad daylight, at 110 degrees, with the sun shining in my eyes? Right?"

"Right," says Pete.

I look at Cooper. He looks at me. He chuckles. Coop has a great chuckle—way back in his throat like an echo. He can't sing, but if he could, he'd be a bass. He doesn't say anything and neither do I. We look at each other and then we both laugh at Pete.

"You've got some good dark glasses, Anderson!"

"Air Corps best," I reply.

"Then you're all set," says Pete.

"Thanks, Pete," I said. Rosie changed the subject. "How do we get to Iran?" Rosie asked.

"We go by ship, with the whole show," said Pete.

"Didn't you fly?" Rosie asks.

"It costs too much to fly us," he says.

"How does a ship get to Iran?" Rosie's enjoying himself.

"Just show up with your stick," Pete says to the conductor. "How the hell should I know? Ask Marc. He's been talking to the Navy."

Marc is smiling. "It's a military secret," he says. "Like Pete said, don't forget the baton."

Hank Henry puts his hand up. Hank weighs about two hundred and fifty pounds. "Excuse me, fellas. Lunch is ready."

Pete has the answer for Hank, putting the comedian on the defensive.

"Pete says. "You shouldn't be allowed to eat. It's costing the country too much."

Hank says, "Listen, skinny, when I read for the part, Mr. Berlin said, 'Don't change a thing!' I'm under orders to eat."

Hank got his laugh and we all went to lunch.

After lunch we have a formation and Marc fills in some details from the Army point of view. "Fellows," he says, very chummy, "I've got a great opportunity for you all for the trip to Iran on a Liberty ship. The United States Armed Forces Institute puts out educational courses which any outfit can use if they want them. I think the trip to Iran is the perfect opportunity. I'm going to hand out a list of courses and you can just check off the ones you want and I'll get the books and material."

Abner Silverstein piped up. "Is it a long enough trip to make it worthwhile?"

"I think so," said Marc.

"Sir," asked Danny Longo, "is there anything else we could get, like movies or something?"

"Nope. It's just a Liberty ship, Danny. There are no movie facilities." Danny looks disgusted.

"We never heard how long the trip it is," says Bill Roerick politely.

"Two weeks," says Marc with a straight face.

"Two weeks — on a Liberty ship!" He had taken Danny to new depths of dismay. "Jeez, we could finish going around the *world* in two weeks."

"That's true," said Marc. "But on a Liberty ship it will take just about two weeks to go down from Port Tewfik, at the southern end of the Suez Canal, through the Gulf of Suez, the Red Sea, the Straits of Yemen, east through the Gulf of Aden, northeast through the Arabian Sea, into the Gulf of Oman and the Straits of Hormuz, and north through the full length of the Persian Gulf, past Abadan to Khorramshahr, Iran."

"Couldn't we drive quicker?" asked juggler Larry Weeks.

"As combatants, I'm afraid that we're not really welcome in neutral countries," Marc said, smiling. "We'd have to shoot our way by land."

"Sorry I asked," said Larry.

Marc distributed application forms which also requested voluntary instructors. We had several responses to a request for faculty members. Bill Roerick, Jus Addiss, John Koenig and several others with useful college backgrounds replied. Among the courses offered were Accounting; Bookkeeping; Dramatics; French; Grammar; Harmony; History: Ancient, Medieval or Modern; also World Since 1914; Mathematics: Algebra, Geometry; Photography; Political Science; Economics; Psychology; Shorthand; Sight Reading for Singers; Singing for Non-Singers; Typing. The ship was known as the "Floating University."

We had spent two weeks in Cairo doing two shows every evening, going to several outdoor, late night cinemas, shopping and prowling in the early morning before the high heat.

On August 31, we played our last two shows. The closing was attended by Navy Captain W.C. Merriweather, Master of the ship that was to take us on our fifteen-day voyage to Persia. He said he loved the show and was proud to be having us aboard his ship.

After our last show, the whole detachment settled into the front seats of the theater to see a special performance which had been arranged just for our pleasure by the Royal Opera House of Cairo. It was a genuine Egyptian belly dance by the all but naked beauty named Tahia. The whole detachment gaped and ogled as she writhed and swirled, twisted and flew, her body lithe and exotic, all the splendors of her arms, legs, breasts and belly moving with the music of her own Takhit orchestra. When it ended, our gang erupted with a tumult of whistles, roars, cheers and applause that could only be produced by profound professional admiration plus considerable sex deprivation. It was a beautiful climax to our month-long visit to the exotic land of Queen Cleopatra.

We spent the next few hours dismantling the show piece by piece and crating everything for shipment. All of Friday, September 1, was devoted to loading the show into trucks. At 5 a.m. on Saturday, we made the eighty-mile journey across the Egyptian Desert to Port Tewfik, at the southern end of the Suez Canal, where we transferred everything into LCT's and ferried to our Liberty ship, S.S. *John Hathorn*. At 7 a.m., Sunday, September 3, we began our fifteen-day educational voyage in a floating oven, clinging to the vanishing memory of Tahia's undulating physiognomy.

Chapter 20

THE WAR

—*Aug 17, 1944: In New Guinea, the Americans make gains.*

—*Aug 20, 1944: Marshal Petain is taken into custody by Germans, refusing to evacuate Vichy.*

—*Aug 26, 1944: General de Gaulle returns to Paris to join the triumphant parade.*

—*Aug 30, 1944: In Italy Allied forces begin attack on the Gothic Line, north of Pisa and Pesaro.*

—*Sep 1, 1944: Allies advance so rapidly in many areas there is difficulty in supplying all fronts.*

The ship's troop commander informed Marc that our detachment would be responsible for assigning two gunner's assistants each day of the voyage to Khorramshahr, Persia. Marc appointed a sergeant each day to choose a corporal or private as his partner. It was the first time we had been given direct responsibility as combatants. The nearest such duty had been as guards on some occasions. However, we also had never been attacked directly while at sea so the boys didn't worry—much.

Again, we were the only passengers on the voyage so we were able to establish certain rules of behavior on our own. Along with Marc's daily schedule, we announced that they could wear what they wanted.

HOWEVER,

read the notice,

DON'T BLAME ANYONE IF YOU GET A SUNBURN.

We had a few cases in the first few days that were painful enough to act as fair warning to the whole company. The bunk rooms were so hot at night we allowed them to take bedding on deck as long as it was removed before wake-up call.

We also posted a class schedule which was revised every few days depending on the popularity of the subject. Finally, there was a schedule of the show for the Persian tour.

After studying the notices for a couple of minutes, Pete made an announcement. "I plan on getting plenty of sleep, Anderson, and if you wake me up to study French or look at the sunrise, I'll break your neck!"

"Maybe you'll put on a little weight and stop calling me Blubber!"

"Not with your willpower!"

"Go take a nap and stop trying to be charming." I started away thinking that for once, he would have nothing to say. I was mistaken.

"I never try to be charming!" he roared, heading for the bunks. "I have never sunk so low." He started away and added, "I thought you wanted to be a writer," with a grin, disappearing before I could speak. The bastard! If I didn't love him so much, I would have hated him.

Of course, there was pleasure in such exchanges between good friends. Oddly it seemed to establish an affectionate relationship with mutual trust. I realized it had started more than two years ago when we started working together and Katie and Nancy became close friends, too. As I headed back to the Orderly Room, I felt a sort of glow. Blubber! It had started with that. The son of a bitch!

Actually, none of us were going to put on weight on the way to Persia. The cooking was uninspired and the intense heat sapped the appetite. Our doctor warned us to drink a lot of water. He was right, of course, but tough guys in their twenties don't think of water as a drink—until they're terribly thirsty.

The second night out, Marc and I were standing on deck enjoying the breeze when Swampy approached us from the forward deck. He leaned down and spoke quietly. "You know fellas, I think there's something going on up there in the dark. I mean, between a couple of . . . *guys*."

Marc's eyes found mine without moving his head.

"Yes, sir," Marc said after a moment. "You're probably right. What would you like us to do about it, Major?"

There was a pause while Swampy thought about it. "Yeah, well, I think I'll just turn in. Good night."

"Good night, Major," we both said. Marc and I kept looking out at the sky. I was trying to make out some familiar constellations. Our latitude was about 26 degrees north, about even with the Florida Keys. I should be able to see Sagittarius and Capricorn.

"We ought to have a course in astronomy," I said.

"How do you think it's all going?" Marc asked.

"I think it was pure genius on your part. It's going great! The guys who usually don't know what to do with free time are all busy."

"Good."

"When does Johnny rejoin us?" I asked.

"He's supposed to meet us in Khorramshahr. I hope it's all going to work. We could never do it without Pete and John."

"That's for sure." I yawned.

"Let's turn in," Marc said.

"Right."

☆ ☆ ☆ ☆ ☆ ☆ ☆ ☆ ☆ ☆ ☆

We ate and slept and wrote letters which we couldn't mail before we went ashore in Persia. The courses continued to keep a lot of guys busy. Artie Steiner had a big following for his calisthenics session every day, and of course, we had daily lifeboat drill to break the monotony. Davie Supple's company diary had little to report each day:

All details to duties.

Ship's captain Merriweather livened up Day 7 by giving a lecture on Navigation. He drew a big audience. We had one heavy rainfall on

Day 9. On Day 11, the captain conducted a tour of the chart room and the bridge, explaining instruments and operation of the ship. Thirty or forty guys showed up for that one. On Day 14, idleness ended. School was over and everyone was busy cleaning up the ship on the last day of the long, hot voyage.

At 5:30 a.m. on Day 15, we were in an area I remembered from my Ancient History class at Lincoln School of Teacher's College in New York City. Miss Elmina Luckey was our revered teacher and with great fervor, she taught us about the bread basket of the world, the Tigris and Euphrates Valley in Mesopotamia, later known as Iraq. The Tigris and Euphrates rivers empty into the Persian Gulf, just below where we were landing, at Abadan and Khorramshahr.

All I could think of that morning in 1944, was how disappointed Miss Luckey would feel if she could see the roasting, barren, impoverished desert that was once civilization's very first, verdant, flowering breadbasket.

Johnny Koenig came on board with the pilot, who was needed to navigate our ship through a winding channel into the harbor of Khorramshahr, which was the location of our first show. Beyond that one-story town, the color of dust and mud, we could see only the endless flatness of desert, roasting in a hellish heat. There was the mysterious sound of unknown language, yelling and rushing about—turbaned heads, bodies clothed variously, wrapped in rags, sometimes a tattered t-shirt, feet protected with primitively constructed sandals (sometimes a piece of rubber tire bound to the foot with rag or rope).

Johnny Koenig, by contrast, was trim and handsome as he returned in his summer khaki uniform, shoulder bars shining, hair smoothly coifed, his peaked cap at a rakish angle. He gave us a welcoming speech.

"Believe it or not, you are in the exotic land of Persia, under the US Persian Gulf Command, whose vital purpose in the war is to transport arms and supplies by trucks from the gulf to our Russian allies. They have assigned thirty of their huge diesel trucks to our show so that we can play for every one of the many thousands of men spread through the Persian Command. We can only give one performance a day because it's too hot to start before 8 p.m. We actually play in the Army camps at each city, in the outdoor amphitheater that they use for showing movies. The layout is exactly as it was described by Bob Sidney several weeks ago. There's room for an audience of 1,800 here in Khorramshahr and we're going to give five shows beginning the day after tomorrow. We won't have that much setup time after the first one. That means our setup will always be in the heat of the day. By the way, while we're in the desert, remember to drink plenty of water and keep your head covered when the sun is out. It gets up above 130 degrees Fahrenheit at this time of year. You're lucky. It gets really hot in the summer!"

"Is the hotel air conditioned, Lieutenant?" said Sergeant Julie Oshins, master of comic bitterness.

"Oh, sure, Julie!" said Johnny. "They've had air conditioning here long before they had electricity. The system was invented by the British decades ago. There's no glass in window openings. There's a webbing of twigs. Little pipes drip water down through the twigs from a tank on the roof. When there's the slightest desert breeze through the wet twigs, it's supposed to cool off the indoors. But wait! You get a daily anesthetic—otherwise known as a half-liter bottle of vodka at lunchtime every day."

This was too good. The detachment broke into laughter, jokes and general uproar. Johnny got their attention again. "Let me explain what is routine behavior every day in this climate. This is serious advice. Except for the day when you're busy setting up the show, take a siesta from one to five." They started again. "Quiet! For siesta—listen carefully—take another shot of vodka, strip to your shorts, lie on your bunk, drench yourself with a helmet-full of water and go to sleep before you dry out and start to bake. One last piece of wisdom: save the rest of the vodka so you can go to sleep at night. Important rule: when you

take a shower, you get three minutes. No more. Water is more precious than vodka.

"Next: the schedule. We're going to play in eight camps over six
weeks' time, and I promise you, these guys are dying to see the show.
They work long hours driving across this desert furnace and their only
relaxation is movies. They've seen an awful lot of those for the past
two years. It's going to be a rugged six weeks but I'm willing to bet the
applause will make up for it. And before you know it, we'll be on our
way to Australia like Mr. B. promised."

Johnny's cheery manner was so infectious that we started applaud-
ing him before we realized that it was lousy news except for the half-
liter of vodka.

We loaded our barracks bags into the trucks and made the short
journey to our barracks in the Khorramshahr Army camp area.

✰ ✰ ✰ ✰ ✰ ✰ ✰ ✰ ✰ ✰ ✰

We began with our daily routine on Monday, September 18, with a
7:00 a.m. reveille and an eight o'clock breakfast. Pete took a large crew
to the docks in trucks and started moving the production into the theater area. Everybody on the crew had to learn how everything that
Johnny and Pete had designed and built was supposed to go together.
I made a rough sketch of it all to send to Nancy in a letter.

Setting up had to be completed on Tuesday so that we could
rehearse the whole show, getting accustomed to the platform, the
changing of scenes; the dancers had to get used to the stage.

For lighting the outdoor show, we needed somebody who was willing to go up an extension ladder to the top of the twenty-foot towers,
clamp the six spotlights on to the tower, tighten them in place and
then, when we were ready, go up again to focus the spots. There was a
bunch of the guys who generally volunteered when Pete asked for
muscle but this wasn't a run of the mill muscle job. Pete's crew was on
stage when Johnny Cooper and I started our search.

"Frankly, guys," I said, "we need a volunteer who isn't afraid of heights, is a good climber and is in generally very good shape." I found my eyes settle on Sergeant Gene Nelson. I looked at Coop and he was doing the same. Gene couldn't help grinning at us. "Okay, guys, what do you want?"

Gene had long since demonstrated his physical strength, skill and balance. Besides his extraordinary athletic dancing, he had become a member of the acrobats, as a tumbler and a lifter. And, of course, he had been our hero as captain of the tug of war team aboard the S.S. *Ormonde*.

Cooper handed Gene a safety belt, a pair of gloves and an adjustable wrench. Gene put on the belt and the gloves, slipped the wrench in his pocket and picked up one of the six spotlights that Coop showed him.

"Before you go anywhere," I said, "let's show you what you have to do to focus these babies once they're mounted in place." We rehearsed Gene on that. The Leko spotlight, the best of that time, had internal shutters to shape the beam top, bottom, left and right. You could also slide the barrel holding the lens back and forth, changing the distance from lamp to lens. Gene listened to instructions from Cooper and went over it twice.

Al Gorta, Coop's assistant, carried the lights up to Gene one at a time and when Gene had them all clamped in place, Al pulled the cables up to him that carried the juice from our mobile anti-aircraft generators.

When the twelve lamps were in place and all wired, we were ready to focus. I climbed up on the stage which was bathed in the noonday sun. I positioned myself on left stage, looking toward Gene who was on the tower to stage right. "Coop, number one left front!" The top light at stage right went on. I put on my sunglasses and stared at the light. "Up a little, Gene, and to your right."

"Whoah!" Pete came out on stage and interrupted. "What are you looking at, Anderson? The sunshine is a hundred times brighter than that little spot!"

"I'm looking at the reflector, jerk! Just what you wanted me to do. Push in a little, Gene. Hold it . . . a touch higher . . . whoah! Tighten."

"How do you know how much it's covering?"

"Like this, knucklehead." I walked back and forth, watching the reflector through my sunglasses. "When I can see the lamp in the reflector, I'm going to be lit when it gets dark. Same thing up and down." I got down on the floor at the front of the stage and looked at the reflector. "I'm getting a little of it here." I got up and turned the palms of my hands to Pete. "Satisfied?"

"It'll do until dark, and then you can make a quick check. You can make corrections after the show in the dark. So what if they can't see anything on opening night?" said my favorite technical director. "Remember, this is a Broadway show, Blubber!"

I yelled, "Number two, Coop!," ignoring my skinny friend. I moved over to my next mark. Pete left me. I had six lights to cover thirty feet. The math was easy. I marked the floor with chalk where I was to stand. When we finished with that tower we did the stage left tower. We did all the focusing on stage the same way, looking into the reflectors, then we thanked Gene and let him go back to dancing and acrobatics while we crossed our fingers and waited for the sun to go down. I crossed my fingers and couldn't wait to see what I was going to get. In the Iranian sunlight, you couldn't see one damned thing where the lights were actually hitting. Opening night in Khorramshahr would be the first test.

The sun went down about six o'clock and the daylight diminished rapidly. At 7:30 our audience began to arrive in their huge trucks. Coop and I had just had a little dinner. I couldn't wait any longer.

"Coop, let's see what it looks like." He revved up the generators. While they were warming up, I went and got Gene out of the dressing room tent.

"Come on, guy! You gotta see this after all you went through today."

"Just bring them up about three points, Johnny. Let's see what happens." Gene and I walked around the side of the platform and out front where we could see what the lights were doing on the front curtain. It looked pretty good—maybe damned good! You could see a fairly even line of lights across the curtain, high enough to light a figure well back of the curtain line. Success! We went back and told Coop. "Save 'em, Coop." He pulled the switches. It was too early to give away the thrill. In another half-hour, it would be really dark and when the soldiers saw the lights come up on the front curtain and the music begin, their blood would begin to flow faster. That's when an audience starts to feel it. Hey, there's gonna be a show! Oh, boy! Out here in this Godforsaken desert look at the goddamn lights on that curtain. Man, something's gonna happen!

The benches were filled—1,900 heads facing a blue-black desert sky, a twenty-four-piece orchestra, with a lot of musicians who had played in number one bands in the States, and in front of them, baton in hand, the erect, confident back of Conductor Milton Rosenstock. Al Gorta had a front spot on Rosenstock as he split the air wide open with the overture. And above the heads of the orchestra, a golden yellow curtain, hanging in soft folds across the thirty-foot stage, a tracing in red brush strokes, the outlines of soldiers in ranks, ranging across the curtain. It was the signature motif of *This Is the Army* just as it had been seen in the New York Broadway Theatre, as President Roosevelt had seen it in the National Theater in Washington, as it was for the Royal Family in the Palladium Theater in London and indeed, in every performance of the show half way round the world.

The overture opened with the glorious sound of the band playing the theme song, "This Is the Army, Mister Jones," and then sliding plaintively into the rich violin section of the warm and loving melody of "I'm Getting Tired So I Can Sleep," and on through all the flavors and colors of every score of the show, except, of course, "Oh! How I Hate. . . ."

From then on through the whole performance, the sparkle, the bright sound, the humor, the pathos, the thrilling dancing and singing and dazzle of a Broadway production miraculously burst in front of this huge, hungering audience clustered together on the desert floor. It was unreal, as we looked around at where we were and looked up to see a midnight black sky, with stars and planets and moon, spread across the heavens.

This audience, all the audiences we gathered from the desert waste through those six weeks, were hungry for home, for surprise, for love. It would take a lot to make them care. But they cared that night and every night. They roared with laughter when Alan Manson as a blue-gowned Jane Cowl sashayed among the soldiers in the Stage Door Canteen, and they stamped and yelled their appreciation when elephantine Hank Henry, a female first sergeant, told her son-in-law Julie Oshins, home on a four-hour pass, that his pass had run out, just as he was desperately trying to get his wife, Lieutenant Bill Roerick, into the sack. And they were as quiet as deer when Earl Oxford sang "I Left My Heart at the Stage Door Canteen" and Jimmy Burrell, "I'm Getting Tired So I Can Sleep."

Mr. B. would have been proud of his show—and of his boys.

We didn't realize how extraordinary their reception of our show was until we learned about others who had been given a very different reception by these men; their behavior had reflected their anger, frustration, boredom and homesickness.

On one occasion, for instance, a well-known Hollywood heavy, with good intentions, came out on stage, glared at them and putting his hand in his pocket said, "All right, you guys, I've got a gat[1] in my pocket!" to which they did not laugh. But one of them responded loudly for all of them with, "Shove it up your ass!" And on another night, when one of our great dramatic actors started to declaim the Declaration of Independence, they rose in a body and threw him off the stage. We were told of several other such responses to entertainers who were either used to night club audiences or mistakenly thought these guys wanted patriotism shoved at them. This was why "God

1. Slang: revolver, pistol.

Bless America," one of Mr. B.'s biggest successes, was included in the Hollywood movie for civilian consumption but was never part of the stage show. Mr. B. wrote the song in 1918, for his World War I show, *Yip! Yip! Yaphank* and then decided it was not right for a soldier audience. In 1938, he pulled it out for Kate Smith to sing in a big radio show. After that, the song was published and Mr. B. gave the rights to the Boy and Girl Scouts. Once again, he started to pull it out for *TITA* and immediately decided it was inappropriate for this war, too.

Actually, we were on thin ice with the closing number of our show for all-soldier audiences — guys that had either been in combat or who were on particularly rugged, lonely duty for long stretches of time, most for two years. But by the time you had seen the whole show and reached the finale, even combat soldiers could accept Mr. B.'s determination, his reminder that the previous generation, those who fought the First World War, thought of it as the end of all wars. "This time," the song says, "we will all make certain that this time is the last time." And the mushroom clouds that would rise over Japan would not only support Irving Berlin's determination but went deep into the heart of all humanity, way beyond patriotism.

☆ ☆ ☆ ☆ ☆ ☆ ☆ ☆ ☆ ☆ ☆

With that first evening of success behind us, we knew it would all work. If the show could perform its magic even on a simple platform, out in the desert, with just a skeleton of the original scenery, with winds that blew the curtains around so that our guys occasionally had to rush onstage and hold onto them, then, once again, we were a hit. The problem now was just to keep doing it, to keep up the energy, the freshness of the jokes, the belief in the lyrics, playing those instruments — and to get from one part of Persia to the next.

Now that Pete knew how much of the production he could use on that little platform, we stored the rest of it in a warehouse in Khorramshahr. As Carl was driving Pete and me back from the warehouse, Carl said very seriously, "Pete, I've got bad news for you, kid."

"I owe you money?" Pete said.

"As Business Manager for the production, I'm afraid we'll have to cut your salary until we leave Persia."

"How the hell do you cut nothing?" Pete asked.

"You see, Pete," Carl continued, "with a little production like that, we can cut your expenses and crew in half and save a bundle."

"You'll never get away with it, Fisher. I'll call the MP's and tell them you stole this jeep."

"Good!" Carl said. "They just sent a general home from here because he built himself a house out of jeep windshields."

"I wonder what I'd have to steal to get home?" I asked.

"First Sergeant, if you don't start feeding us better, they should court martial you."

"You told me to lose weight," I said.

"I told you to lose weight. Guys who work need food!"

The trouble was, the merchant marines on the Liberty ship had spoiled us. We weren't used to C-rations. Besides, Pete was irritable. He could see what was coming: put up the show, take it down, load the trucks, stay up all night—and then eat cold corned beef hash fresh from the can. Sure enough, when we finished the five days in Khorramshahr, we had to strike the show and load trucks immediately after the last show. We ate what was called breakfast at 1:00 a.m., boarded trucks at 2:00 and arrived in Ahwaz at 4:40 a.m. in a howling sandstorm. We set up cots in barracks and slept through the storm, ate a meal at 12:45 p.m., which might logically have been lunch but they called it dinner, then worked on setting up until 6 p.m. As we hit the sack that night, Pete caught me making notes for the Morning Report. "Okay, Anderson, I give up. What day is it?" I looked at my notes. "Monday," I said. "When do we open?" Pete asked. I thought I'd better get this right. I checked again. "Tuesday," I said. "Good," he said and fell into bed.

It was an outdoor theater again with 1,900 seats, rows of wooden benches about as basic as possible. They'd had a lot of abuse in two years, as had everything in the Persian Gulf Command.

Setting up got easier and easier. The lighting was working fine for Coop and me and our peerless tumbler-dancer-pole climber, Gene. In Ahwaz, we did four shows, Tuesday through Friday, then the crew went into the same twenty-four-hour turnaround: strike the show, load the trucks, leave at midnight. The rest of the company left on Saturday, September 30 at 7 a.m. and arrived at Andimeshk three hours later. The crew worked at setting up and that evening we were able to do the focusing in the dark. We were so used to doing it in the sunlight that it seemed like cheating.

While we finished setting up on Sunday most of the detachment went on a tour of a neighboring village called Dizful, otherwise known as the City of the Blind. We had to set up in an outdoor theater of 2,500 seats, the biggest we'd been in. Our sound man had to turn up the amplifier to the limit. The troops loved us.

Monday, the rest of us toured Dizful and found out why it got its name. Approaching the so-called city we encountered a long meandering stream, one bank of which was gouged out, forming hundreds of caves cut deep into the mountainside by the river's action. Many of the caves went back for great distances. In the dark, foul air were hundreds of people in the big caves. They were not totally blind, but eye diseases were widespread. Of those who could see, many could not focus.

Dizful was also noted for being "the hottest place in the world" by virtue of being the hottest city in Persia. In the summer, temperatures were known to get to 170 degrees in the open desert. Even in September, when we were there, it was common to reach 140 degrees in the sun. In the winter, many of the residents ventured into the cold wearing blindfolds to protect their eyes from the painful experience of daylight.

Our guides told us that the birthrate was high. Women averaged twenty-five pregnancies but only three or four babies would survive childbirth. Of those who lived to wander the streets, naked, many with swollen, distorted stomachs, like pregnant pygmies, few lived to be adults.

Our MP guide took us to a cave where they were smoking opium, which they offered us as we walked past.

"They can squat that way for hours, perfectly happy," the MP told us. "A pipe full costs them about nine cents. That much in the States would cost you about forty-eight bucks." He stopped us before we got far. "A bunch of GI's came here without us and went in too far. We never found a trace of them."

As we headed for the trucks, a skinny native boy offered to jump from a high cave into the river for five rials, about fifteen cents. Danny Longo gave him the money and off he went. We watched him climb up to a ledge about sixty feet above the water and jump into the stream. He climbed out, grinning and laughing with his hand out, begging to do it again.

As our trucks began pulling away, and as happens in every Persian town, crowds of children ran behind us shouting and screaming for money.

This was our last chance to sightsee until we reached Teheran (as it was then spelled). As we drove north, we saw the wildlife that lives in the desert—wild boar, foxes, gazelles and jackals. A sad sport for some of the soldiers when they had time off, was to tear across open desert in a jeep or small truck shooting at the gazelles, sometimes killing them, sometimes just wounding the poor devils. It was an unhappy indication of their boredom.

We played two shows at each of the next four camps—pronouncing them reminded me of mashed potatoes: Andimeshk, Khurramabad, Hamadan, Kazvin. Almost half the audience were British and Russian soldiers. The ground was higher and the desert heat lessened with each move northward.

The last miles to Teheran over great mountains were a geologist's delight. The mountains gave us our first green in Persia—trees, vegetation, mountain flowers.

Our truck convoy had left Camp Stalingrad, Kazvin at 8 a.m. October 13. At noon, we were entering Teheran, the first modern city we'd seen in Persia. We were gaping at the almost total contrast with the rest of the country. There were still a few destitute and sick people in evidence, but they were a scattered intrusion. Well-dressed affluence dominated much of the city. Many buildings were new, many of the cars late models — German, French, British, mostly small, a few bigger Mercedes or Peugeots. We saw colorful bazaars and very inviting food stands. Poverty and illness had been pushed aside into other parts of the old city to make way for the wealth of the country, to give them room to enjoy the money that flowed out of the ground, black oil turning into gold for the powerful few.

Our convoy kept rolling and we were soon out of the city center and into another mashed potato name, Camp Amirabad. This was where the Persian rulers and British power and wealth had established the military center of the country. We were pleased to find we were billeted in an Army Service Club in two huge rooms and were playing in an outdoor theater with benches for an audience of 2,400. We had the weekend to set up our show, which was more than enough time, thus giving us time to explore Teheran.

It appeared that the first economic law of the ancient city of Teheran, and indeed of many ancient communities in the third world, was that it have available a river or stream supplying it with water. Water flowing downward through a city affords clean water upstream. As the affluence of the residents diminishes step by step downstream, so does the quality of the water. They use it for drinking, cooking, bathing, washing and finally as sewage disposal. The poorest live at the bottom of the river in filth and shacks, or simply lying on the ground. And so it was in the capital city of Persia, or what we now know of as Iran.

We discovered, too, that with the concentration of money in Teheran there were many good shops and restaurants, although the sight of an American Army uniform seemed to raise the prices dramatically.

Rosie was pawing a belt with a nice silver buckle. There was no tag on it. He held it up to the storekeeper. "How much?"

"I give you good price. Two hundred American dollars. Real silver."

"You're kidding!"

"No. No kid. This one only one hundred." He pointed to a plain belt with what looked like a brass buckle.

Rosie dropped the silver belt and after pricing some belts and shoes turned to us. "I think I'll buy a couple of sheets and get Tony Paglia to make me a costume,"

"Why don't you trade in your Algerian cape?" Carl asked him.

Rosie gave him a look of utter disbelief. "Never!" he said and led the way out of the store.

☆ ☆ ☆ ☆ ☆ ☆ ☆ ☆ ☆ ☆ ☆

We were startled by a brief notice on the bulletin board on the morning of the opening performance:

> LIEUTENANT DANIELS ON TEMPORARY DUTY TO HEADQUARTERS,
> PERSIAN GULF COMMAND.

I went to the Major. "I don't know any more than you do. Marc came to me an hour ago and showed me an order which just said he should report to Command. So I said, well, you better get on over there and find out what they want. He's gonna let me know."

Everybody was busy getting ready for the opening so I never had a chance to investigate. Marc wasn't around that night when the show opened. The 2,400 seats were filled. Again the audience was almost half British and Russian, and the response wildly enthusiastic. Obviously, a Broadway musical variety show was a unique experience even in the capital city. On the other hand, in order to amuse our detachment, we showed them a movie at 10:15. When they had finished entertaining others, they were delighted to watch Pin Up Girl. I can't remember what it was like now. The title is not promising, it doesn't appear in historical references, but our guys were hungry for any distraction.

The next morning, Swampy called me into his office and handed me a telegraph copy of an official Army order.

> FIRST LIEUTENANT MARC DANIELS IS RELEASED FROM
> ASSIGNMENT AND DUTY WITH THIS IS THE ARMY DETACHMENT
> AND TRANSFERRED TO HEADQUARTERS, PERSIAN GULF
> COMMAND. THE SIGNATURE WAS, MAJOR GENERAL
> DONALD H. CONNOLLY, ON THE AUTHORITY OF THE WAR
> DEPARTMENT.

This could mean anything. The order could have come from the European commander, General Eisenhower, or it could have come from Washington.

Ben and John knew nothing about it. It appeared that either Marc was transferred as the result of his own application for a change in assignment, or perhaps—and many thought this more likely—that Mr. B. was behind it, thinking that it would be safer if Marc were not in a position to cause another Naples fiasco.

Bob Sidney had his own theory. "He couldn't have done it on his own. He would have needed a recommendation and who would give him one?"

I said, "He knew he wasn't going to get any further staying with us."

"But if he just wanted a transfer, he was trained as an infantry officer. He'd be sent right into combat," Pete said.

"Maybe," I said. I thought he'd been completely wrong in his behavior in Naples but I hoped he'd be all right. He and Meg had been good friends of Nancy's and mine once.

We never heard from him, but I saw him in Hollywood after the war when I was touring with a show. He told me he had requested the transfer.

"When we were in Italy, after the debacle with Bob Sidney, I met a guy in Fifth Army Headquarters who tried to get me to transfer to his special unit. He needed someone with infantry training who had been a teacher. The job with him was to give replacement troops some special training. It wasn't mainly technical—it was attitude, to make them more useful officers when they went into combat. I turned him down at first, but then he contacted me in Khorramshahr and I said yes. I didn't enjoy working on the show with Bob. The orders came through a month later. It was a great job and I got promotions which I never would have had with Berlin."

Without Marc, it meant more administrative work for Swampy and John.

☆ ☆ ☆ ☆ ☆ ☆ ☆ ☆ ☆ ☆ ☆

We played five shows in Teheran and every seat was filled. That meant we had played to 12,000 people in five days. The last show had in its audience an extraordinary gathering of high ranking representatives of the Allied forces: Mikhail A. Maximov, Soviet ambassador to Iran; Major General Ivan Kravgin, Chief Soviet Transportation Director; Leland B. Morris, American ambassador to Iran; Sir Reader Bullard, British ambassador to Iran; Mohammed Saed, Prime Minister of Iran, representing the Shah; and, of course, Major General Donald H. Connolly, Commanding General of the Persian Gulf Command. After the show they all came backstage and made speeches, expressing their appreciation in such glowing terms and variety of languages and accents that it was very like a meeting of what would later be the United Nations. We shifted from one foot to the other, trying to keep smiling politely.

We were happy to hear Staff Sergeant Ford Carr speak on behalf of the enlisted men drivers who had taken us through all of Iran. "Basically, my guys said working with your outfit was the best time they've had in two years! And I second the motion!" That meant more to us than everything we heard from all the brass.

The next morning we took down the show, loaded everything on trucks, had dinner, watched a Hollywood offering, *Till We Meet Again*, had a good night's sleep, and loaded the show and ourselves onto a special train for the short trip to Arak. The rail bed was smooth, the train was comfortable and fast. Obviously the government had invested a lot of their oil in an efficient railroad system.

After a brief lunch stop in Qom at 11:05, we detrained in Arak at 4 p.m., unloaded and set up the show in their outdoor theater which held only 1,200 people, half the size of Teheran. After two shows in Arak, Monday and Tuesday nights, again with Russian and British troops making up about half our audiences, we took down and loaded the show as usual and boarded the train again for the long ride south to the blistering heat of Khorramshahr, where we arrived on October 26 at 7:00 a.m.

Royal Opera House

Cairo.

IRVING BERLIN'S

"THIS IS THE ARMY"

Gala Performance

Thursday 17th August 1944.

*in aid of the Mohamed Aly El-Kabir and the
Red Crescent Societies.*

Chapter 21

THE WAR

— Oct 24, 1944: In the Philippines, US 1st Cavalry Division units cross
from Leyte to Samur. Complex battle ends in sinking of most of
Japanese naval strength.

— Oct 26, 1944: US sinks three more Japanese cruisers. Decisive epic
battle. US Navy has no more serious opposition in the Pacific.

— Oct 27, 1944: During next few days about 100 Japanese aircraft are
destroyed at bases in Luzon.

The train was rumbling through the longest tunnels I've ever seen,
under the many mountain ranges from Teheran to the center of the
country where it all flattened to desert. Of course, they didn't have to
pay much for their labor, but the engineering must have been incredibly difficult.

The foursome was together as usual. The subject: where we were
going and how we were getting there. How does one get from
Khorramshahr, Persia, to Australia? Pete was at his disputatious best.
"You keep telling me we've got a great library, Blubber. Do we have any
maps? An atlas, for instance?"

"Don't ask me, Skinny. I'm just a dumb top kick. Our librarian is sitting right behind you."

Pete turned on our librarian-baritone, Private First Class Bill Aubin
with his bully voice. "I suppose all our maps are in the baggage car just
when we need them, dummkopf."

"Just a minute, mein Herr," Bill said in his genuine middle-European
accent.

"I'm Czechoslovakian, goddamn it, not German."

"I was speaking Austrian, Sergeant." As he said this, he was pulling
an International Atlas out of a large knapsack. He opened it to Persia
for Pete and laid it on his lap. Pete managed to twist his appreciation

into a barb for authority. "Why the hell isn't this guy a sergeant, Anderson!"

We spent the next half-hour studying the atlas, tracing our route. Pete narrated.

"Down through the bloody hot Persian Gulf again, across here—the top of the Arabian Sea—and look, that's just the north end of the Indian Ocean. There's Bombay! That's where we wait for a ship to Australia. And then we go way the hell down and all the way around Australia. Christ is that the best we can do? The whole south shore of Australia and then up the east coast to Sydney and then to Brisbane? Do we stop in Sydney?"

"I think so. We have to buy some stuff there, and then we get off this ship in Brisbane."

Swampy walked by at that moment. Pete looked up.

"Major, how long do we spend in Bombay?"

"I wish I could tell you, Pete. The cable I got from Washington says we go to Bombay and wait for a troopship that has room for us. Nobody's got a timetable." He smiled at his joke.

"Well, I've got a lot of work to do just crating everything for the ship before we leave for Bombay. And there's more I should do before we start playing again."

"You may have plenty of time," Swampy said. "We don't do any shows in India, except maybe hospital shows, and we'll try to get you anything you need. I'll promise you one thing, Pete: waiting in Bombay will be better than waiting in Khorramshahr." And he left Pete with another smile.

The train ride to Khorramshahr took twenty-four hours. The train had no dining car. We made one hour stops at Army camps for lunch and then for dinner—first at Doroud, then at the best mashed potato sound of all, Andimeshk.

We pulled into Khorramshahr at 7 a.m. on October 26, and the Port Command told us we were booked to leave for Bombay on the S.S. *Sontay*, a British transport, on Tuesday, the 31st. That gave us six days to repair and crate everything for the voyage to Bombay.

We weren't giving shows. That gave Swampy a chance to be in charge. Every rifle had to be cleaned, oiled and packed.

Pete was in the middle of the crating job when I checked in on him.

"Anderson!" he roared. "I hope you've got plenty of money. These crates are falling apart. Busted casters. Every time they lower the crates into a ship or out again, they manage to break something."

"You keep telling me you win at poker. Buy some casters."

"Screw you. Anything I win at poker goes to the Feller Foundation."

☆ ☆ ☆ ☆ ☆ ☆ ☆ ☆ ☆ ☆ ☆

At 1 a.m. on October 31, we started loading everything on board the S.S. *Sontay*, which could only be called a troop ship instead of a freighter because they had put hammocks in the two forward holds. To eat, we had to take down our hammocks, put up tables and carry the food from the galley. We spent most of our time taking things down and putting things up. There were eight hundred fifty other passengers, all members of the US 352nd Engineers. This gave the cooks over one thousand mouths to feed every day, plus ship's crew and officers.

We were traveling in convoy again and had two very slow ships with us. There was no room to do laundry so we saved that for Bombay. Before the nine days were up, we got to be a pretty grungy lot.

It was a crowded ship with little room for activity. We gave daily afternoon shows in the only open space on board: the forward deck. The shows were a double blessing. As they were on so many occasions, they gave the audiences something to do and they did the same for us.

At 2:35 p.m. on the fifth day, our destroyer escort alerted us to put on life jackets and go to boat stations. The escorts dropped depth charges and remained in the area for about twenty minutes. We kept staring at the water. Our escort rejoined us; no oil slicks were reported.

We had another submarine alert the next day. Again no torpedoes and nothing surfaced. Seven days out the captain announced over the loudspeakers that the two slow ships were leaving the convoy and going in to Karachi. We immediately increased the convoy speed and everybody cheered. Crawling along had made us feel like sitting ducks.

On Day 9, all passengers cheerfully stowed their hammocks and we exchanged our money for rupees.

☆ ☆ ☆ ☆ ☆ ☆ ☆ ☆ ☆ ☆ ☆

Bombay is at the end of a peninsula, with the Arabian Sea on the west and south. To the east is the Bombay Harbor. Seven or eight miles of water lie between the mainland of India and the eastern side of the peninsula where we landed. As the S.S. *Sontay* rounded the south end of the peninsula, it then turned northward into Alexandra Dock in Bombay Harbor at 12:45 p.m. with the sun shining brightly. We stared in amazement at the richness of the scene: beautiful ships and sailboats and handsome buildings along the shoreline. After six weeks of the squalor, disease and heat of Persia, I had been prepared for the squalor of India. There is plenty of it, but we didn't have a chance to see that side of the ancient country. What we saw was the reflected wealth of the British Empire and the mystery and grandeur of India, old and new.

Lieutenant Koenig, who had flown ahead to arrange our quarters, came on board in his customary mood, bringing a pile of mail.

"Greetings, kiddies! I hope you've been saving your money. While we wait for a ship to Australia, relax and enjoy Bombay. It's a rich city, with great shops and dandy restaurants. You can spend all the money you have and more. However," and he lowered his voice and abandoned his frivolous tone, "one serious reminder: While we're here, *do not* reveal our identity from now until we reach New Guinea and start giving shows. You're just an infantry outfit on your way home. News travels fast in this part of the world and now that we've left Axis Sally, we've got Tokyo Rose looking for us. Otherwise," he said, "you might as well enjoy yourself. Besides the shopping and eating, the Bombay race track is a gem, with spectacular horses and elegant Indian women strolling in the rich green grass in their splendid saris, with smart, open sandals and brilliant red toenails!"

"Cut it out, Lieutenant, you're makin' me horny!" Rosie said.

Pete broke in. "Before they start looking for broads, Johnny, I've got news for them. We've got plenty of work to do."

"Peter," John replied, "don't be such a party-poop. At least give them something to look forward to."

"Just check the bulletin board for your name. The party-poop needs a big work crew for the rest of the afternoon. So if your name's on the list, forget about the red toenails for a couple of days."

"Any news about Berlin's schedule?" I asked.

"I don't think we'll hear 'til we get closer to the Pacific," Johnny said.

"That's too bad. I think it would buck them up. I know it would buck me up."

The crew began unloading everything from the ship into trucks. The rest of the outfit boarded British Army trucks for the short drive to our quarters, the British transit camp in Colaba, a suburb of Bombay, way at the south end of the peninsula.

☆ ☆ ☆ ☆ ☆ ☆ ☆ ☆ ☆ ☆

Everyone, including the officers, was in tents. The daily schedule was posted on a bulletin board outside of the Orderly Room tent. We paid some native dobies, as the British called them, to catch up with our laundry. They did a great job. The British had trained them well.

To keep the guys from going berserk with all the free time, we had daily formations at 10 a.m., daily inspections, regular workouts, regular care of equipment, including the gun-cleaning chore and cleaning of all our gear. We didn't want to get caught looking slovenly in case some local GI commander dropped in. That still left most of the afternoons and evenings free, except for Pete's crew.

Johnny was right about the shops in Bombay. A lot of packages were being mailed home from our outfit, items that were great gifts to American wives and sweethearts—beautiful leather sandals, saris, bracelets, rings—a vast assortment of Indian artifacts. And then there were the restaurants. Of course, we all went often to the ones that served steak—a forbidden food for the native citizenry, but a big treat for us. When we drove into Bombay in our jeep we discovered we had to watch carefully for the sacred cows who had the right of way no matter how long it took them to cross an intersection.

The most popular picture postcard view of Bombay is the "Gateway to India," similar but smaller than the Arc de Triomphe in Paris. The gateway was the arch through which the new viceroy or members of the British royal family would walk when they arrived in Bombay. Directly opposite was Green's Hotel, known for the most elegant dinners in the city. The cocktail terrace of Green's afforded the best view of the beautiful harbor. Pete, Rosie, Carl and I grabbed the jeep several times and splurged for a cocktail hour and dinner.

☆ ☆ ☆ ☆ ☆ ☆ ☆ ☆ ☆ ☆ ☆

Johnny took me aside coming out of the Orderly Room. "How are the guys taking it? It's a long time without shows."

"For the most part, they're enjoying the city. Mostly they're okay. I worry about Barclift," I said.

"There's nothing we can do for him. He's been bitter about Bob dominating the show from the beginning. He wanted a bigger role.

"What worries me is I think he picked up some pretty heavy stuff somewhere. He seems to be half there at times."

"Really? Lordy, I just hope he doesn't overdose or something. He could really make a mess for us. Can you talk to him?"

☆ ☆ ☆ ☆ ☆ ☆ ☆ ☆ ☆ ☆ ☆

I found Eddie Barclift at breakfast next morning. He was all by himself in a corner of the mess hall. I took a cup of coffee and sat down next to him.

"How're you doing?"

"Oh, I'm all right."

"Do me a favor, Eddie."

"What?"

"Don't take any chances. This isn't forever, you know, and you've got a whole fuckin' life ahead of you."

"Don't worry about me, baby. I won't do anything foolish. I just can't stand being altogether . . . connected. I can handle it better if I can be somewhere else."

"Okay—as long as you can handle it. There are a lot of us who care about you."

He didn't say anything for a minute. "Thanks. Don't worry. I'll be careful." And then he smiled a little. "I promise."

Bob Sidney caught up with me when I was leaving the mess.

"What did she want?" he said with some disgust. "Bitching about me?"

"He never mentioned your name."

"So what *did* he call me?"

I laughed in spite of myself. "Bob, for Christ's sake, you know he has a tough time. Rise above it, babe. As long as he does his job."

"Don't worry. Deep down, I'm a very sympathetic person."

I couldn't help smiling at that. Actually, it was quite true. Bob constantly covered his sentimentality with sarcasm. Barclift's problem was too much idle time, too little challenge. But when he was onstage, when he was working, he was fine.

On Sunday, November 19, our tenth day in India, we gave our only entertainment in Bombay: a special show at the US Station Hospital for about four hundred patients and staff. As usual, getting a reaction from an audience made everybody who was involved feel better. Unfortunately, it only involved a few of the guys.

We got a bag of mail on the following Saturday, November 25. There was a letter in it from Mr. B. addressed to "All the guys in 'This Is the Army.'" Swampy asked me to read it to everyone before lunch on Sunday if it was good news. I took a quick peep at it. It was perfect.

> "Dear Boys: I have been hearing great things about your performances in Egypt and in Persia. You have been commended highly by Washington for the work you've been doing, including the hospital shows you've given in your spare time and the radio show you did in Persia. Incidentally, King Farouk sent word to the President praising the show in the Cairo Opera House. I wish I could have been with you. I've just received a message from the White House thanking me for what you did. So I thank you, too.
>
> I have plans to meet you in New Guinea and I may even beat you there because I've discovered a quicker means of transportation than you're using.
>
> My best to you all. Sincerely, Mr. B."

I hardly got the last word out before there was a roar from the guys and then applause. At moments like that, I was reminded that Mr. B. had one hundred sixty-five men under his control, in partnership with Uncle Sam. This letter at that moment was a unique tonic. I posted it on the bulletin board. We noticed that the guys kept stopping to read it again for the next couple of days. Rosie, Carl and I were walking past the bulletin board on the way from the mess hall two days later. Rosie looked at the letter and chuckled.

"Funny thing, I haven't heard anybody bitch about anything for two whole days! You'd think it was the second coming!" We laughed, because although I had doubts about how much faith any of us had in the second coming, we sure as hell weren't bitching either, except maybe Pete who tended to thrive on complaint. Or maybe he didn't want to lose his identity.

He'd say things like, "Why the hell can't Washington come up with a few more ratings, especially for my guys. You're the First Sergeant—do something! Get 'em off my back!"

I looked for Eddie Barclift. He was sitting in the sun, reading a letter. "Hey, Boobalah. Any word from Cole?" I don't know how long Eddie had been living with Cole Porter, but it was the only family he ever mentioned. And, of course, it was because Cole Porter and Irving Berlin were good friends that Eddie was assured a role in the show.

He smiled, "Yeah, pretty good. You know Cole gets depressed for long stretches. He's never without pain entirely. But he has good periods, too."

"Good," I said. "I got a couple of good letters from Nancy."

"Good," Eddie said. He put his hand on my arm, "Hey, don't worry about me. I'm okay."

☆ ☆ ☆ ☆ ☆ ☆ ☆ ☆ ☆ ☆ ☆

The next few days and nights went quickly, and suddenly, it was time to load the show onto the comparatively huge S.S. *General H. W. Butner*, a US Navy Transport, and set sail for Australia.

Since the letter from Mr. B., the morale was high. We were nearing the reality of what General Eisenhower had promised on the stage of Her Majesty's Theatre in London eight months earlier: we were getting closer to the guys who were fighting the Pacific war.

☆ ☆ ☆ ☆ ☆ ☆ ☆ ☆ ☆ ☆ ☆

Our ship departed Bombay's Alexandra Docks at 3:30 p.m., Friday, December 1, 1944, bound for Brisbane, Australia. It would be a twenty-one-day voyage, and as we had discovered from the International

Atlas (thanks to Bill Aubin and our traveling library), would take us 9,000 miles.

Our travel direction, mostly southeast until it curled eastward and then very briefly north, would take us through temperatures first very warm as we approached and crossed the equator, then cooling considerably as we reached the 44th southern parallel.

But, where was the war in the Pacific? Not in Australia. Bits of news came to us through the ship's officers. The US 32nd Division was having trouble on the island of Leyte, in the Philippines. Our huge new bombers, the B-29's, were hitting Tokyo. The planes must be based somewhere. The Navy was scattered everywhere. Our submarines were sinking Japanese warships. Word was, we sank their aircraft carrier Junyo in the China Sea and another one near Formosa. All of our Army, Marines, Navy and Air Force had bases. In other words, US service men and women were scattered all over the Pacific.

"But, Pete, how would we get to all these scattered groups? We can't wait for convoys. We can't fly the show."

"Stop wondering, Anderson! We'll find out soon enough."

"One vision I have of us is on LCM's."

"Landing Crafts? The whole show?"

"Maybe a fleet of them."

Temporarily, the answer to our question was postponed. Captain C. S. Isgrig, commander of the *Butner*, said he would be very grateful if we could provide some entertainment throughout the voyage. So we worked out a schedule similar to the one on the *Monarch of Bermuda*: two shows every evening and small units in various parts of the ship every day.

There was an announcement on Monday, December 4, 1944 at 10:35 a.m. over the loud speakers that we were crossing the equator. Nothing happened. There was no bump or sound. No celebration. It was smooth as anything.

"I think the brass should have popped a cork or something," Rosie said. "After all, we're crossing the fuckin' equator! We should be drinking champagne!" But that was it. Not even a 3.2 beer.

On my twenty-seventh birthday, Saturday, December 9, at 6:15 a.m., just as we were getting up, the ship's engines stopped and then reversed. We went out on deck and discovered that a Chinese student—actually an Air Force Cadet pilot on the way to the US—had fallen overboard. They had to lower a lifeboat to rescue him. Underway once more, we were at breakfast when I pointed out that the cadet had obviously gotten drunk in my honor, which was more than I could say for my travel companions.

"Jesus, Blubber, you're not only fat, you're getting old," Pete said.

"Never mind doing anything special," I said. "Just a cake and a little ice cream. You can skip the champagne."

Suddenly, all the ship's guns started firing. The sound was impressive.

"At least the captain remembered!" I said. I started to get up. Immediately, the ship's loud speakers crackled and a voice came on.

"As you were! That was a practice firing. There is no emergency."

"Sit down and eat, Blubber! We'll buy you a drink in Sydney."

☆ ☆ ☆ ☆ ☆ ☆ ☆ ☆ ☆ ☆ ☆

On December 18, as we pulled into the docks at Sydney, patrol planes flew over the harbor, checking all ship movements. Obviously we were now in Tokyo Rose's territory.

The next day, Ben Washer, Carl Fisher and I went ashore on temporary duty to purchase things needed for the show while the ship headed north for Brisbane. We had a list of electrical equipment, makeup and other miscellany to find. The three of us would then all fly to Milne Bay, New Guinea, to meet the detachment.

Carl and I checked into the American Red Cross facilities. Ben found a hotel. We spent the next few days shopping. Christmas was coming and we were hungry for mail, waiting to connect with Mr. B. and to find out how we would travel the Pacific. The detachment would be in Brisbane by now, and loading onto the Navy Transport

U.S.S. *General Mann*, for the short voyage to Milne Bay. Calling from Brisbane, Holmgren reached me at the ARC and said I had been chosen to fly up to Finschhafen, New Guinea, to board our new ship.

"What new ship, sir?"

"I don't know much about it, Alan. I just received orders that they've found a ship we can use to take the show all over the Pacific."

"And I'm going to be the first to travel on her?"

"Looks like it."

The Major gave me all the directions to find the ship in Finschhafen.

"You just deliver these orders to the captain and sail back down to Milne Bay, where Pete will have to remodel the ship so we can all live on it."

Ben ran into an officer friend who invited us all to a Christmas Eve party. We accepted. We drank a lot, feeling sorry for the guys in the company who were looking forward to a turkey-less Christmas. We drank to Mr. B., hoping he would join us soon. I drank to my wife and son. When we ran out of people to drink to, we just drank.

Carl and I spent Christmas with the Red Cross. It wasn't exactly like being home but we had turkey and a glass of red wine.

On December 26, the day before taking off for Finschhafen, I talked to Holmgren, who said the whole detachment had been screwed out of the 11 a.m. Christmas dinner the Red Cross had prepared for them in Brisbane. It seems the port of embarkation guys wanted more time for *their* Christmas. Our orders mysteriously changed. We had to board the General Mann at 8 a.m.

The detachment ended up with a tasteless beef stew on board the U.S.S. *Mann* at 4:00 p.m., while our officers shared a turkey dinner with the ship's officers. Merry Christmas!

☆ ☆ ☆ ☆ ☆ ☆ ☆ ☆ ☆ ☆ ☆

On December 27, I flew to Finschhafen and went aboard a very plain little freighter named *El Libertador*. The ship, destined to be our home for several months, had been leased from the Dutch East Indies Maritime Office by the US Navy, after discussions between Washington and Mr. B.

The Dutch captain greeted me at the dock, and speaking relatively good English showed me around the ship, assigned me a cabin, gave me a good lunch and informed me that they would be fueled and ready to leave at 5:30 the next morning for Milne Bay.

Pete had loaned me a one hundred-foot steel tape and a clipboard. I spent the afternoon wandering about the ship, having been informed that I could go anywhere except into the Indonesian crew quarters in the stern. That was their domain. I drew diagrams of the ship's deck, examined the cabins that the captain said would be available to us, and then examined and measured the two forward holds. Clearly it would be a challenge to Pete to make these dank caverns habitable. Once he had built a stairway, painted the interior white and built enough bunks in tiers, he would have to install lights, air ducts and fans. He would also have to leave room for the storage of the production. The freighter's cranes would be necessary to handle the unloading and loading of the show. It was going to be a challenge, even for Pete Feller!

The distinctive aroma of curry grew stronger as I went further aft. I climbed the ladders to the gun turrets, both port and starboard, introduced myself to the US Navy gunners in each turret. They seemed happy to know there would be Yanks aboard and I said I was glad there were to be Navy gunners protecting us all. I didn't ask them if they felt capable of holding off the Japanese Navy.

After my dinner with the ship's officers, I wrote a short letter to Nancy, describing my whereabouts in vague terms, phrased to avoid the censor's pen.

I awoke at 5:15 a.m. to the clanking of a winch. They fed me royally with melon, boiled eggs, ham, toast and coffee as we chugged out to sea.

I learned how to pronounce the Dutch names of Captain Voss and his chief officer, G. H. Van Hoope. They were very friendly and full of questions about *TITA* and Mr. Irving Berlin, the great songwriter. It was going to be quite a change for them, instead of hauling freight and having no one to talk to except each other. I discovered that Dutch officers did not converse with their Indonesian crews.

It was a very relaxing trip, without incident until the third and last day. It was close to noon, we were in open ocean, out of sight of land. I was up on the bridge, enjoying the breeze. Captain Voss called me over to the port side and then pulled me back into the shadow of the bridge cabin.

"I don't want him to think we are interested in him. Now you can look." He handed me his binoculars, pointing to a small object far to port. I looked at it with his glasses. I kept trying to see details. It looked like a submarine plunging through the waves, not moving very fast, floating deep, most of the hull submerged.

"Isn't that a submarine?"

"Oh, yes. Fortunately, he is not interested in us."

"It's Japanese?" I asked in alarm.

"Of course."

"Shouldn't we go further away from him?"

"If he thought we were worth a torpedo he would probably go under, run closer and let one go! I'd rather he'd just sail along lazily watching us. I'm quite sure he would not give away his position just to go after us."

I remembered hearing that the ship was chosen for us because it would not be worth wasting a torpedo to blow it out of the water.

The submarine kept up the same pace, going north. Finally, we could see him no more.

Two hours later we slowed our engines and drifted toward the Milne Bay harbor. I felt relieved to be near a friendly port. That submarine had given me a chill.

☆ ☆ ☆ ☆ ☆ ☆ ☆ ☆ ☆ ☆

Mr. B. was so anxious to see the little ship he had worked so hard to get for us to live on that he was standing on the dock as we slid alongside and I stepped off. We hadn't seen each other since he had left us in Bari, Italy, five months ago.

When I stepped on the dock, he put out his hand and grasped mine with both hands, smiling warmly.

"The last Andersons I saw were Nancy and young Alan. He's a handsome boy. I wish you could have been with me—"

"Me, too."

"She misses you. I hope it's not too long before you're together." He gave my arm a squeeze and I put my hand on his, struggling for composure. I had the feeling it was not easy for him to demonstrate emotion.

I pulled myself together enough to smile. "It's already been too long."

A moment later, my pals showed up and Pete managed to change the atmosphere with his greeting.

"Where the hell did you get this thing, Blubber?"

"Never mind! This *thing* seems to float—and it's all yours!"

"Thanks a lot!"

☆ ☆ ☆ ☆ ☆ ☆ ☆ ☆ ☆ ☆ ☆

When we all got to the theater in Milne Bay, Jus and Hayden caught me up on what had happened in my absence.

Ben had found a brief story in the Brisbane paper about Mr. Irving Berlin who had been "entertaining wounded troops at the hospitals in New Guinea and was expected to join up with his show in the next few days."

That joining had taken place on December 30, while I was at sea, when the detachment arrived on the S.S. *General Mann*. Mr. B. was at the dock to meet them also.

"Mr. B. gave every one of his boys a warm greeting," Jus said.

"Warm?" said Hayden, the more effusive of my two assistants, "Half the guys were all choked up! I mean it was like father and sons meeting after all this time."

☆ ☆ ☆ ☆ ☆ ☆ ☆ ☆ ☆ ☆ ☆

Pete and his crew went to work on our modest little ship, making the holds habitable and putting counters and cupboards on the main deck, so that our newly assigned Army cooks could serve us three meals a day.

Pete's improvements took eleven days. While this was going on, we continued to give shows. We played for thousands of Allied service men and women that were stationed all over this east end of New Guinea—US, British, Australian—nurses, Red Cross, WAC's. We did short shows and long shows. The audiences were huge and hungry for us—thousands, from every imaginable service; 8,000 one day, 10,000 the next. These shows were all unscheduled, arranged within hours, put on just anywhere they could gather an audience. Give Rosie room for his whole band, no scenery, nothing but a platform to stand on. We had no place to put on makeup or costumes. We had no sleep, no time to set up. Sudden rains would pour for a few minutes and then stop. The dancers could hardly find a dry place to put on dance shoes and get onto whatever platform existed. It was madness. They didn't care what we looked like, they just wanted to hear the orchestra and the singers and the jokes and the songs and Mr. B. And Mr. B kept going and going, acting as though he were ten years younger, he drew such energy from the joyous response he got from these audiences.

January 2, 1945. From a letter to Nancy:

> This is the first letter I've written this year. Two letters from you came bouncing in today, full of love. But I must talk about the commonplace things that are around me. We've begun giving shows under impossible difficulties—small stages out in the

open with thousands of boys on the benches, on the ground, in trees or trucks—trying to give them a Broadway show out of nothing, our guys hovering around a lantern in a small tent, putting on makeup and costumes without seeing, me running up homemade ladders focusing what lights we can operate fifteen minutes before overture. All sorts of hurried measures by everyone to do as much show as possible. And the amazing thing is, it is a Broadway show and they go crazy watching it. God, they shout and laugh and beat their hands in applause and our boys play as they never played. I haven't written for days, busy keeping the frantic guys calm and the bewildered ones confident—and Berlin reassured. I haven't been able to think, nor has anyone. Meanwhile, there's been New Year's Eve with us apart again. The only good things I can tell you are that with the sympathy we feel for the boys who are fighting or have fought or will fight, I am so grateful when they pour out their appreciation of this show. It gives it just that much more point to be doing it at all. There is nothing more terrible to undergo than three years on one of these Pacific islands. I can't conceive of how they've borne it. Most of them have done so and then they turn to us and say, 'Christ, I'd hate to have to knock around the way you guys do, never having any kind of base, always going somewhere, never knowing where.' God, they're sorry for us! Then I realize how lucky we are. I always seem to come back to that if I talk enough, don't I? The most amazing thing happened on New Year's Eve. We've all been together for two and half years and most of the time we're pretty bored with each other, but after the show we pooled our beer ration and had a party—just the company—and in our common loneliness we worked up such a tremendous feeling of friendship, everyone felt grateful for the warmth and cheerfulness that came out of it. It sounds sentimental—and as a matter fact, that's what it was.

☆ ☆ ☆ ☆ ☆ ☆ ☆ ☆ ☆ ☆ ☆

The eleven days ended. The squat little *El Libertador* was ready. We loaded the production and the whole detachment into our own private ship and began our island to island life. Mr. B. moved into a cabin for this first leg, one hundred fifty guys moved into their bunks in the second hold—we top grades—and the officers moved into cabins and our cooks prepared our first dinner on board. The beginning was a two day voyage from Milne Bay to Oro Bay, New Guinea.

When we came aboard I was greeted by Captain Voss, but when I introduced him to Major Holmgren and Lieutenant Koenig, he did a double-take. He suddenly realized that he had been fraternizing with a noncom on my solo voyage. I couldn't help smiling at his sudden embarrassed consternation. He was distinctly cool to me for a few days. But when he saw that Mr. B. fraternized with a whole company of noncoms, and he began to get bored with Swampy, we began to resume our friendly relationship.

When the dinner gong rang, Mr. B. asked me to gather the boys so he could talk to them. "Before we eat our first meal on board, I have a message for you from the Pentagon. You know I've been trying for months to get Washington to improve the ratings for the company and they kept telling me that we had higher ratings than any companies our size. Well, they finally came through with what I'd call a goodwill gesture. Several Tech fours, and Tech fives and the rest Pfcs.[1] Forty-five guys who are now privates will be promoted to private first class."

Hayden Rorke started clapping and the whole outfit joined him. Mr. B. put up his hands to finish.

"Thank you, Hayden. I'm sorry I couldn't get more, fellows. You deserve a whole lot more than we'll ever be able to get."

I decided I ought to speak up. "Mr. B., I think we all agree on one

---

1. Technical Sergeants, Technical Corporals, and Privates First Class. None of these are command rankings, but they represent an increase in pay.

thing: we've missed you, we're glad you're back and we're all grateful for everything you've done on our behalf."

They cheered and clapped. He smiled at me and then waved at our on-deck kitchen.

"Let's dig into that dinner. It smells great."

☆ ☆ ☆ ☆ ☆ ☆ ☆ ☆ ☆ ☆ ☆

When we anchored off Oro Bay, the cranes lifted our production, crate by crate, out of the forward hold and into the LCM's which were tied up to the ship, and then we were ferried ashore to set up the show.

Our first performance in the Pacific Ocean island-to-island campaign was in the Lattimore Bowl Theater in Oro Bay, New Guinea, setting a pattern we followed for five months. We lived on board our ship, went ashore to set up and then played one show each evening, moving the show from one theater to another every two or three days, then on to the next island to repeat the pattern. The audiences varied from 6,000 to as many as 12,000 for each performance.

Our first performance at the Lattimore Theater started in a downpour. In this case, the stage was covered. The audience didn't budge and the show continued. Finally the rain stopped and we played the whole show, with all the lights and costumes and makeup and the sound of a twenty-four-piece orchestra. Broadway in New Guinea!

After the finale, Mr. B. asked us to turn off all stage lights. He then asked the whole audience to light matches, flashlights or just cigarettes and sing with him "God Bless America." The impact of this song in that setting was overwhelming.

I wrote Nancy something of that moment:

> How did he know it would be appropriate? Because they were
> not in foxholes. They were not stuck in the heat of Iran. It had
> just been a long, long time and they were homesick and they
> could sing "God Bless America" and it would help them—

against the background of the quiet, lush beauty of the New
Guinea forest, a lazy homesick atmosphere, and a picture postcard loveliness in each sunset. Life is deadly dull and madden-
ingly routine for the men who must stay here for a long period
of time. Many have served three years in this Theater of
Operation alone. Their responses to that song went deep into
their hearts. Their mental and emotional vulnerability cried out
for the sentimental.

Chapter 22

THE WAR

—Jan 2, 1945: US Landing force bound for the Philippines leaves Leyte: 6 battleships, 16 escort carriers, 10 cruisers, dozens of destroyers and support vessels.

—Jan 19, 1945: B-29 aircraft from Marianas Base destroy aircraft production in raids on Japan.

—Feb 22, 1945: In Germany, US Third Army advances threatening to isolate many troops of the German Seventh Army.

—Feb 26, 1945: Corregidor is secured. More than 5,000 Japanese dead, many trapped in tunnels all over island.

—Apr 12, 1945: President Roosevelt died.

After playing for five days in amphitheaters near Oro Bay, New Guinea, we made our first extended voyage on El Libertador, a distance of about five hundred miles, north from New Guinea for two days to Manus, the largest of the Admiralty Islands. We made the journey at full speed—a breathtaking twelve knots per hour.

When we reached the open ocean of Bismarck Sea, Bob and I were standing at the bow enjoying the fresh breeze. There was a small object on the northwest horizon that reminded me of the one Captain Voss had shown me less than a month earlier.

"Take a look, Bob," I said, pointing.

"What's that?" he asked.

"I think it's a submarine."

"One of ours?"

"I don't think so. We saw one off of Finschhafen when I was sailing down to meet you guys. The captain thought it was Japanese."

"Shouldn't we tell him?"

I looked up at the bridge. Voss and Van Hoope were standing just back in the shadow of the bridge cabin. Voss had his binoculars trained to northwest.

Bob followed my look. "I hope the Navy's right. Didn't they tell us that we don't need to travel in convoy because our ship isn't worth the price of a torpedo?"

"Uh-huh. Of course, if Tokyo Rose knew we were here, I wouldn't bet on it. We'd make big headlines if Irving Berlin and his boys were blown out of the water."

We kept watching and so did the officers. A few minutes later, the object had disappeared to the west. So far so good.

☆ ☆ ☆ ☆ ☆ ☆ ☆ ☆ ☆ ☆ ☆

After playing three days in the Manus Naval Base theater, we moved the show to another theater on Manus Island. We played there for five days, commuting from our ship each day, then we raised the anchor and doubled back to New Guinea to play ten days in the Finschhafen area. There were many thousands of troops there, working day and night keeping the ships loaded with supplies bound for the front lines of Samar, Leyte and Luzon. The Japs had battled long and hard to hold them; they were losing but not without many American casualties. The hospital wards near Finschhafen had hundreds of patients every day. Mr. B. and our boys entertained wherever they could and Mr. B. talked to scores of the casualties individually, as he had in Italy. After the hospital wards, we did two shows in the evenings in the amphitheaters. That was hard work for our boss.

Our objective was to play in the Philippines as soon as we were allowed. For the present, we had to keep busy back of the lines as we had in Naples, before the final assault on Rome.

Orders came on February 15 to proceed to Hollandia to join a convoy bound for Leyte. The voyage was too dangerous to attempt, even for our old bucket. Reaching Hollandia on the 19th we found that by some snafu we had been left off the convoy list. We had to wait.

It wasn't easy. Hollandia harbor was blacked out at night. No mail was reaching us at this point; the APO didn't know where we were.

But Mr. B. was with us, so it seemed pretty certain they'd keep track of us.

After dinner we invited the crew and the Navy gunners to share a little of our homemade liquor. That was an added luxury we enjoyed—having our own kitchen and cooks and a medical officer, Captain Eddinger, who was the expert in charge of the dispensing so it never got out of hand. It was a treat he allowed us all to enjoy now and then as a social benefit. It reminded me of the Army allotment of vodka in Persia. The quality was high enough to prompt Mr. B. to request a portion now and then when he was on board. A boring wait for a convoy prompted Doc Eddinger to prescribe a Libertador Cocktail for all.

On February 25, we departed Hollandia from the north shore of New Guinea in a convoy of thirty-four ships, including destroyer escorts, bound for Leyte Island, Philippines. We were ordered to wear life jackets and helmets at all times during the voyage.

Ben and Mr. B. went by fighter plane. While he waited for us, Mr. B. put the finishing touches on "Heaven Watch the Philippines," a song that was to be his gift to the Filipino people, who had been taking such a crushing blow in the war.

The convoy took seven days. I assigned some of our men to a regular watch with the gunners—four hours on, eight hours off. Our Navy gunners were ordered by the convoy commander to do some practice firing with our two guns. We were surprised to find that our guns made a hell of a noise and the shells landed smack on target. We all cheered and for a change, the gunners took a bow.

March 4: 7:15 p.m., we anchored in Tacloban Harbor, Samar Island.

March 5: 4:10 a.m. air-raid alert sounded. All up to stations. 4:30, all clear. 9:30, Koenig and Washer came aboard with mail! General elation! LCM's each carrying a truck tied up to ship. Started loading show into trucks. Another crew went ashore to start setting up. At 11:00 a.m., Mr. B. came aboard. At the same time, crew began refueling ship.

✩ ✩ ✩ ✩ ✩ ✩ ✩ ✩ ✩ ✩ ✩

We set up the show in what was proudly called "The Little Theater off Times Square." After Mr. B's songs he stepped forward and announced that when he first came to the Philippines, he heard the children singing "God Bless the Philippines" to the melody of "God Bless America." Mr. B. said, "I decided they should have a song of their own so I wrote one which they rehearsed this morning. They're ready to join us singing, 'Heaven Watch the Philippines.'"

We opened the curtains to reveal a huge Philippine flag filling the whole rear wall of the stage. Mr. B. and our group sang the first chorus of the song and the Filipino Boy and Girl Scouts — the girls in colorful evening gowns, the boys in dark trousers and white blouses — sang the second chorus with him, to thunderous applause. Mr. B. then announced that he was giving the song to the Filipino Boy and Girl Scouts in memory of General Teddy Roosevelt, who had been one of the director's of the Scouts when he was governor of the Philippine Islands.

The same ceremony and special songs were repeated over several days, in several theaters, attracting other notable members to the audience, including Colonel James Roosevelt, the President's son, and a parade of all the highest ranking generals serving in MacArthur's theater of operations.

As the days and nights went by, there were rainstorms that slowed but did not stop the shows and Red Alerts, which sometimes made us pause briefly. But Mr. B. and the Scouts and our cast went on and on, playing to huge audiences. You would have thought, from the response, that Berlin had already won the battle for the Philippines!

A week later, after our last performance in Leyte and Samar, on Saturday, March 24, Mr. B. dismayed the audience and sent a chill though the whole detachment by making his farewell speech. Leaving behind a song for the Filipino people and a series of letters and speeches of commendation for the detachment, he promised to be in touch with our families and to welcome us back to New York when we returned home.

"I'm going to make a few appearances and sing your new song in and around Manila before I fly home," he said as he threw the audience a kiss and left the stage to a torrent of tears and applause. We were reminded of Bari, Italy, when the boss said good-bye for five months. This farewell sounded dismayingly permanent.

☆ ☆ ☆ ☆ ☆ ☆ ☆ ☆ ☆ ☆ ☆

We played another three weeks in Tacloban, on Samar, then on Mindoro Island. We played Manila following Mr. B.'s last appearance, and then went on to other huge audiences on Luzon Island.

A week after he left us, I received a letter from Mr. B. As usual, he typed it himself, on a plain sheet of white paper. It read in full:

> March 30, 1945. Dear Alan: Ben will tell you in detail of my few
> days in Manila. Everything is all set for the opening here,
> which is much sooner than I thought. The temptation to stay
> for the opening is great, but that nervous breakdown I've
> promised myself seems to be just around the corner. Besides,
> Paramount has cabled asking when I was leaving. Please write
> me soon and give me the news. I know everything will run
> smoothly—no doubt more smoothly without me around. Best
> to you all. I. B.

☆ ☆ ☆ ☆ ☆ ☆ ☆ ☆ ☆ ☆ ☆

The day before we finished playing in the Manila area, on Friday the 13th of April, the whole world was shaken by the death of President Franklin Delano Roosevelt. It was not altogether unexpected and yet it so depressed us that it was hard to respond properly to Colonel

Harry Disston, Chief of Special Services in the Western Pacific. He praised the detachment and then pinned the Philippine Liberation Ribbon on each and every one of us. We undoubtedly failed to adequately show our appreciation, our minds were so occupied by the sadness we were feeling. We felt that FDR and the First Lady belonged to us after our visit to the White House. No doubt there were Americans who did not share our feeling, but the great majority of men and women in uniform had a near worship for FDR.

Also, coming so close on the heels of Mr. B.'s departure, we were especially vulnerable to feelings of loss and uncertainty. Fortunately, we were occupied day and night with a continuous schedule of moving, setting up, playing, doing hospital shows and moving again. Sending our guys into hospitals to buoy the spirits of the lonesome wounded was both heartbreaking and gratifying. The wounded were particularly susceptible to the humor of irony and cynicism at which Hank, Julie and Dick were masterful. They were live versions of the Bill Mauldin cartoon characters, Willie and Joe, who were familiar to the guys in wards on stretchers with wounds from being—as in Mauldin's title—"Up Front."

Our job was morale, and the busier we could keep our whole company, the better it was for *their* morale. Back in the US, Mr. B. did his part by making phone calls and writing letters to most of our families. He wrote to Nancy as he had promised:

April 9, 1945
Mrs. Alan Anderson
St. Helena Island
Frogmore, So Carolina

Dear Nancy: I returned from the Pacific this week and tried to get you on the phone but was told that you were still in South Carolina. This note is to tell you that Alan is fine, considering how homesick he is for you and the baby. He seems to have a better hold on himself than most of the boys and manages to take the hardship of being away in stride.

The trip through the Pacific was very much more rugged than the others. They are starved for entertainment there and as a result, the show seemed to go much better there than anywhere else. They will be in Manila by the time you get this. I'm off for California in a few days. I understand that Alan's father is there, so I will get in touch with him. With my best to you and the boy. Alan showed me a recent picture and he is getting to be quite a guy. Sincerely yours, Irving Berlin

I wish I'd known then what he had said in that letter, that he felt I had "a better hold" on myself than "most of the boys." He did say something of the same sort later on in a letter to me and it was certainly good for my morale, there was no question about it. He had secured a kind of additional father role for many of us, including me, and he continued to write several of us. We also wrote him, keeping him up-to-date.

Living aboard ship continued to help our morale, too. We had a home. When we pulled anchor on *El Libertador* and sailed for another island or another port, there was time to lie in the sun, write letters home, get into calisthenics with Artie Steiner. Or just stand at the bow, watching the ship slice through the sea, endlessly peeling the water, rolling it over to leave a trail of white foam all day long and into the night, searching the horizon and wondering at the stars. There's nothing more magical for passing time than being on shipboard, mesmerized by the movement, the blowing air, with time to read a book or write a letter or just fall asleep, lulled by the motion of the ship and the rhythm of cresting waves. When we finished a performance, we were back home, on board.

There were heroes among us. One I just mentioned: our calisthenics leader, Staff Sergeant Artie Steiner—dancer, athlete, good friend to all. I knew Artie for four years in the war and another forty-five years afterward, and I don't remember him frowning. Unhappily, he died after a long bout with Parkinson's disease, a bitter end for a physique and a spirit that were centered on motion and joy.

Some of the names of the harbors and centers we played in the Philippines resonate still in my mind—Tacloban, Mindoro, Manila, Alangapo, Dagupan, San Fernando, Batangas.

We were in dock on board *El Libertador* on May 2, in San Fernando on Luzon, the biggest island in the Philippines, when we heard on the ship's radio that Adolf Hitler was dead and Berlin had fallen.

Four days later, on May 6th, we pulled into harbor at Batangas, a large city on the south end of Luzon. The next day we heard by radio that representatives from the US, Great Britain, France and Russia were present at Eisenhower's headquarters at 2:41 p.m. as General Jodl and Admiral Friedeberg signed the unconditional surrender documents. We played the opening performance in an unbelievable atmosphere of joy on both sides of the curtain. The Allies proclaimed the 8th of May as V-E Day—Victory in Europe—celebrated as Churchill, President Truman and King George VI broadcast speeches to the world.

Johnny Cooper and I were checking our spotlights as we listened to the radio, when I saw a familiar figure in Navy uniform walk past my ladder and look up at me, holding out a bottle and smiling. I found myself staring at a longtime childhood friend from South Mountain Road, Lieutenant Dr. Quentin Deming. The Demings lived two miles down the road from the Andersons and I had played tennis on the Deming court every summer since Quentin and I were about twelve.

"I read in the paper this morning that the show was here, and I decided you and I had better celebrate together!" he said.

"Quentin! Out of the blue!"

"Actually, out of the briny. My ship just docked here."

"You have a ship?"

"I'm the doctor on board a battleship. Our news this morning said your show was playing here."

I told Coop we could finish our check-up later and after thumping each other on the back, Quentin and I went next door to our barracks, found two cups, settled on my cot and popped the cork off a bottle of the best cream sherry.

"This was all I could find," he said, peering into the liquid. "But I decided it was better than 3.2 beer for this occasion." We started by talking about friends, family and home, and then made toasts to them all, then to victory in Europe, to FDR, and to our new President, Harry Truman, "May he fill some mighty shoes!" We carried our precious bottle to the Orderly Room and I introduced Quentin to everybody there. We finished the sherry on more toasts and Doc Eddinger declared open bar for Libertador Cocktails. By dinner time, Quentin and I were happily crocked.

We played the following week in Manila and then, after the many thousands we had played to in those islands, backtracked southeast to Morotai.

Our doctor, Captain Eddinger, assigned to us while we were in the West Pacific, did a checkup on the company and surprised me with his diagnosis.

"Sergeant, it acts like virus pneumonia and there's not much we can do except get bed rest, eat good food, and drink lots of fruit juice and water." With those words, he sent me to the Army hospital in Morotai. They signed me in and before I knew it, I was being examined while lying on a hospital cot.

"I feel okay, Doctor. I only have a little fever in the afternoon."

"You've got virus pneumonia and it can get really serious if you don't get rid of it," he said and went about more pressing problems—like treating wounds and replacing legs.

I had a rough idea of the *TITA* schedule. They were scheduled to play Morotai until the end of May and then go to Biak for about ten days. I wanted to be released before they left Biak because I had no idea what they were doing after that.

I lay in bed day after day. There were some Japanese prisoner patients down at the end of the ward. There was always an MP making sure they didn't try to leave. I had the impression that was the last thing they wanted to do. When their wounds were healed, they'd be in a prison camp and out of combat.

One of the nurses was taking my pulse, sitting on my bed.

"How long have you been here?" I asked her.

"I don't know. It's over two years."

"How do you stand it?"

"I don't," she said, letting go of my wrist. "Your pulse is normal. Time for you to get another chest X-ray." She turned back to me, speaking with quiet resignation. "None of us can stand it. If we didn't have a needle to fall back on, I think we'd go nuts."

I tried not to look surprised. "What's in the needle?"

"Morphine," she said. She stood close to me and spoke quietly. "None of us could function if we didn't have it around."

"The doctors?" I asked.

"Not when they're on duty. But God, without it we'd all go nuts. I'll get you an X-ray and we'll see how the chest is doing."

It had been fifteen days. I'd just had my third X-ray. Dr. Sullivan said, "You're clean, Alan. I'm going to let you go back to duty." So they put me in a casual outfit. Casual means you're temporarily not where you belong but you might as well relax and enjoy it.

I reported to the headquarters of the casual outfit and they found out by radio that the detachment had sailed from Biak headed for Hollandia and I should meet them there. When I landed in Hollandia the next day, Johnny Koenig and Pete Feller met me at the plane.

"They told us you were coming. Are you all well?"

"Certainly he's all well," Pete said. "He's fatter than ever."

"My lungs are clear. But I lost weight, slave driver," I said to Pete. "The food was not only hospital. It was *Army* hospital."

"Good. You can help us set things up." Johnny said. "And you can help us find a new ship!"

"What?"

"Our lease is up on *El Libertador*. The Dutch shipping company wants it back."

"You can also help me get everything out of storage," Pete said. "We stored all the stuff in good old Milne Bay, because the ship wasn't big enough."

"I want to find a ship that will hold everything!" Johnny said. "And by the way, Doc Eddinger wants the whole outfit to get X-rayed, since your problem."

The detachment landed the next day. By then Johnny had a line on a new ship for us from a Hawaiian touring company. Pete had arranged to have everything taken out of storage and put in a big shop where he could work on the production, and I had barracks space reserved.

☆ ☆ ☆ ☆ ☆ ☆ ☆ ☆ ☆ ☆ ☆

When the ship had been unloaded, Doc Eddinger had an X-ray schedule set up for everyone. He started with the orchestra, and then everyone Pete wasn't browbeating. My company clerk and our medical assistant, Corporal Hank Ohlandt, kept track of who was being treated. Doc Eddinger checked on every result as they came in.

At dinner time, Doc Eddinger said he wanted to see the officers and the committee after dinner. We met in our newly assigned orderly room.

"I've got a lot of the reports in already and I have one disturbing piece of news: Rosie has a problem. That's why he's not here. He's in the hospital. He has a bad lung. I don't think he can do any more work until he gets over it. And I would estimate that his treatment could not be accomplished in less than a month—and maybe longer."

Pete couldn't speak.

"Where do you think he can be treated, Doc?" Swampy asked.

"I think he has to go home," Eddinger said.

"New York?" I said with alarm.

"Right." No one said anything for a moment. Eddinger went on. "Frankly, since Alan's problem, I thought we'd better be sure we didn't have any other incipient lung problems. I think we caught Alan's early. Rosie may have been carrying his around for some time. But it isn't safe for him to go on working until he gets rid of it, and we just have to hope that he can get rid of it."

I wanted to say "shit." That's what Rosie would say.

"What's his schedule, Major?" I asked.

"He's having more tests. I expect he can fly home tomorrow morning."

"No chance of fixing it here?"

"Nope."

Carl, Pete and I picked him up at the hospital with his stuff and drove him to the airport. It was one sad son of a bitch of a day. In a way, we were jealous of him—getting to go home. But on the other hand, we would miss Rosie like the devil. It just wouldn't be the same, damn it.

"Who do you think could take your place, Rosie?" I asked.

"Willard," he said. "Willard could do it just fine. He knows every note and he can handle the guys."

"Isn't Max theoretically the Assistant Conductor?

"Max is okay for an emergency, but he can't handle the guys the way Willard can. They all respect Willard. Max isn't tough enough."

"Okay, buddy," I said. "We'll be losing a damned fine trumpet, in addition to the guy with the stick."

Rosie didn't say anything for a moment. "I know. I wish I thought I could make it. But I think the Doc is right. I feel lousy. Got no pizzazz!"

"What do you need pizzazz for? Just beat their knuckles with your little white stick!" He grinned at Pete. "Yeah? Who do you think taught me to beat them!"

We watched Rosie's plane take off, then we got back in the jeep and Carl drove back to the company. When we had been going for a few minutes Carl said, "We've lost our music director, our composer, our father figure, our producer and our home. What the hell have we got left?"

"I guess the only thing left is our show. We may be sick of it, but every time we put the damned thing on, they love it!"

I got a letter from Mr. B., written on July 10.

> I have your letter of June 23rd and hope you are completely well now. I am sorry to hear that you had been in the hospital. —I knew about Rosie. He sent me a nice letter. I hope his condition isn't too serious. I am glad he is getting out of the Army. Please let me hear from you again soon. Good luck to you all. My best.

The committee agreed to follow Rosie's recommendation, even though it meant giving up the lead trumpet.

We performed shows in several outdoor theaters in the Hollandia area for ten days until June 21. Willard Jones did a great job—Rosie was right. Pete rebuilt the scenery, repainted everything, built new crates. We were ready for a ship and convoy to take us to the Marianas, where there was a tremendous concentration of Air Force and Navy men and women waiting for us.

After one of our last shows before we boarded, Swampy called a detachment meeting.

"I know you guys have earned and acquired a lot of service ribbons and bronze stars for the theaters of operation in which you have all served. Ribbons and stars for Europe, the Middle East and now the Pacific, and tonight I've got some more for you that the War Department requires me to give you. Your Southwestern Pacific Ribbon will now be adorned by two Bronze Service Stars, plus a very special one—the Philippine Liberation Bronze Star for serving in the combat region of Luzon. You can be very proud of all these symbols, added to all the good conduct ribbons you got in the states. Someday they'll help you to remember when your kids ask, 'Where did you go when you were in the war, daddy?'"

When he had finished presenting them all, I startled the hell out of Swampy and the detachment by snapping to attention and saying, "Major Holmgren, on behalf of the detachment, thank you, sir!" And snapping off a salute, which he returned, almost blushing.

On July 1, 1945, three days before *TITA*'s third anniversary, we boarded the Liberty ship *Furnifold M. Simmons*, which was to take us in convoy to Saipan Island. Dr. Eddinger came on board to say farewell and handed me a package in front of everyone.

"Alan, I am entrusting you with a prescription for the whole company, to be taken judiciously when the morale is low — or when needed for celebrations!"

"Sir?" I said blankly.

"Libertador Liqueur, Sergeant. Several bottles — for medicinal purposes, of course."

Chapter 23

THE WAR
—May 2, 1945: Hitler's death reported by German High Command.
  Berlin falls.
—May 7, 1945: German generals sign unconditional surrender to
  General Eisenhower.
—May 8, 1945: V-E Day. Victory in Europe celebrated.
—May 11, 1945: US forces begin concerted attack on Japanese on
  Okinawa.
—July 16, 1945: First test of an atomic weapon at Los Alamos.
—July 20, 1945: A US test flight from the Marianas simulates delivery of
  the atomic bomb.

The desire to have our own ship again was overwhelming. Johnny flew ahead of us once more and continued negotiations with the Hawaiian Cruise Ship Company. He wanted a contract giving us the ship from Saipan until the end of our Pacific duty, an event that suddenly seemed a reality. Now that the war was over in Europe and we were bombing the Japanese mainland daily, the war had done a one-eighty. Nevertheless, our Liberty ship did have a destroyer escort for the voyage north. The Japanese submarine fleet was still alive.

The 1,500-mile trip took seven days. We docked in Saipan at 10:00 a.m., Sunday, July 8, and from there spent seven weeks on the three main Mariana Islands, playing almost every evening to huge audiences, mostly Air Force and Navy. Our shows were often interrupted by enormous rainstorms that forced the orchestra to quickly crowd under whatever shed or shelter was available. The audiences, protected by rain gear, stayed put, determined not to miss a moment of the show.

Guam was the biggest of the three islands, about thirty miles long and eight or nine miles wide. Saipan and Tinian were tiny in comparison. We played first on Saipan for two weeks, then were supposed to have our new ship to live on—but it didn't appear. We made the short move to Tinian by LCM. That island had nothing for us but tents, which seemed to be just at water level. Mud was everywhere. No sooner had we moved in when torrents of rain began to swamp us. In Jus's words to his father:

> This is an old story to our outfit, and surprises no one. I hon-
> estly believe that if they told us to live in trees next week, the
> only reaction would be, 'Okay, which one is mine?'

We finished in Tinian and moved to Guam by LCM, where we dried out gradually and began living in barracks.

On our fifth day on Guam, August 6, 1945—unknown to almost everyone in the world but a few people, including President Harry Truman—Colonel Paul Tibbetts, flying a B-29 bomber he had named the Enola Gay, after his mother, took off from Tinian at 2:00 a.m. Fortunately, the airport on Tinian, unlike our tent area, was above water. At 8:15 a.m., when the Enola Gay was directly over the Japanese city of Hiroshima, Tibbett's bombardier released a uranium 235 fission weapon, commonly referred to as an atomic bomb. The moment of release resulted in the weapon impacting the ground pre-cisely where the resulting explosion would achieve the maximum damage to all that was within range of the detonation. No one truly understood then what lay beyond the immediate human slaughter of more than 80,000 people from the resultant blast and the firestorm which followed instantly, laying waste to more than half the city's pop-ulation. Nor did anyone truly conceive of the many thousands more that were to be maimed and burned and of the many more who were to suffer for decades the horrifying long range effects of the radiation, condemning bodies to painful, crippling physical distortion and destruction, and gradually, to excruciatingly torturous deaths.

It was expected Japan would certainly surrender after the first immediate effects were realized. In fact, it took a second atomic bomb,

dropped three days later on the city of Nagasaki, plus fierce bombardment of the mainland and of the islands by conventional bombing, to
force an unconditional surrender.

The war was over! And at that point, so little was understood of the
real impact of the atomic bombs, that the enemies of Japan and
Germany were simply overwhelmed by the profound satisfaction in
the end of the war. We were at peace. For the United States and her
allies, life could go back to normal.

However, there was much work to do. Hundreds in military hospitals had to be transferred to medical care in the US. There were many
thousands of troops and masses of equipment and weapons of all
sorts spread over a vast area of the Pacific. It was going to take some
time.

Swampy was informed by General MacArthur's headquarters that
we had a lot more to do. "They want you guys to keep playing to the
troops until most of them are on the way home." We had to write letters home that would explain why the end of the war was not the end
of *TITA*.

We had one compensation: our cruise ship was delivered to us in
Guam. We boarded the *Haleakala* two weeks after the surrender.

No more stuffy hold in our little Dutch coffee grinder. *Haleakala*
had enough cabins to house the whole detachment in first class facilities, three to a cabin. It also had sufficient freight area to hold the complete production. This would improve the shows and make it easier to
load and unload from island to island. It also had a large dining room
and kitchen, complete with expert cooks and a store of fresh foods.
The chief cook told me confidentially that he had a meat locker full of
steaks. He proudly proved it to us with our first dinner on board.

"Damn," Carl said, when we sat down to eat with plates and silverware and glasses of water. "I wish to hell Rosie could have been here to
see this."

"He'll never believe us when we tell him," Pete said.

Swampy was on his feet rapping on his glass.

"Gentlemen! Your attention for a moment! Just one short toast—to Johnny Koenig for our new home!" He raised his glass and everybody roared approval.

Johnny took a bow. "Thank you, Major! Here's to you all for doing a great job under all kinds of crappy conditions. You earned a steak dinner!"

Before we left Guam, the ship's speaker system broadcast President Truman's radio address announcing the final acceptance of the unconditional surrender by Japan and the appointment of General Douglas MacArthur to Supreme Commander of the Allied Powers to rule over Japan.

The coming of peace resulted in joyous bedlam all over the harbor. Hundreds of ships competed in blowing whistles, horns, sirens and bells. The ships' rails were lined with men and women waving and shouting with joy. Fighter planes did "victory rolls" over us all.

☆ ☆ ☆ ☆ ☆ ☆ ☆ ☆ ☆ ☆ ☆

We started work. Okinawa was our next goal for the show. There were thousands of Navy, Army, Seabees and Air Force, but because the fighting had just ended on Okinawa, there were no movie amphitheaters yet. We detoured to do some shows in the Ulithi Islands and left for Okinawa three days later in a twelve-ship convoy. A tropical storm made it a heavy rolling, rough trip. Several of the guys lost an excellent dinner.

On September 2, the official Surrender Terms were signed on board the U.S.S. *Missouri* in Tokyo Bay. President Truman announced "V-J Day." All gun crews were relieved of duty and blackouts were canceled the following day.

On September 4, we dropped anchor off Okinawa but discovered that we were still early.

"They aren't ready, Pete," the Major said. "They're short of skilled carpenters."

"Tell them we'll come and help," Pete said. The Major got an affirmative to that one and Pete took a big gang ashore with all their tools. They joined the work of knocking out platforms and benches, then we started setting up for the first show.

These guys were hungry for a laugh. There were 10,000 men and women at every performance of the show.

At our second performance, on September 10, two great heroes attended and came backstage to talk to us: Major General Merrill (of Merrill's Marauders) and General Joseph Stilwell (Vinegar Joe). Vinegar Joe had been Chief of Staff to Chiang Kai-shek in China's battle against Japan. In 1944, Stilwell and Merrill joined forces side by side with Chinese troops in the Burma campaign, and they were still together—Merrill was commanding the Tenth Army and Vinegar Joe was his Chief of Staff.

Our guys were literally in awe, hearing praise from these two men. Their speeches reminded us that Mr. B. should be hearing them, too.

The *Haleakala* was pitching badly when we returned for the night. Captain Curtice warned us that there was a typhoon about three hundred miles off, moving toward Okinawa.

☆ ☆ ☆ ☆ ☆ ☆ ☆ ☆ ☆ ☆ ☆

We had our own family POW experience when Hayden Rorke made contact with a living member of the Corregidor Death March, who confirmed that Eddie Rorke, Hayden's brother, had survived the march. The march had become a symbol of the wanton cruelty of the Japanese to prisoners of war. Of the 15,000 US and Filipino troops who surrendered to the Japanese on Corregidor on May 6, 1942, it appeared that an enormous number had not survived.

Hayden's search for his brother really began when he and several Catholics in our detachment managed, at the end of a service, to kiss the Pope's ring in Rome and asked that the Pope pray for the safety of Eddie Rorke. The Pope put his hand on Hayden's bowed head and assured him he would pray for Eddie. Once we reached the Pacific, whenever we pulled into a new harbor, Hayden was focused on finding his brother. He would give his brother's name to every outfit we met in the hopes that he was still alive. Mr. B. had made inquiries to Washington, and what leads they had he relayed back to Hayden. When we reached the Philippines, Hayden had queried every surviving prisoner he could find, saying "Eddie Rorke" over and over again wherever we went.

When we were near Manila he had his first miracle. He found a master sergeant who had prepared a list of men being sent for transfer to the States, and he remembered Eddie's name being on it. Then a corporal, hearing the discussion, popped up and said to Hayden, "Is your brother Eddie Rorke, 803rd Engineers?"

Hayden could hardly speak. "You know his name and his outfit?"

"Eddie was my best friend." The corporal shook Hayden's hand eagerly and introduced himself. A sergeant overheard them and calmly interrupted. "Hey, fellows, if you want Eddie Rorke, what I last heard, when he got out of the hospital, was that he had been sent to Camp #11 and they're going to send him home from there."

Hayden began to relax. He was sure that Eddie was alive and on the way home.

Then we almost lost Hayden. When we returned to the ship after the September 15 show, the typhoon was just eighteen hours away. The path of the typhoon was sixty miles wide and we were dead center in the path. We had to scramble up rope netting from the LCM's to reach the deck. Hayden lost his footing and slipped into the water between the LCM and the ship. In the high, crashing waves, Jus and Dick Reeves yanked Hayden up and into the boat seconds before the steel LCM slammed into the hull of the ship. Captain Curtice gave Hayden a shot of bourbon when he heard what had happened.

The crew dropped three anchors which held the *Haleakala* through the night. We had to cancel the show the 16th and 17th; there was no way to get to shore. Besides, it was raining buckets in a seventy-five-mile wind.

We finished playing in Okinawa a week later and made our voyage to tiny Iwo Jima. We came into the harbor, looking up at the column of volcanic rock dominating the whole scene—the peak upon which three American soldiers raised a flag in triumph, a dramatic moment caught in a news photographer's photo which was to become famous.

The picture captured a mixed atmosphere of grim nostalgia and celebration with the battle won, and that barren monument dominated the scene of a costly victory. Some of the last blood spent in the war had been just prior to that celebration.

We played for four nights on Iwo Jima, filling the 8,000 seats at each performance. The next morning, September 29, we set out for Eniwetok and the Marshall Islands, the first leg toward home.

Eniwetok did not have facilities for us to do regular shows so we played variety shows in three different locales to audiences again numbering 10,000 each.

We were instructed to throw all ammunition overboard once we were at sea, on the way to Kwajalein. The Navy gunners supervised. All weapons were neutered by lack of ammunition, including our own rifles.

We did two full shows on Kwajalein with no rainstorm, and far from typhoons. They were good performances, full of energy. There was a kind of elation in the guys, as though they could feel the end coming. They could hardly wait for the speeches of praise after the curtain to finish so we could start our last trip.

The voyage to Honolulu took seven days. We did a show on shipboard for ourselves and the crew on our next to last day. It was put on by Artie Steiner and he called it the "Haleakala Smoker." It consisted of boxing bouts, a wrestling match, a variety show and impromptu music by the band. It was energetic, enthusiastic, bawdy and entirely undisciplined.

There was a whole new sense of elation in our last shows in the Hawaiian Islands. We knew that when we finished them, we would be going home — somehow. In the meantime, we had six days of shows ahead of us, from Wednesday through Monday, when we would give our final show. We started with Oahu at Fort Shafter, then two shows at the Perry Bowl, and two more at Hickam Field with several speeches by high ranking officers. I think we could have written them ourselves. I'm sure they thought the smiles on our faces were because of their gracious words. They didn't know we were smiling most of the time because we were almost home.

No one mentioned the silence from the boss. Would we see Mr. B. before it ended?

On Sunday, October 21, we moved the show into the Schofield Barracks Bowl for our next to last show — another huge, grateful audience of 10,000. With the echo of their applause in our ears, we started striking the show for the move to the Honolulu Stadium, where we would give our final show the next night.

Johnny Koenig came running backstage, yelling to us, "Come here, you guys! I've got news for you!"

Everybody swarmed on to the stage. Johnny was holding a piece of paper up and waving it around over his head. Everybody got quiet.

"This is a telegraph message to *This Is the Army* which arrived a couple of hours ago. They just got it to us.

> 'Dear Boys, I am flying in and will be with you on October 22nd for the last show. Please make sure my costume is pressed. Irving Berlin.'"

Every face was grinning when we went to work on the move to the Honolulu Stadium. Pete didn't have to yell once.

The next morning, Monday, October 22, the entire detachment was on board the *Haleakala* waiting. A motorboat came alongside with one passenger. Looking dapper in his official correspondent's uniform, Mr. B. climbed up the ladder to us with a smile on his face, his dark eyes shining, as eager as a kid. It was an emotional meeting for all of us, with much joking and laughter. We spent the day, chatting, relaxed and joyful. Papa was with us.

We gave him time for a nap and then at 6:00 p.m. we all went to the stadium to prepare for the evening performance. The huge sea of faces included Army, Navy and Air Force personnel and a great many civilian leaders. There were many speeches after the show thanking Mr. B. and all of us for the work we had done and the pleasure we had given to so many thousands around the world. And then there was absolute silence. All eyes from those thousands of faces followed Mr. B. as he stepped to the edge of the stage, his cap in his hand.

The excitement had been building inside us all for days, and finally, for this whole day with Mr. B. at our sides. But it wasn't until this moment when he walked forward to the edge of the stage to give a final speech after a final performance that it struck us in the gut: When he finishes his words, it will all be over—ended.

He began by telling them all how glad he was to be here once again, raising money for the Army Emergency Relief. Many more gracious words were spoken and then he said, "This is a really important night. It is our last night, one of great relief and great joy, too. We started as a team and pulled together as a team up to this final performance. It has been a glorious thing for me—to help in the only way I could to win this war. My prayer now is, as a songwriter, I hope to God I'll never have to write another war song."

The End

THE UNITED STATES ARMY

presents

THE FINAL PERFORMANCE OF

IRVING BERLIN'S

All Soldier Show

"This is the Army"

Sponsored by

HONOLULU JUNIOR CHAMBER OF COMMERCE

For the Benefit of

THE ARMY RELIEF FUND

and

THE COMMUNITY CHEST

HONOLULU STADIUM

22 OCTOBER 1945 · 8:00 O'CLOCK

Epilogue

After that last performance in Honolulu on October 21, 1945, Mr. B. said good-bye to us backstage and then he and Ben were on a plane within minutes, headed for Hollywood. Suddenly Mr. B. was gone, and before we knew it we were at an enormous ending. We were all so happy and relieved, we weren't thinking about endings. We were going home and we were dazzled by a monumental beginning.

The next morning we climbed into the empty shells of B-24 bombers, lugging our barracks bags, scrunched down on the mats, occupying the space that had so recently been filled by the bombs that had helped to end the war. We fastened safety belts around us and before we knew it, we were landing on Hamilton Field in San Francisco. There we were directed to troop trains to the various forts and camps nearest our homes. My destination was Newark, New Jersey, the closest to Fort Dix, where I was inducted.

I got off the train with my bags and wondered how I would find Nancy in that mass of welcomers. Suddenly I saw a blonde head with a familiar beautiful brow and then a hand waving at me — unmistakably, my golden darling: gently rounded cheeks, open smile and wondrous blue eyes — actually within a car's length from me. Before I could move she was there with her arms open and we were clutching each other with a combination of disbelief and ecstasy. We kissed and hugged and kissed over and over, unable to stop, and then we just stood swaying, holding on for probably ten eternal seconds.

"Car?" I said dumbly.

"Right outside." She pushed keys into my hands. I shoved them in my pocket and swinging one bag on my shoulder, we both grasped the other bag and waddled down the platform.

We reached the parking lot with all the others, not knowing or caring how we got there, just wanting to go where we could be away from it all and be together.

Closing the doors of our '38 Plymouth, we headed for New York and her father's house. We had dinner with Byron and Betty, went to bed early and got up late.

When we got to the barn in the morning, I held the door open for her so Kett could see her first, and then I stepped inside and we saw each other across the room. I was smiling and he was staring at me and then immediately sought the safety of his mother's arms. She knelt down to him.

"This is your Daddy, Kett. Do you want to give him a hug? He came all the way across the ocean just to be with you and me." He buried his face in her neck.

"That's okay," I said. "Wait until we get a chance to get used to each other."

I had to keep myself from wanting to scoop him up and hug him and kiss him. He was such a beautiful kid.

"I can see you've been taking good care of your mommy. She looks so pretty, doesn't she?"

No smile, but a little nod after a moment to think about what I said.

I had to face the fact that he didn't have any memory of me. He was so young when he saw me last, in August, 1943 — two and a half years ago. I would have to be patient.

☆ ☆ ☆ ☆ ☆ ☆ ☆ ☆ ☆ ☆

Hayden wrote me after he was home that he first heard Eddie's voice on the phone from San Francisco just a week before Hayden landed there himself. He saw him when he walked into their mother's apartment in New York. Hayden, of course, insisted that it was because of his appeal to the Pope that his brother had made it home. No one argued with him.

☆ ☆ ☆ ☆ ☆ ☆ ☆ ☆ ☆ ☆

The first *TITA* reunion was on July 4, 1967, our twenty-fifth anniversary. It was held at the famous theatrical restaurant in the heart of New York's Theater District, Sardi's, for which we all had fond nostalgia. Vincent Sardi loved us all and gave us a break on the cost, and we repeated the party every five years on July 4th. The self-appointed alumni chairman was Alan Manson, no longer playing Jane Cowl in a gorgeous blue gown—not even Sergeant, just Alan Manson, host to us all. His hearty flamboyance made him a natural to be chairman, eagerly and efficiently, and also to act as Master of Ceremonies at every reunion. I had saved a list of the whole company and we gradually reached most of them, although there were some we never saw again after the show ended.

Sadly, Mr. B. never came to a reunion. I feel sure that the show meant an enormous amount to him and that he wanted to have his good memories of it remain intact, rather than re-live the disappointments brought on by seeing Ezra Stone. No matter how ardently we appealed to him, his depression had set in and he couldn't bear the idea of getting together. His colleague, Sammy Cahn, wrote a parody of the song "This Is the Army" for Mr. Berlin, to try to cajole him into attending one of the gatherings. It didn't work. His attempts to write new songs were being called out of date—but that's another story, which has been told by all his biographers. This book is about the war years, when he was confident and vigorous, traveling with the show, sometimes in Hollywood finishing *Holiday Inn* and other movie commitments. Everything he wrote had a big audience when he was there with us, going around the world, either in person or in spirit. He was always there somewhere, keeping us going.

There were many others who never missed July 4th at Sardi's, even in recent years, when some were on crutches. The fiftieth was the last one that found a large number still ambulatory. The fifty-fifth should never have been attempted: there were so few who could even get there, except on crutches, that we had to invite the wives, to make it a party.

Now that it is hard to find more than two dozen of us still alive out of the three hundred twenty-five or more who were involved in the show at one time or another in its history, it is doubtful that we will risk another attempt at reunion. Before anyone knew what it was, we lost several guys to AIDS, and by the time that tragic scourge became well-known, more of our number died. Dear Jus Addiss was one of the first to go.

In 1984, when I decided to write a book about *TITA*, I interviewed about fifty of the company. Nancy and I went on trips to Florida and California, with stops along the way. The rest were in the New York area where we were living. When I finished the interviews, I began to plan the book. During that first year, Hayden died, also of AIDS. He was still living in the San Fernando Valley. I had a long phone conversation with him from our home in New City, New York, shortly before he died. He told me he knew he had only a few days left. We talked about many of the guys in the show and many of the things we remembered and cherished. Knowing that it was our last conversation, Hayden talked about what it was like, knowing that it was about to end. He sent his love to us all and said he was sending me all their files from the show, including a copy of the letters Jus had written his father. A few days later he was gone. Silence. It was unreal. Somehow the people in the show couldn't disappear. I guess I feel that they never will.

One of my greatest regrets is that I didn't write this book in time for Mr. B. to see it, or Pete, Rosie, Carl, Henry Jones, Bill Roerick, Jus, Hayden, or so many more.

List of TITA Members

Overseas	Occupation	Last Name	First Name
O	Stage Manager	Addiss	Justus
O	Singer	Agnello	Michael
	Singer	Albert	Irving
	Dancer	Allen	Earl
	Dancer	Alton	Leon
	Commanding Officer	Ambraz	Simon P.
O	Stage Manager/First Sgt.	Anderson	Alan H.
O	Dancer	Anderson	George
O	Saxophone	Arthur	Lawrence
O	Singer	Arthur	Zinn
O	Singer	Atkins	Arthur
O	Singer	Aubin	William
O	Company Clerk	Bachner	Arnold
O	Dancer	Bacior	Charles
	Singer	Baker	Larry
O	Actor	Bandler	Alan
O	Choreographer/Soloist	Barclift	Nelson
O	Finance Clerk	Bass	Joseph
O	Actor	Bates	Kenneth
O	Acrobat	Bednarcik	Louis
	Dancer	Beller	Herbert
	Singer	Benson	Samuel
	Dancer	Berchman	Leonard
O	Comedian	Bernie	Dick
	Projectionist, Electrician	Bettelli	Frank
	Actor	Blake	Charles
	Head Usher	Bloom	Leonard
O	Singer	Bonasera	Frank
O	Dancer	Bowlby	Bill
	Assistant Treasurer	Bowman	John J.

	Role	Last Name	First Name
	Assistant Treasurer	Brassil	George
	Bass	Braun	Lester
	Cartoonist	Breger	Dave
O	Dancer/Singer	Brodnax	Jack
	Actor/Stage Manager	Brooks	Howard
O	Carpenter	Brousseau	Howard
	Dancer	Brown	Frank
O	Dancer, Specialty	Brown	Marion
O	Actor	Brown	Robert C.
O	Singer	Browning	Dick
O	Acrobat	Buono	Angelo
	Writer/Sketch	Burdick	Richard
	Pianist, Rehearsal	Burian	Kurt
O	Percussionist	Burke	Girard (Judy)
O	Singer, Soloist	Burrell	James
O	Actor/Stage Manager	Bush	Joe
	Singer	Campbell	Vance
	Singer	Canavarro	Ray
	Singer	Canzano	Arturo
O	Dancer/Wig Dresser	Capuozzo	Carmine
	Assistant Treasurer	Carlin	Alexis J.
	Banjoist	Carr	Samuel
	Singer/Clerk	Case, Jr.	Spencer T.
	Secretary	Case, Sr.	Spencer T.
	Personnel Clerk	Chaney	Ralph
	Medical Officer	Chartock	Hyman
	Singer	Chetlen	Thomas
	Singer, Soloist	Churchill	Stewart
	Singer	Collier	William
	Specialty Performer	Cook Jr.	Joseph
O	Electrician, Master	Cooper	John
	Singer	Coppola	Tony
	Acrobat	Cristiani	Belmonte
O	Dancer/Soloist/Comedian	Cross	James (Stump)
O	Dancer	Culley	Randolph
O	Singer	D'elia	Frank
O	Dancer/Soloist	Danieli	Alfred

O	Officer	Daniels	Marc
	Violinist/Asst. Conductor	Dann	Elias
	Singer	David	Fred
	Singer	D'Elia	Frank
	Percussion	de Milt	Charles
	Actor	de Milhau	Louis A.
	Dancer	Deming	Fred
	Singer	Dempsey	John C.
	Publicity Man	Denenholz	Reginald
O	Singer	Deutch	Irving
O	Singer	Deutch	Murray
	Music Publisher	Devore	Alexander
	Actor	Dexter	Alan
	Singer	Diamond	Aaron
O	Dancer/Soloist	Dickson	Charles
	Stagehand	Didonato	Jose
O	Stagehand	Donley	Robert
	Stagehand	Donovan	William
	Singer	Douglas	Harold
O	Dancer	Draper	Paul A.
	Dancer	Dutton	William
	Dancer	Ecconomou	Hercules
O	Medical Officer	Eddinger	Dr. Leo
	Cellist	Ehrlick	Jesse
O	Actor	Elliott	Ross
O	Acrobat	Erbisti	Geno
	Dancer	Fairman	Derek
	Dancer	Farnsworth	Scott
O	Singer	Farrell	James
	Violinist	Feldman	Louis
O	Technical Director	Feller	Peter L.
	Singer	Ferlora	John
	Dancer	Ferre	Clifford
O	Stagehand/Drill Sergeant	Ficarra	Anthony
	Singer	Fiorella	Mario
O	Business Manager	Fisher	Carl
	Musician	Fisher	Phil

	Dancer	Fluker	Herbert
	Singer	Frank	Bernard
O	Singer	Freeland	William
	Violinist	Freeman	Nathan
O	Costume Designer/Dancer	Fretwell III	Joseph
O	Singer	Fried	Leonard
	Staff Officer	Fuller	James W.
	Dancer	Gagnon	Chick
O	Stagehand	Gardner	Harold
	Pianist, Rehearsal	Garf	Gene
	Publicist	Gendel	Max
O	Dancer	Gengo	Larry
O	Singer	Gertz	Edward M.
O	Actor	Gilmour	Arthur
O	Saxophone	Giudice	Joe
O	Singer	Glenn	Paul
	Music Publishing	Goldstein	David
	Ticket Taker	Goldstein	Harold
O	Unknown	Goode	Richard
	Singer	Goodis	Marvin
	Music Publishing	Goodman	Gene
O	Electrician	Gorta	Al
O	Dancer	Goss	Ray
O	Trombone	Greene	Seymour
	Sound Technician	Griffin	John
	Singer	Grubman	Murray
	Dancer	Hampton	Thomas
	Treasurer	Handy	George
O	Trumpet	Harmon	Paul
	Singer	Harr	Warren
	Dancer	Hatchett	Arthur
O	Singer	Hawkins	Louis
	Dancer	Hearn	Fred
O	Actor/Singer	Hederman	John J.
O	Comedian	Henry	Hank
	Singer	Higuchi	Francis
	Singer	Hoha	Harold

O	Commanding Officer	Holmgren	Clifton
	Singer, Soloist	Horne	William
	Singer	Horowitz	Hyman
	Violinist	Horton Jr.	Walter H.
	Dancer	Howell	William
	Record Clerk	Ickes	Franklin D.
O	Dancer	Irving	Richard
	Viola	Israel	Paul
	Singer	Ives	Burl
O	Singer	Jackson	Robert A.
O	Dancer	Jaeger	Cassie
	Singer	Jarrett	Jerry
O	Dancer	Jarvis	Eugene
O	Dancer	Johnson	Charles
O	Dancer	Johnson	Kevin Joe
O	Dancer	Johnson	Orlando
O	Singer	Johnston	George
O	Actor	Jones	Henry
O	Singer	Jones	Phillip
O	Trumpet/Conductor	Jones	Willard
O	Staff Officer	Josephy	Willard
O	Piano	Kahn	Morton
	Dancer	Kapner	Fred
	Oboe	Kaufman	Benedict
O	Singer/Actor	Kearney	James
O	Dancer/Soloist	Kelly	Fred
O	Dancer	Kelly	Maurice
O	Trumpet	Kessler	Ralph
O	Dancer	King	Phil
	Singer	Kingsley	Charles
O	Singer	Kin Ne	Roger
O	Singer	Knapp	Johnny
O	Set Designer/Officer	Koenig	John
	Actor	Kogan	Edward
	Viola	Kolstein	Harry
O	Trumpet	Koven	Jake
	Music Copyist	Kratt	Bill

	Role	Surname	First Name
	Percussion	Kraus	Phil
	Violin	Kraut	Oscar
	Dancer	Lamarr	Stephen
O	Singer	Lane	Al
O	Viola	Lanese	Tom
	Dancer	Langdon	Richard A.
	Electrician	Lauter	Harold
	Carpenter	Lavaia	Rocco
	Makeup Artist	Le Goms	Jack
O	Dancer	Lee	Thomas
	Singer	Lefshetz	Hyman
O	Dancer	Lenny	Jack
	Flute	Levanda	Ed
	Publicity	Levine	Jules
	Saxophone	Levy	Saul
	Arranger	Lipman	Joseph
O	Singer	Lippy	Earl
	Music Publishing	Lissauer	Robert
O	Singer	Livecchi	Joseph
O	Additional Direction	Logan	Joshua
O	Dancer	Longo	Daniel
O	Singer	Lowell	Allan
O	Singer	Lynch	William
	Actor/Writer/Director	Maccoll	James
O	Singer/Soloist	Magelssen	Ralph
O	Actor	Manson	Alan
O	Singer	Marcus	Robert
O	Dancer	Martin	Al
	Supply Sergeant	Maruca	Francis J.
	Singer	Matterazzo	Mike
O	Trombone	Matteson	Don
O	Singer	Mccray	Donald
O	Singer	Mccutcheon	William
	Writer	Mcdonnell	Tom
	Singer	Mcgee	Anthony J.
O	Actor	McIlhargey	William
	Assistant Stage Manager	Mckelvey	Lige

	Assistant Stage Manager	Meister	George E.
	Writer	Mendelsohn	Jack
O	Magician	Mendes	John Prince
	Violin	Merlin	Ving
	Actor	Merrill	Gary
	Violin	Mesrobian	Peter
O	Violin	Miller	Max
O	Clarinet/Saxophone	Mince	John
O	Comedian	Mitchell	Pinkie
	Unknown	Mitek	John
	Singer	Monteux	Claude
	Dancer	Montgomery	Howard
	Actor/Comic	Moore	Robert E.
	Piano, Rehearsal	Moorin	Edward
	Trumpet	Morreale	James
O	Dancer	Nelson	Gene
O	Piano, Rehearsal	Newman	Murray
O	Singer	Nicholas	Carl
O	Dancer/Choreographer	Nugent	Pete
	Dancer/Drill Sergeant	O'Brien	Chester L.
O	Guitar/Singer	O'Connor	Edward
	Actor	O'Rear	James
O	Singer	O'Rourke	Gerald
	Assistant Stage Manager	Obbereich	Robert L.
O	Singer/Medical Assistant	Ohlandt	Henry
	Souvenir Programs	Orian	John
O	Comedian	Oshins	Julie
O	Violin	Ottobrino	Carl
O	Singer/Soloist	Oxford	Earl
O	Wardrobe Manager	Paglia	Tony
	Piano/Arranger	Pahl	Melvin
	Publicity	Palca	Alfred
	Dancer	Parker	Ivery L.
	Music Publishing	Parr	Allen
	Cello	Pascarella	Cesare A.
	Actor	Perry	Tileston
	Singer	Pesce	Cosmo

O	Dancer	Pillich	William
O	Trombone	Plattner	Herbert
O	Dancer	Prael	Harvey
	Specialty/Donald Duck	Propst	Joedene A.
	Singer	Race	Orville
	Dancer	Ramos	Steve
	Officer/Camp Upton	Rankin	Ainsworth H.
	Dancer	Reade	Charles
O	Singer	Reeves	Richard
	Dancer	Riley	John
	Staff Officer	Ritchie	A. W.
	Music Publishing	Robbins	Buddy
	Actor/Lyricist	Robin	Sid
	Singer	Rodick	Karl U.
O	Actor	Roerick	William G.
	Piano, Rehearsal	Rogers	Milton
O	Actor/Stage Manager	Rorke	Hayden
	Singer	Rosenblatt	Henry
O	Property Master	Rosenman	Herbert
O	Conductor	Rosenstock	Milton
O	Violin	Rosoff	Harry
	Actor	Ross	Anthony
O	Comedian	Ross	Irving
	Singer	Ross	Winston
O	Carpenter	Rubencamp	George
	Artist	Rubens	Albert
	Unknown	Rubens	Gerald
	Violin	Rubin	Gerc
	Music Publishing	Sack	Victor
O	Singer	Salmon	Louis
	French Horn	Salomon	Lester
	Actor/Comedian	Salomon	Stanley
O	Dancer	Salzer	Sidney
	Violin	Samel	Martin L.
	Music Publishing	Santly	Harry
	Dancer	Sassi	Nicholas
O	Singer	Savitt	Marvin

O	Singer	Scadden	Frank
	Publicity	Schenker	Nathan
	Music Librarian	Schlisserman	Herman
	Singer	Schoenfeld	David
	Officer/Music Publishing	Schumann	Walter
O	Dancer	Scott	Melbourne
	Arranger	Segure	Roger
O	Singer/Soloist	Shanley	Robert
O	Wardrobe Assistant	Shapiro	Bernard
	Bassoon	Sharrow	Leonard
	Singer	Shettle	Arthur
O	Violin	Shifrin	Joe
O	Actor/Singer	Showalter	Max
O	Director/Choreographer	Sidney	Robert
	Bass	Siegel	Abe
	Music Publishing	Siegel	Irving
O	Violin	Silverstein	Abner
	Violin	Silverstein	Harold
	Singer	Simini	Gerald
	Civilian Consultant, W. D.	Simon	Louis M.
	Dancer	Sirois	Stanley B.
	Company Clerk	͵Skarda	Emil
O	Unknown	Smith	Bill
	Trumpet	Snyder	Bunny
	Violin	Sorkin	Herbert
	Music Publishing	Stein	William
	Assistant Treasurer	Steinberg	Harry
O	Dancer/Specialty	Steiner	Arthur
	Souvenir Programs	Sternberg	Jonathan
	Music Publishing	Sternfels	Julian A.
	Porter	Stewart	Sam
	Director/Actor	Stone	Ezra
O	Actor	Stuart	Norman
O	Singer	Summerlin	Robert
O	Company Clerk	Supple	David A.
	Comm, SS, 2nd Corps Area	Supplee	H. Clay
	Singer	Tamber	Sid

O	Dancer	Tate	Charles
O	Cello	Tekula	Joseph
O	Dancer	Thomas	Hampton
O	Sound Technician	Tolbutt	John
O	Saxophone	Towne	Jack
	Actor	Truex	Philip
O	Singer	Turner	Clyde
	Singer	Vanemburgh	Norman
	Carpenter	Vanburen	Raymond
	House Manager	Vroom	Paul A.
	Assistant Personnel Clerk	Wally	Franklin
O	Singer	Walti	Faul
	Publicity	Wardell	Mike
O	Publicity, Warrant Officer	Washer	Ben
	Dancer	Watson	George
	Guitar	Watson, Jr.	Claude R.
O	Juggler	Weeks	Larry
	Singer	Weill	Harry
	Dancer/Comic	Weill	Larry
	Saxophone	Weissfeld	Emil
	Singer	Welansky	Bernard
	Singer	Welsh	Michael
	Dancer	White	Al
O	Actor/Makeup Handler	Whitley	Bert
O	Singer	Wiggins	James
	Publicity	Wilk	Max
	Dancer	Williams	William
O	Singer	Willins	Al
O	Dancer	Wocjikowski	Joseph
	French Horn	Woehr	Chris
	Singer	Wright	Lloyd D.
	Photographer, Signal Corps	Wurzel	David
	Singer	Yacopi	Americo
	Carpenter	Yaeger	Robert
O	Singer	Yakim	George
O	Singer, Dancer, Solo	Yates	William
	Assistant Supply Clerk	Zaino	Vincent J.

Index